INSURGENT DIPLOMAT

INSURGENT
DIPLOMAT

CIVIL TALKS OR CIVIL WAR?

AZIZ PAHAD

PENGUIN BOOKS

First published by Penguin Books (South Africa) (Pty) Ltd, 2014
A Penguin Random House company

Registered Offices: Block D, Rosebank Office Park, 181 Jan Smuts Avenue,
Parktown North, Johannesburg 2193, South Africa

www.penguinbooks.co.za

ISBN 978-0-14-353885-1
eISBN 978-0-14-353134-0

Text design and typesetting by Triexie Smit in 10.5/13 pt Cambria
Cover design by Hanneke du Toit
Cover photograph by DIRCO
Printed and bound by Paarl Media, Paarl

This book is dedicated to all those striving to achieve a peaceful
and prosperous South Africa, Africa and world.

Contents

Foreword by Thabo Mbeki

I have known Aziz Pahad for more than five decades. Our lives in the struggle for South Africa's liberation have intersected in ways personal, political and intellectual, starting before either one of us went into exile.

I have, therefore, shared a deep and abiding sense and spirit of comradeship with Aziz during our long and challenging years in exile. This continued on our return to South Africa when we were involved both in our complex process of negotiations, and in successive governments of a free and democratic South Africa.

In these journeys, we have been moulded by the ethos, traditions and philosophy of the African National Congress (ANC). Indeed, the ANC has been the organisational and normative lodestar that guided and informed all our activities and thought processes in the course of the struggle and later on when we became the governing party.

The ANC has thus provided the centre of gravity for the disparate social forces and personalities that constituted our Movement, and this is a very important dialectical thread that runs through Aziz's narrative in this book.

The book represents something of a hybrid: it is a richly textured cross between autobiography and memoir. Here we experience the profound influence of Aziz's family lineage, especially that of his parents on his formation as a fighter for liberation. However, there is also the temporal environment of his early years in South Africa and the wide spectrum of characters who populated it, and with whom he interacted. This treatment is often punctuated by humorous anecdotes – a manifestation of Aziz's humane and sunny disposition and common touch.

The autobiographical part of this book is very much a prelude to Aziz's political immersion and intellectual growth in the cauldron of the struggle, at home and abroad. His university studies at Sussex University in the United Kingdom, military training and political activism in the internal South African struggle and the international solidarity movement were all part of the larger script that would take Aziz into important leadership positions in both the ANC and the South African Communist Party (SACP).

At the insistence of the ANC, in 1989 the Organisation of African Unity (OAU) and the United Nations (UN) General Assembly adopted the Harare Declaration. The ANC had foreseen that sooner or later the apartheid regime would be obliged to enter into negotiations with the democratic movement. It therefore proposed and drafted the Harare Declaration as a framework for these negotiations.

The developments that informed the need for the Declaration provide the impulse for the core of this book, as well as for Aziz's close involvement and participation in wide-ranging talks with a cross section of South African interlocutors and other non-South Africans.

It is particularly with respect to the operational and substantive complexities of the secret talks that took place in England, Switzerland and South Africa where this book breaks new ground. This is the first account of these secret talks, written from a purely ANC perspective, to enter the public domain. Moreover, the tensions, disagreements and ambiguities that both sets of talks generated in the ANC are laid bare.

The detail with which Aziz approaches the thematic coverage of the talks provides great understanding and rare insight into how the actual contours of South Africa's negotiated settlement were shaped. This includes the onset of the negotiation process attendant on our return from exile, hammering out both the technical and political frameworks of the negotiations that led to the Convention for a Democratic South Africa (CODESA) process and beyond, right up to the country's transition to democracy, which became irreversible.

With the passage of two decades of democracy under the guidance of the ANC and its electoral victories, this reflective narrative helps us to recall the difficult and arduous path South Africa had to travel on its road to freedom and liberation.

This is an account that, therefore, takes on added authenticity since it chronicles the author's life in the struggle and the many selfless sacrifices that were made under very trying personal and political circumstances.

Unfortunately, too few of those at senior levels of the ANC who participated in the complex struggles leading up to our liberation, which Aziz discusses, have written about this period. This task has been left to people who were outside observers, who approach the task of storytelling informed by their own political and philosophical predilections. Thus do problems arise about the authenticity of such accounts.

We must, therefore, be very grateful that Aziz took the trouble to write this book, proceeding as he does from his vantage point as one of those who helped to make our history.

Accordingly, this is a book that must be read as representing both the rich tapestry of the liberation struggle and the great legacy of South Africa's transition to democracy – a reminder, especially to the younger generations, that freedom was not free!

Thabo Mbeki

Preface

In 2014 South Africans celebrated the twentieth anniversary of democracy. This coincided, on 8 January 2014, with the ANC's commemoration of its 102nd anniversary.

Since 1994 South Africans have, against all odds, achieved many impressive successes in strategic areas of public policy that address the deprivations and scourges of our apartheid past. The record of such achievements can be seen in education, health, housing, labour law, welfare and social services, and in the general improvement of the quality of life for millions of ordinary South Africans.

However, South Africa still faces a litany of challenges. We continue to experience major deficits and shortcomings in the lack of progressive leadership at every level of society. And there is a distinct lack of human and institutional capacity to deliver on the ambition of addressing the hard legacies of poverty, unemployment and inequality, as well as the growing disparity between the 'haves' and the 'have-nots'. This is compounded by the violation of the letter and spirit of the *Batho Pele* principle of serving the people and the rising crescendo of popular dissatisfaction with the quality and non-delivery of services. At the level of governance, there are worrisome symptoms of cronyism, abuse of state resources and growing levels of systemic corruption.

These developments all exercise a serious negative impact on our commitment to democracy, non-racialism, non-sexism, anti-tribalism and reconciliation, as well as the crafting of a true South African patriotism. Indeed, they are all ingredients of a recipe that fosters conditions ripe for instability and violence.

To deal with the challenges of the present and the future, all South Africans have to appreciate an incontrovertible fact of our struggle. In the fight against the apartheid system – which the UN declared a Crime Against

Humanity – we would do well to remember that thousands of Africans, South Africans of Indian origin, coloureds and whites joined the struggle, knowing that it would result in arrests, imprisonment, torture, deaths in detention, impoverishment and exile.

It was the collective sacrifices of these individuals that ensured that South Africans of all races and creeds succeeded in finding a peaceful negotiated solution, which averted a catastrophic racial war. It is thus incumbent on all South Africans today to assume joint responsibility for consolidating our young democracy in the greater quest to achieve a better life for all our people.

In this broad narrative of our liberation, I am but one player in a struggle that involved thousands of men and women of great character, integrity and commitment. However, the demands and imperatives of the struggle for democracy required that we worked strictly according to the 'need-to-know rule'. I cannot, therefore, pretend that I am telling the complete story; there will invariably be gaps that others must and should fill.

I must be quite emphatic that this book is not only about my life; it is also an attempt to represent my involvement in a dialogue and negotiation process that broadly followed and was faithful to the liberation philosophy of the ANC, as well as its enunciated policies, decisions and directives. My main purpose is to demonstrate how matters of principle and practice served to guide the ANC team, of which I was a part, through a very difficult and demanding journey that took us to the ultimate destination of a free and democratic South Africa.

The result is that what follows is not only a chronicle of historic developments within the country and the run-up to formal negotiations towards an all-inclusive democracy, but also how those often complicated and protracted events impacted on – and were influenced by – my own life and the part I was able to play. This narrative is, then, part autobiography, part memoir and, most importantly, part historical record – one that I hope will contribute to a better and more comprehensive understanding of what transpired in those pivotal years that led up to 1994, and how those developments were informed by ANC policies established since the formation of the organisation.

With that said, my life and experiences – like those of so many other activists – cannot be separated from those of the ANC and the SACP. I was privileged to grow up and interact with many outstanding leaders of the Congress Movement who drew their inspiration from both the ANC and the SACP.

Quite significantly for my own political development, I was especially fortunate that I had the privilege of working under the guidance and leadership of Thabo Mbeki from the early 1960s in South Africa, and later in the UK, Zambia, Zimbabwe, Angola and many other countries of the world.

In this book, I set out the context in which my political consciousness, awareness and learning evolved over the course of the 1940s and 1950s. Naturally, those personal memories and anecdotal experiences cannot be separated from the broader picture. What was happening within the politics of the time and the all-important interplay of those events exercised a strong influence on how I was growing as an individual, an activist and a member of the ANC. As it transpired, I was but a humble contributor to the turn of events that would free South Africans from decades, even centuries, of oppression. In this light, I also chronicle the circumstances in which I, along with many other comrades, went into exile, as well as cast the spotlight on those causal factors that led to the intensification of the struggle in South Africa and internationally.

A critical and essential part of my story is about how South Africans of vastly different political and ideological persuasions, as well as socio-cultural backgrounds, managed to find a negotiated solution. This was not the 'miracle' so widely advertised, but a result of the sacrifices of thousands of deeply committed individuals and the outcome of outstanding leadership at the most decisive moments of our struggle.

I focus here on the significant overt and covert talks that were an integral part of the story, and the intense discussions and debates with representatives of the apartheid regime and ordinary South Africans in which I was involved; but these were only one strand of other talks that took place. These include, most importantly, 48 secret meetings with Nelson Mandela while he was in prison, and almost 200 other meetings between the ANC and South Africans that took place secretly and openly in Africa and many other parts of the world.

Our approach to a peaceful negotiated solution was always based on ANC policies, those put in place at the party's founding in 1912 and reflected in all major policy documents since, including the Atlantic Charter/African Claims, in response to the victorious powers meeting to set up the League of Nations after World War II; ANC president Chief Luthuli's letter to the government in 1957; Mandela's article in *Fighting Talk* in 1961; the All-In African Conference call in 1961, which called for a national convention; the ANC Conference in Kabwe, Zambia, in 1985; and the Harare Declaration in 1989.

I was deeply involved in many of the significant developments of the time, and in a variety of different capacities over the course of my life: as a member of the Transvaal Indian Youth Congress (TIYC), the ANC

Youth and Student Section (ANC YSS) in London, the ANC's National Executive Committee (NEC), the Central Committee (CC) of the SACP, the Revolutionary Council (RC) and the Politico-Military Council (PMC). I have also held important strategic positions, including Deputy Head of the ANC International Relations Committee (1990–1994), representative of the ANC in the Transitional Executive Council (1993–1994) and, finally, Deputy Minister of Foreign Affairs during the presidencies of Nelson Mandela and Thabo Mbeki (1994–2008).

If there is a common theme that runs through my life experiences, it is that there is a delicate balance between insurgency and diplomacy. Thus, when President Mbeki was recalled by the NEC of the ANC in 2008, we were at a crucial watershed in our efforts to fundamentally change the structural problems that characterised South Africa's political, economic and social landscape. I was extremely concerned that this dangerous – and unacceptable – decision would have serious consequences for the ANC, our nascent democratic institutions and the country at large. As is well known, six other cabinet colleagues and I resigned as a result.

President Mbeki's unfortunate 'recall' points to the need for all South Africans to deal with the contradictions and challenges of governing a new democratic South Africa and what needs to be done to sustain this collective endeavour so as to prevent us from falling into the many pitfalls of failure, cynicism and despair.

And so it is that my story, my memories, are set against this significant backdrop – South Africa's emergence as a fledgling democracy and what that came to mean to the country and its people.

Aziz Pahad
Johannesburg
September 2014

Acknowledgements

Over the course of my life and this book's long gestation period, there are several people to whom I owe a debt of deep gratitude and it gives me great pleasure to acknowledge the different roles they have played.

I wish, first and foremost, to thank my wife, Professor Angina Parekh, for giving my life new meaning and for being the constant in my life. Without her perseverance, encouragement, support and constructive insights, I would not have completed this book.

A special word of gratitude is reserved for my brother, Dr Essop Pahad, who went into exile with me. Despite our many arguments and disagreements, he has always been a source of political guidance and encouragement. I wish to especially acknowledge my sister-in-law, Meg Pahad, for her friendship and guidance over the years.

I remain deeply grateful to other members of my nuclear family – Ismail and Kulsum, Nassim and Isa, Juned and Farida – for the support they gave Essop and me when we returned from exile.

I wish to acknowledge my sons, Sam and Zayren, and my nephew, Mayur. Their generosity of spirit has been a constant reminder that familial bonds can, and will always, transcend time and space.

This book has its origins at the Institute for Global Dialogue. As such, I would like to record my appreciation to its Board for inviting me to be a Senior Fellow in order to write my memoirs. I am grateful to Dr Garth le Pere, the former head of the institute, who played an invaluable editorial, substantive and advisory role in ensuring that this project came together.

I also wish to thank Dr Anver Saloojee for his useful and insightful comments on the manuscript, Hanlie Griesel for her research support and Malcolm Ray for his initial involvement with this project.

My ANC and SACP families have been a central part of my life and a constant source of inspiration in times good and bad. I therefore want to thank all my comrades for their solidarity and friendship over our long and difficult decades of struggle.

Finally, I would like to acknowledge the support and cooperation of Janet Bartlet of Penguin Books South Africa, Frederik de Jager, as well as Penguin's freelance editor, Sean Fraser.

Chapter 1

The early years

The first wave of Indians came to South Africa in 1860 as indentured labourers and settled in what was then the Crown Colony of Natal. They were predominantly from the south of India. Indentured labourers were followed six years later, in 1867, by 'Passenger Indians' or 'Passage Arrivals' who came to South Africa to seek greener pastures. They were mostly Hindus and Muslims – like my grandparents, who came from the state of Gujarat in North India – and were, in the main, traders or those who came to work in Indian shops. Most settled in Natal, but soon moved to other regions in order to set up businesses, thus becoming the main competitors of white traders. Fearing competition, the government of General Jan Smuts intensified anti-Indian legislation that, among other prohibitions, prevented Indians from trading in certain areas or attempted to curtail their movements from one area to another. Despite these restrictions, many among their number went on to become independent traders and joined professions within the bounds of those occupations they were allowed to enter.

I was born on Christmas day 1940, the third of five sons. My brothers were Ismail, Essop, Nassim and Juned, and our early years were spent in the small town of Schweizer-Reneke, in what was then the Western Transvaal and is now part of the North West Province. My father first worked in the family business, but later opened his own small general dealership. In 1945 my family decided, for economic and political reasons, to move to Johannesburg. We moved to a two-bedroom flat in No. 11 Orient House, Becker Street, in Ferreirastown. One bedroom was used by my parents, while Essop, Nassim, Juned and I shared the other. There was a dining room and a living room, which at night doubled as a bedroom for my eldest brother, Ismail. Friends would often stay over and somehow we ingeniously managed to create more sleeping space.

The move to Becker Street was fortuitous but fateful, since it had a profound impact on my political development; Ferreirastown turned out to be a hive of political activity. Rather importantly in this regard, Orient House was flanked by the offices of the ANC and the Transvaal Indian Congress (TIC). The Tambo-Mandela law offices were in Chancellor House, on the corner of Becker and Fox streets, and thus close to where we lived. Then there was Kosi Café, which was directly below the Tambo-Mandela offices in Chancellor House. In the absence of any public recreational facilities, Kosi Café became our regular gathering space. We also took advantage of the billiard room across the way from the café where many of the top gangsters of the area used to hang out. I knew those gangsters well and under their 'protection' felt safe and secure from other competing gangs in the area. These connections led me to join the 'Becker Street Gang' and we earned a healthy respect from the community.

Another interesting feature of our neighbourhood was the Johannesburg Magistrate's Court, which was also in Becker Street. Not only was this court the scene of many of the political trials, but in the absence of sporting facilities we used to play football on the lawns of the courthouse where we were constantly harassed by the police and, if caught, even beaten up.

Given the strategic location of our flat, it became a hub of political and social gatherings. Senior ANC leaders, as well as those from the Indian Congress, the Congress of Democrats and the Coloured People's Congress (CPC), all of which became stalwarts of the liberation struggle, frequently visited for lunch, supper or meetings. They included Nelson Mandela, Walter Sisulu, Oliver Tambo, Robert Resha, Duma Nokwe, JB Marks, Moses Kotane, Alfred Nzo, Thomas Nkobi, Mendi Msimang, Yusuf Dadoo, the brothers Molvi and Yusuf Cachalia, Zainab Asvat, Ama and her husband TN Naidoo, Jasmat Nanabhai and others.

My mother, Amina, was born in July 1918 in Klerksdorp in the then Transvaal. She spoke very little English, while we only had a nodding acquaintance of Gujarati and Hindi. Yet she was able to communicate with us and the many visitors to our flat. Her lack of knowledge of the English language was no obstacle to her being what Ahmed Kathrada describes in his memoirs as a 'humanist who displayed immense strength and courage in the face of adversity ... to all her strengths were her kindness, her generosity of spirit, her selflessness and her commitment to community'.

My mother was extremely kind and caring, not only to her family but to everyone she encountered – even to the Special Branch who frequently raided our flat in the early hours of the morning. We were often rudely awakened as Special Branch police searched the flat and interrogated our parents. Even though we objected, my mother ignored us and insisted on offering them refreshments. As a measure of her magnanimous spirit, she always told us that we must share what we had, even if it meant depriving ourselves. She saw no contradiction between her commitment to family and community, and her commitment to fighting oppression and discrimination.

Reflecting on my mother, Nelson Mandela writes in his autobiography, 'I often visited the home of Amina Pahad for lunch, and then suddenly this charming woman put down her apron and went to jail for her beliefs. If I had once questioned the willingness of the Indian community to protest against oppression, I no longer could.'

In their biography, Albertina and Walter Sisulu write that Goolam and Amina Pahad at Orient House provided 'a home away from home in the city centre'. Sisulu noted that he initially believed that Indian women were 'conservative and unwilling to involve themselves in public life'. But that opinion had changed after he met my mother and other women involved in the Passive Resistance Campaign. My mother was a woman with a vision. She never sought publicity or accolades for her participation in the struggle, and she maintained a strong belief in creating a non-racial, democratic South Africa. Her commitment did not derive from book knowledge but from her own life experiences and her constant contact with activists and leaders of the Congress Movement.

My father, Goolam, was born on 21 September 1912 in Kholvad, Gujarat. He came to South Africa in 1919, but then returned to India in 1922 to further his education, which is when he met Dr Yusuf Dadoo and developed a lifelong friendship. After my grandfather's death in 1926, my father returned to South Africa. He was a stoic character of great fortitude and self-control. He was also active in the Indian Congress, which strove for independence in India, and he continued his political activism when he came to South Africa. He later rose to become an executive member of both the Transvaal and the South African Indian Congress (SAIC). When a state of emergency was declared in the wake of the Sharpeville massacre in March 1960, my father was detained and imprisoned for five months. As a result, his business collapsed, leading to financial ruin. On his release, he made the difficult decision to leave South Africa for the UK.

It was rather ironic that the luxurious headquarters of all the major institutions representing white capital and finance were also located in our neighbourhood. Even today the massive Anglo American corporate buildings continue to dominate the landscape. I recall vividly how many of our leaders pointed to these buildings to explain the inequality of the apartheid system and the extent to which big capital complied with it, offering early exposure to the complex tensions between exploitative capitalism and the promise of socialism. This area also housed one of the main 'pass office' buildings in Market Street. The 'pass' was emblematic of the dehumanisation of African men and women, and I grew up witnessing daily the humiliation and ill treatment of hundreds of Africans as they queued for hours outside the pass office. The Marshall Square Police Station was another landmark where many political detainees were imprisoned.

In later years the notorious John Vorster Square Police Station was built on Goch Street, two blocks away from Becker Street. We had many fights with young white policemen, especially on Friday nights, when they returned to Vorster Square after drinking sprees in town. If the fights were serious, we had to stay off the streets because they were sure to return with reinforcements. Fortunately, they were often too drunk to identify anyone.

Ferreirastown, its spatial environment and the various landmarks were, therefore, not only an important part of my growing up, but also formative in my socialisation and my growing awareness of political life. Indeed, the cumulative experiences of Ferreirastown provided the driving impulse that made politics part of my DNA. This environment, and particularly my early encounters with so many Congress leaders, shaped my understanding of the world in which I grew up. This was a world animated by important events, key figures, daily activities and a particular understanding of history that became deeply woven into the rhythm of my life.

The Indian Congress

Many TIC executive committee meetings were held in our flat and, as young children, we were fortunate to have interacted with many of its leading members. These almost daily interactions greatly enhanced my education and insights about the South African Indian community.

Mahatma Gandhi was an important figure in shaping my world view, largely because we were constantly told that we should aspire to emulate him. In 1880, when Gandhi was still a young lawyer, he came to South Africa for a legal assignment after which he was to return to India. When he learnt of the intentions of the Natal Legislative Assembly (NLA) to disenfranchise Indians, he postponed his departure and led the struggle against discriminatory legislation and proceeded to organise numerous petitions and protests.

He founded the Natal Indian Congress (NIC) in 1894, and in June 1903 started a newspaper, *Indian Opinion*, which survived until 1960. Years later, he was criticised for setting up an ambulance corps to help the British during the Bambatha Rebellion in 1906, leading to an allegation that he was a 'British loyalist'. Clearly, Gandhi had not grasped the relationship between the struggles of South Africans of Indian origin and the majority of the oppressed in South Africa, but I do not believe that the criticisms were justified, nor properly contextualised.

When the Asiatic Law Amendment Act was introduced in 1906, every Indian over the age of eight had to register and be fingerprinted. This certificate of registration was effectively a 'pass' that had to be produced on demand. Gandhi went to the Transvaal to lead the campaign against this law. He formed the Passive Resistance Association and launched the passive resistance *Satyagraha* campaign in order to defy the law. The campaign was highly successful and only 500 of an estimated population of 13 000 registered – although many were arrested.

In 1908, General Smuts, with the connivance of the British government, negotiated a deal with Gandhi whereby Smuts promised to repeal the Act if the Indians registered voluntarily. As a result, the campaign was called off, but Smuts did not repeal the Act as promised. This was not the first time that Smuts and the British had reneged on an agreement with the oppressed people of South Africa as they went about consolidating white power in the country. Gandhi's experiences in South Africa and his impact on the local political landscape provided the crucible for the major role he went on to play in India's struggle for independence after his return there in 1914.

The experiences of Gandhi and the *Satyagraha* campaign taught us the importance of non-violent but militant struggle, and the necessity to be vigilant about compromises that were not necessarily made in the interests of the people, but rather in the interests of the colonial masters and the ruling establishment. Most importantly, I learnt that British colonialism would conspire with minority white interests to defeat the objectives of our struggle. This lesson has been repeated throughout our struggle, as well as other anti-colonial struggles.

Dr Dadoo played a critical role in these unfolding dynamics – such that he became a well-known and highly respected household name in South Africa. Popularly known as 'Mota' or 'Doc', the life story of Dadoo represents a tapestry of struggle against imperialism and apartheid, the mobilisation of South Africans of Indian origin and the unity of all anti-apartheid forces in South Africa. In 1929 he went to Edinburgh to study Medicine, and it was here that he was exposed to Marxist literature and was deeply influenced by the *Communist Manifesto*. After completing his medical studies in 1936, he returned to South Africa and, as a close family friend, political leader and constant visitor to our home, Dr Dadoo had a profound impact on my parents – and in later years on us as children and adults. My father and Dr Dadoo had been friends in the Kholvad village in Gujarat in the 1920s, and they now rekindled their friendship.

On his return Dr Dadoo found that there was no unity among the oppressed and their representatives. The Communist Party of South Africa (CPSA) had been weakened by sectarianism and the Indian Congress was led by moderates who were determined to strike dubious compromises with the ruling regime. Dr Dadoo became actively involved, and with progressive Indian activists, such as Molvi Cachalia, Yusuf and Amina Cachalia, Zainab Asvat, my father Goolam Pahad, Nana Sita, TN Naidoo, Jasmat Nanabhai and PS Joshi, formed the nationalist bloc of the TIC in 1939. There was intense debate between the nationalists and conservatives in the Indian Congress movement about how South African Indians should relate to the evolving legal and political architecture of apartheid in the country on one hand; and the need to fight for a non-racial democratic South Africa on the other, which would demand involvement and solidarity with the struggles of the African and coloured people. It was clear to the progressive elements that the Indian struggle could not be separated from the context of the broader struggle of the African people.

The Passive Resistance Campaign

In 1946 the Ghetto Act was introduced in order to curtail Indian property ownership in so-called 'controlled' 'white areas' in Natal. This provided the catalyst for Dr Dadoo to lead a passive resistance campaign and, in the process, drive the militant transformation of the Transvaal and Natal Indian congresses.

In the two years of the campaign, from 1946 to 1948, over 2 000 men and women defied the writ of the Ghetto Act and were imprisoned, with Dr Dadoo jailed twice for his role. My mother, Amina, was one of the six women from the Transvaal who went to Durban to participate and was detained twice. I was six years of age. In later years, when I fully understood the repercussions and implications of the campaign, it added another vein of understanding to my evolving political consciousness and fuelled my growing hatred of the apartheid system and its regime. While the campaign did not result in the repeal of this restrictive law, it did help to further mobilise the broader Indian community and brought the issue to the attention of the international community.

In this period, another major event was set to take place: the independence of India in 1947, a struggle led by Mahatma Gandhi. Through their collective energy and commitments, Indians had defeated the might of British imperialism despite the boast that 'the sun would never set on the British Empire'. In solidarity with India's struggle for independence, the TIC organised a number of demonstrations outside their offices, because leaders even then realised the importance of Indian independence for anti-colonial struggles in Africa. Since the TIC offices were just a block away from our school and our flat, we took youthful delight in participating in the demonstrations. I recall the excitement of seeing the ANC flag and independent India's flag flying side by side outside the TIC offices, and the singing of South African and Indian freedom songs. When India's Interim Government was formed, one of its first major actions at the UN was to introduce a resolution on the South African regime's mistreatment of 'South African Indians' – this was my first concrete exposure to the unity of anti-colonial and anti-imperialist struggles.

However, I can remember that even at the young age of seven how saddened I was by the fact that, because of British colonial manipulation and opportunism by some Indian leaders, the territory of India was divided and the Islamic state of Pakistan had been created. This led to a number of communal riots, which resulted in thousands of deaths. The British had created divisions that widened religious and sectarian cleavages. My father, however, was adamant that few people supported the partition of India and based his argument on the fact that his family were all members of Congress, and Congress was opposed to partition. The significance of this experience drove home the need to oppose any attempts to divide people on the basis of religious or ethnic differences and reinforced my embryonic understanding of the imperatives for a non-racial, democratic and secular South Africa.

It was all these events that conspired to empower the nationalist bloc to take control of the TIC and the NIC. From a rather moderate and servile opposition, the congresses became militant organisations and provided the bridgehead for decisive change in the way that South Africans of Indian origin related to the broader democratic struggle. My parents took me to many meetings and events to celebrate the victory of the nationalist wing of the Indian Congress and our flat became a centre of such celebrations. The high-water mark was the signing of the 'Doctors Pact' in 1947 between Dr Monty Naicker representing the NIC, Dr Yusuf Dadoo representing the TIC, and Dr AB Xuma representing the ANC. This was the first concrete manifestation of cooperation in working towards a non-racial South Africa and became the foundation and symbol for unity of the oppressed.

One special person who became our mentor and the equal of an elder brother was Ahmed Kathrada, or 'Kathy' as he was affectionately known. Our families were close friends, perhaps because the Kathrada family also came from Schweizer-Reneke and were originally from Kholvad. Kathy's life has been one of political activism in the Congress Movement, punctuated by banning, detention and imprisonment.

Kathy lived at No. 13 Kholvad House, which was around the corner from our flat in Orient House. Kathy's flat, like ours, was a hive of political and social activity. However, Essop and I were never invited to join these activities since this would have been inappropriate given Kathy's *de facto* older-brother status. Moreover, Kathy was a strict disciplinarian and did not take kindly to young activists, including myself, who did not carry out their political tasks with vigour and commitment. He strongly believed that social, sporting or cultural activities should not interfere with political tasks and would sternly ignore my protests, if only to remind me and others that the struggle for freedom was the most important task in life. We did not complain when he was around, but in our circles we always questioned his strict political discipline.

Kathy took every opportunity to explain the politics of the SACP, ANC and Indian congresses and their common objectives and visions. He was the quintessential role model and we aspired to be like him, a difficult if not impossible task. Even though he was charged in the infamous Treason Trial, he continued to work underground after his acquittal and banning. This led to his arrest in July 1963 during the raid on Lilliesleaf Farm and his subsequent life imprisonment with Mandela and others after the Rivonia Trial.

Amid all this political combustion, my active and formal political life was moulded in the trenches of the TIYC. Here I was deeply influenced by comrades such as my brother Essop, Babla Saloojee, Essop Jassat, Abdulhay Jassat, Moosa (Mosie) Moolla, Farid Adams, Suliman (Solly) Esakjee, Herbie Pillay, Indres Naidoo, Shirish Nanabhay, Laloo (Isu) Chiba, Reggie Vandeyar, Ahmed Timol and Yusuf (JoJo) Saloojee. In all campaigns, the TIYC was actively involved in distributing leaflets, putting up posters, selling Congress newspapers and mobilising the Indian community in support of the struggle. These activities added another dimension to my political maturity and enabled me to interact with people across the spectrum of political, cultural, racial and ethnic groupings.

The Durban riots

A deeply disturbing and traumatic occurrence was the African-Indian riots in Durban, which erupted in 1949 when I was nine years old. The ostensible cause of the riots was a sense of economic marginalisation, inferiority and exploitation experienced by Africans at the hands of Indians. The scale of violence left a deep impression on me: 142 people died, over a thousand were injured and 58 Indian-owned shops and more than 250 houses were destroyed. There was a general fear that South Africa would be engulfed in racial conflict between Africans and South Africans of Indian origin. Despite many reports of white incitement of such attacks, the Riots Inquiry Commission found that there was no white involvement.

I remember being rather nervous and scared, especially as stories of ethnic violence in India were still raw and fresh. I was totally confused and could not understand what drove sections of the oppressed people of South Africa to attack one another. Indian leaders from Transvaal and Natal joined with ANC leaders and campaigned vigorously to end the riots. When this was successfully accomplished, they issued a joint statement in which they explained that 'the fundamental and basic causes of the disturbances are traceable to the political, economic and social structure of this country'.

I was fortunate to be able to listen to many of our leaders explain the root causes of such ethnic violence and the need to always 'look for the hand of the enemy'. Congress leaders put the violence into proper political context and showed how agent provocateurs could exploit the poverty and deprivation of ordinary people. This lesson – to always look for the root causes of conflict – served me well throughout my life and political career.

The Durban riots also gave greater meaning and urgency to the need for unity in action, built on the foundations of grassroots activity. The prompt response of congress leaders and the massive efforts undertaken to put the riots into a proper political context, as well as the ANC's emphasis on non-racialism, goes a long way to explain why such xenophobic riots have not been repeated in South Africa.

The riots pointed to the need to promote growing unity in struggle among our people, and the challenge of confronting white monopoly control of the economy to prevent conflicts over scarce resources.

The working class in struggle

In our political discussions, we learnt that the 1940s and '50s made up a period of unprecedented trade union activity. During World War II, African workers provided two-thirds of the labour force in strategic industries such as agriculture, clothing, gold, coal, cement, iron ore, chemicals and explosives. Their working terms and conditions were appalling and, as a consequence, union organisation and membership grew considerably. In 1941, an important development was the formation of the African Mine Workers' Union (AMWU), which proved successful in recruiting African miners. The government's response was the introduction of War Measure No. 1425, which prohibited meetings of more than 20 persons on mine property without a special permit. Repetitive War Measures were being used as state instruments to outlaw strikes, but strike action continued – and, in fact, increased – despite police brutality and the killing of union members.

On 4 August 1946, a public conference of the AMWU, attended by over

1 000 delegates, took place at Johannesburg's Newtown Market Square. This conference resolved to embark on a general strike from 12 August by Africans employed in the gold mines. It is estimated that over 70 000 African miners went on strike over three days, resulting in the closure of several mines. Police attacked miners indiscriminately and some were badly injured and killed. On 26 August, over 50 people were charged in the Johannesburg Magistrate's Court with conspiracy and infringement of War Measure No. 1425. The group included leading members of the Communist Party, such as Moses Kotane, Dr Dadoo, Hilda Watts (née Bernstein) and Brian Bunting. Many of the accused pleaded guilty and were sentenced to imprisonment.

The court where those arrested appeared was situated in our street and I remember my friends and me joining the crowds as they emerged from the court, singing freedom songs and shouting ANC and CPSA slogans. I revelled in the festive but militant atmosphere without, however, fully understanding the significance of what was happening. Unwittingly, the relevance of the dialectical nexus between working class and national struggles was being inculcated in me. Years later when I was in my early twenties I began to understand the leading role of the working class in the struggle, and the reality of how racism was often used by powerful interests to subvert the class consciousness of the white workers.

Many members of the CPSA and trade-union leaders were also ANC and Indian Congress leaders, so it was inevitable that working-class militancy would have a direct impact on the ANC. The CPSA organised the Pioneers Club and we became very friendly with several of its members, such as Barbara Harmel, Ilsa Fischer, Tony Bernstein, Mark and Sheila Weinberg, Max Sisulu and other 'children of Congress'. The club presented one of the few opportunities for children of all race groups to socialise, and these encounters proved thoroughly enjoyable and exciting. Our friendships were to blossom further when we attended the University of the Witwatersrand (Wits). But importantly, in the Pioneers Club we learnt not only about the political situation in South Africa and Africa, but also about national struggles in the United States of America, China, the Soviet Union and India. Ruth First and Hilda Bernstein had visited China and India and they gave us fascinating comparative accounts about developments taking place in these countries. I cannot claim that at this stage I or my contemporaries fully grasped the subtlety of this pedagogy, but it undoubtedly nurtured the seeds for my future political orientation.

This then was the environment that provided the gravitational pull for being politically involved. While we were products of our family background and history, the congress environment became equally prominent in challenging an increasingly repressive political regime. Political discourse swirled around us almost on a daily basis in our flat, in the congress offices and on street corners. I was thus very privileged to have grown up in a 'Congress base'. In a real sense, while I had a nuclear family, the Congress Movement and the many personalities who animated it had also become family and an integral part of my existence.

The Suppression of Communism Act

Against the background of a politically ascendant and ideologically hegemonic apartheid state, the struggle intensified and became more militant. In response, the National Party government introduced a new law, the Suppression of Communism Act of 1950. This must be one of the most draconian laws in modern history, perhaps only comparable to those of Nazi Germany. This legislation became the state's main instrument for attacking the freedom and liberties of all anti-apartheid forces, communists and non-communists alike. My brother Essop and I were to feel the sting of this law when we were banned under its provisions in January 1964.

The definition of communism was ludicrously wide and included, for example:

- Clause b – which aims at bringing about any political, industrial, social or economic change within the Union by promotion of disturbance or disorder, by unlawful acts or omissions or by the threats of such acts or omissions or by means which include the promotion of disturbance or disorder, or such acts or omissions or threats.

- Clause d – which aims at the encouragement of feelings of hostility between European and non-European races of the Union, the consequences of which are calculated to further the achievement of any object referred in paragraph a (i.e. dictatorship of the proletariat) and paragraph b.

The Act provided for the appointment of a liquidator who was authorised to compile a list of former members or supporters of the Communist Party. Activists appearing on the list were subjected to any number of outrageous restrictions, which included having to resign from any organisation or public body, even Parliament. The Governor-General was authorised to ban any publication that promoted the spread of communism. Under Section 9 of the Act, anybody, whether listed or not, could be banned from attending a gathering and, under section 10, prohibited from being in 'defined' areas. The Minister of Justice, CR Swart, was also given powers to ban meetings.

Before the law could be enacted, however, the CPSA dissolved itself and leaders such as Moses Kotane and Dr Dadoo played an important role in establishing underground structures of the party. Fully understanding the far-reaching totalitarian implications of the Act, the ANC, the SAIC, the African People's Organisation and the Communist Party met to discuss its consequences. As Oliver Tambo presciently observed, 'today it is the Communist Party, tomorrow it will be our trade unions, our Indian Congress, our African People's Organisation, our African National Congress'.

At this critical moment, which demanded solidarity and unity among the opposition forces, many leading figures – especially in the ANC Youth League – were suspicious of working with the Communist Party, particularly its white and Indian members. There were serious objections from Youth League members, including Mandela, Tambo and some 'African Nationalists'. They argued that attention was being diverted from the ANC's 1949 Programme of Action and that the campaign was being 'hijacked' by communists and non-Africans.

To its credit, the ANC conference in 1950 rejected their opposition and resolved that a campaign of mass action should be organised against the Act and its associated repressive measures. A day of mourning was called for those killed by the police during the workers' strikes and protests on 1 May, and the conference further called for a national strike on 26 June 1950.

The Defiance Campaign

The Defiance Campaign was driven by protest action against a cluster of repressive laws and regulations: the Group Areas Act, the Separate Representation of Voters Act, the Suppression of Communism Act, the Bantu Authorities Act, the pass laws, and the stock limitation and rehabilitation schemes. Dr JS Moroka, president of the ANC, was to head the Joint Planning Council, while Walter Sisulu and Dr Dadoo played a major role in preparing a document on the methods of struggle to be adopted in the campaign. Nelson Mandela was elected volunteer-in-chief with Molvi Cachalia as his deputy. JB Marks and Yusuf Cachalia also served on the council. The council's declaration expressed its conviction that: 'All the peoples of South Africa, irrespective of race, colour or creed, have the inalienable and fundamental right to participate directly and fully in the governing councils of the state.' This in the face of the National Party government's attempts to crush legitimate protests with ruthless and brutal police action.

Our flat was again the epicentre of activity since many of the preparatory discussions for the Defiance Campaign took place within its confines. I also regularly visited the ANC and TIC offices and could not help but be caught up in the excitement of this new phase of our struggle.

The organisation creatively used various forms of struggle to publicise the campaign, including demonstrations, pickets, rallies, strikes and study groups. It was launched in Johannesburg, Boksburg, Durban and Port Elizabeth on 26 June 1952, and it was not long before some 8 000 volunteers were detained for defying various laws. My mother was one of the first to volunteer and was duly arrested. At that time she was suffering from rheumatism, a result of previous detentions, but she rejected all advice not to join.

The Defiance Campaign made a tremendous impact on me. I was then 12 years old. The task assigned to us young comrades was to distribute leaflets, write slogans on walls and put up posters. We worked in groups of five or six. One person carried the bucket of home-made glue, another the brush and posters, and three or four had the task of putting up the posters and acting as lookouts to alert us of any police presence. In many ways these activities were a wonderful and meaningful adventure for us.

The ANC had created a 'Volunteer Section' called the *Amadelakufu* (those who dare defy death) and to this day I have no idea whether our adventurous pursuits fell under its remit! I could not fathom how the activities we were carrying out constituted a defiance of death.

An important part of the Defiance Campaign narrative was deepening and widening the unity among artificially defined racial groups and spurring them to concrete action as part of a gathering chorus of voices that rejected the legal underpinnings of the apartheid system. At the operational level, it transformed the ANC and Indian congresses into mass-militant organisations. Moreover, the campaign had a salutary and defining effect on the formation of the South African Coloured People's Organisation (SACPO) and the white-led Congress of Democrats. All these organisations came together to constitute what became known as the 'Congress Movement'. Unity in action was thus being forged in the cauldron of struggle, and representatives of all racial groups were unequivocal and selfless in their willingness to make supreme sacrifices for a non-racial and democratic South Africa.

During this time, I was attending the Ferreirastown Indian Primary School in Becker Street, in close proximity to the Johannesburg Magistrate's Court. People arrested during the Defiance Campaign were tried in the Magistrate's Court and Congress organised a daily demonstration at the end of each day of a trial. These demonstrations took place in an open field opposite the court, which was used for sporting activities by the students from Ferreirastown Primary during their breaks. While some students were incensed that our sports were being interrupted by Congress Movement demonstrations, many of us took active part in them. The speeches were militant and inspiring, and when the demonstrations were over my friends and I would accompany the demonstrators as they marched in song from the playing field to Park Station, from where Africans had to board their trains to return to their dusty and inhospitable townships.

All this had a politicising effect on me. Marching together with our African compatriots and listening to the songs and speeches was not only exhilarating, but it also helped me to better understand the political dynamics and organisational logic of the Congress Movement. One of the most pernicious and negative aspects of the apartheid system was that by law we had to live in different areas, attend different schools and even socialise separately. The joint activities inspired by the Defiance Campaign gave real meaning, content and context to non-racialism. Indeed, the Congress Movement provided an effective platform for challenging the artificial racial categories imposed on us by the apartheid system.

There was a general sense of satisfaction that the campaign marked a historic watershed in shaping the philosophy of 'Unity in Action' for all South Africans under the leadership of the Congress Alliance. Consequently, we celebrated 26 June as 'South Africa Freedom Day'.

When analysing the historic importance of the campaign, Govan Mbeki (Thabo Mbeki's father, who was one of the Rivonia trialists) trenchantly wrote: 'Firstly it gave an opportunity to the rank and file of the ANC membership to be involved in a political way in the struggle against oppression ... Secondly, the people realised that the way to freedom passed through jail. Thirdly, the campaign inculcated the idea and spirit of sacrifice of personal interest for the public good. Fourthly, out of the campaign came a disciplined volunteer corps of men and women who gave unstintingly of their time and energy without remuneration in order to build and strengthen the ANC. And finally, the Defiance Campaign put an end to the era of deputations to and pleading with the government.' The citadel of white power had been shaken.

In August 1952, the police, using their powers under the Suppression of Communism Act, arrested many Congress leaders, including Nelson Mandela, Walter Sisulu, Nana Sita, Dr Yusuf Dadoo, Nthato Motlana and the Cachalia brothers, Yusuf and Molvi. They were charged with leading a campaign to change the political situation in the country through unconstitutional and illegal methods, and all 20 defendants were finally found guilty and sentenced to nine months imprisonment with hard labour, suspended for three years. More ominous for the Congress Movement was that the judgement created a new category of offenders, namely 'Statutory Communists'.

At an underground conference held in 1953, the CPSA elected a new CC. Moses Kotane was elected General-Secretary and Dr Dadoo a member of its CC. The CPSA was also renamed the SACP. Its leadership – which included Bram Fischer, Joe Slovo and Ruth First, Michael and Ray Harmel, Rusty and Hilda Bernstein, Rica and Jack Hodgson, and Ben and Mary Turok – represented a potent intellectual strain that helped to educate me about what was later to be termed 'colonialism of a special type'. This related to the specific features and conditions of the racial character of South African settler colonialism and the dialectical relationship between the national and class struggles. It was only several years later, however, that I began fully appreciating the political and ideological significance of this concept.

It was always exciting to listen to the leadership of the SACP discussing the struggle in general, but also their delving into the dialectical nature of national and class struggles. The point is that leading communists correctly understood the dangers of sectarianism and factionalism and accepted the critical role of the ANC in helping to transcend such divisions. In a non-dogmatic manner, they explained the differences between progressive nationalism and reactionary nationalism. As such, they argued that the SACP had a crucial role to play in using the tools of Marxism-Leninism to give progressive content to the National Democratic Revolution (NDR). In this regard, personalities such as Ben Turok, Rusty Bernstein and Michael Harmel were important catalysts in developing my understanding of Marxism-Leninism and the complex interplay of dialectics in a society such as ours.

The Congress of the People

In the aftermath of the Defiance Campaign, there was growing concern in the ANC leadership about how the momentum and enthusiasm generated by the campaign could be sustained. As the National Party tightened its repressive grip on state and society, in August 1953 at a provincial conference of the ANC, Professor ZK Matthews proposed a broadly representative national convention to consider issues and problems of national importance. This would include drawing up a Freedom Charter that would chart the path for a democratic South Africa. The idea and concept were fully accepted and endorsed at the ANC Annual Conference in September of that year. This was followed by a highly significant gathering in Durban in March 1954 when executive members of the ANC, the Indian Congress, the Congress of Democrats and the CPC gathered to take forward plans for a national convention. They crucially decided to establish a National Action Council for the Congress of the People, made up of eight delegates from each organisation that endorsed and supported the Congress of the People.

Besides provincial committees, which were modelled on the council's membership, the motor force would be a massive army of 'Freedom Volunteers'. They would become the foot soldiers in promoting popular appeal for the congress and collecting demands that would form the basis of the Freedom Charter. Literature for this auspicious occasion was specifically developed for different racial, ethnic, religious and occupational groups and was widely distributed. The final phase would be the election of delegates from every urban and rural locality in South Africa who would come together to assist in formulating and drafting the Charter as the metaphorical voice of the people.

In similar fashion to the Defiance Campaign, I became actively involved in the preparations for the historic Congress of the People, which took place in June 1955 in Kliptown, a township south of Johannesburg. Once again, I was part of the team that put up posters, wrote slogans on walls and distributed leaflets. I also accompanied more senior comrades who went house to house canvassing people's demands so that these could be incorporated into the final document of the Congress of the People. It was a remarkable and historic process and without precedent among liberation movements anywhere in the world at that time.

Indeed, we were creating a people-driven Freedom Charter, which was an extraordinary document in itself, calling for a democratic, non-racial, non-sexist and united South Africa. It also situated our struggle in the context of the organic linkages we shared with the African continent and progressive forces throughout the world. The demands in the Freedom Charter, so lyrically expressed, thus reflected the aspirations of millions of South Africans, and its contents have guided all major ANC policies since. The normative elements of the Charter form the bedrock of our Constitution and the basis of much of our public policy today.

The memorable Congress of the People was attended by thousands of delegates from all over the country. They included my parents, my brother Essop and many of my comrades from the TIYC. In one of my moments of monumental folly, I decided not to attend this historic gathering and was severely criticised for doing so. I had inexplicably acted in an apolitical and spontaneous manner and had made a decision that I regretted throughout my life.

The 1956 Treason Trial

Following the successes and achievements of the Congress of the People, it was hardly surprising that our leadership would suffer high-handed reprisals at the hands of the apartheid regime. This occurred with military precision in early December 1956 when 160 senior leaders representing all national groups, classes and religions throughout the country were summarily arrested and put on trial for treason. The main charge involved the active participation of the arrested leaders in the campaign to draw up the Freedom Charter. But if the regime had intended to use this as a show of force to intimidate Congress leaders, they miscalculated badly. As Chief Luthuli commented: 'One thing stood out: the resistance has long since ceased to be a matter of race. It is not the dark skin against the light but a loose confederation of people of all classes, creeds and colours, lined up against adherents of the Master Race and the injustice it lives by.'

Leaders who had been banned and separated for years were now suddenly able to rekindle old friendships and develop new ones in The Fort, the Johannesburg prison where they were held. It also enabled the establishment of a Joint Executive of the Congresses. When the trial opened, thousands of people gathered at the Drill Hall and it was exciting to be part of the demonstrations that took place. The strains of 'Nkosi Sikele' iAfrika' defiantly reverberated throughout the Johannesburg city centre even while the police attacked the demonstrators. The treason trialists joked that the prosecution was unimpressive and was intent on killing them with boredom.

The preparatory hearings for the trial lasted months and before the prosecution could even mount its case, charges were withdrawn against 73 of the 160 accused. The actual trial, involving 90 leaders, started in August 1958. The defence was led by a highly competent and senior team made up of Vernon Berrangé, Bram Fischer, Issie Maisels and Sydney Kentridge. They were truly outstanding and, consequently, the three judges withdrew one of the two charges under the Suppression of Communism Act. In October the prosecution was forced to withdraw the entire indictment and two months later the state announced that the trial would proceed only against 30 of the accused. In August 1959, two years and nine months after the arrests, the trial of the 30 leaders started in Pretoria.

It was interrupted on 21 March 1960 by the massacre at Sharpeville near Johannesburg, which left 67 people dead and 186 severely wounded, many of them shot in the back. The police had opened fire on Africans during a campaign that had been launched by the Pan Africanist Congress (PAC), which had broken away from the ANC in 1959, against tha pass laws. As protests across the country mounted and the international community expressed its dismay, the government reacted viciously: it declared a state of emergency, banned the ANC and PAC and rounded up more than 15 000 individuals.

Meanwhile the Treason Trial continued in the vortex of this tense at-mosphere, with Nelson Mandela and Duma Nokwe taking charge of the defence case. Finally, on 29 March 1961 the accused were found not guilty. I was one of the hundreds of Congress supporters who had gone to Pretoria to await the verdict, and when it was announced there was jubilant singing and dancing all round. The unexpected and humiliating defeat for the regime closed another chapter in our struggle. From that day onwards, the regime would never again allow independent judges to conduct any major political trial. All the judges agreed that the state had failed to prove that the ANC or the Freedom Charter were communist-inspired. The final affront to the government was Justice Frans Rumpff's opinion: 'On all the evidence presented to this court and on our findings of fact, it is impossible for this court to come to the conclusion that the African National Congress has acquired or adopted a policy to overthrow the state by violence, that is, in the sense that the masses had to be prepared or conditioned to commit direct acts of violence against the state.'

The Treason Trial was again an important opportunity for me to get to know our leaders, not only from the Transvaal, but from other parts of the country, and I was privileged to interact with many of them. Chief Albert Luthuli spent a lot of time in Orient House and so did other leaders from Durban, such as Ismail Meer and Chota Motala. Moreover, the trial helped me develop a better understanding of the importance and contribution of every section of the community to our struggle. This was consistent with much of the thinking at the time since many ANC leaders, including Mandela and Tambo, commented that the Treason Trial was another experience that convinced them of the commitment of other minority groups to the struggle and their willingness to make great sacrifices. The trial also galvanised the international anti-apartheid movement, which, for example, gave birth to the Defence and Aid Fund that in later years played a major role in funding defence lawyers and supporting political prisoners and their families.

Central Indian High School – The 'Congress School'

When the National Party came to power in 1948, they campaigned on a policy of *swart en rooi gevaar* ('black and red danger'), which provided the political rationale to entrench the apartheid system as never before. Among the catalogue of repressive laws was the Group Areas Act, and the National Party government put extreme pressure on Indians to locate to areas reserved for them and to move out of those designated as 'white areas'. One of the ploys was to limit the entry of students in Indian high schools in urban areas and thus force them to attend schools in Lenasia, which was the newly designated Indian Group Area approximately 30 kilometres from the city centre.

A year after completing primary school, we attended the Booysens School, which was previously a white school and had since remained unoccupied. Within a year of settling down there, we were instructed that the school would be closed immediately and that we had to move to a school in Lenasia. Many parents succumbed to government pressure and relocated. But in defiance, the Congress Movement decided to resist this new form of social engineering, which further entrenched apartheid, by establishing the Central Indian High School (CIHS), commonly referred to as the 'Congress School'. Hundreds of Indian pupils, including myself and my brothers, Essop, Nassim and Juned, decided to attend the CIHS in Central Road, Fordsburg. The school became the 'finishing school' for our political development and an important terrain of struggle.

Many of our teachers were leaders in the ANC, TIC and the Congress of Democrats. They included prominent figures such as Duma Nokwe, Alfred Hutchinson, Molly Fischer, Thandary Naicker and Molly Anderson. Michael Harmel, a leader of the then-banned Communist Party and still active in the Congress of Democrats, was the first principal. Because of the presence of such high-profile movement leaders, the school was subjected to constant police raids and our schooling was continuously interrupted, with violent confrontations avoided only because of the timely interventions of our teachers and student leaders.

The school infrastructure was sparse and austere. We had no science laboratories or equipment, and textbooks were in short supply. Classrooms were overcrowded, the buildings too hot in summer and too cold in winter, and there were no recreational facilities. These shortcomings, however, were more than compensated for by the commitment and dedication of our teachers. Many of us also understood that we were attending a 'school of resistance' and did not, therefore, expect a 'normal' education. Much of the lessons in History, Geography, English and Afrikaans were given within a political context, which meant that we were receiving different interpretations of standard textbooks compared to students at government schools.

Alfred Hutchinson, a gifted writer, was our English teacher. I recall how he used the literature textbooks to frame the discourse on the political situation in South Africa and Africa, and from this drew appropriate lessons for our struggle. Our Afrikaans teacher was Molly Fischer, and whenever she became exasperated with us for not fully grasping her Afrikaans lessons, she jokingly told us in Afrikaans that her task was like throwing 'pearls to swines', adding that 'alles sal reg kom – jy sal sien' ('all will be well – you will see'). To which we replied, 'die agter os kom ook in die kraal' ('the last ox also comes into the pen').

Hutchinson and Molly Anderson, another English teacher, had an affair across the colour line, and because of the lunacy of the Immorality Act, Hutchinson escaped to Ghana and Molly later joined him in exile there. I was saddened to learn of their sudden departure because I had grown close to both and found their friendship and advice invaluable.

The school essentially survived on contributions from parents and other donations. However, many parents were indigent and could not afford to pay fees and, consequently, many of our teachers often had to survive without monthly salaries. It helped a great deal that the school came rent-free because the property belonged to the Hindu community. As such, Congress managed to sustain the school for many years.

Ongoing police harassment and the force of the Group Areas Act, however, made it difficult for many of the ANC and Congress leaders to continue teaching at the school; and when I was in Standard 9 (today's Grade 11), Congress was informed that the school had to find new premises. It was subsequently relocated to a property adjacent to the Newtown mosque in the same area, but the conditions were even worse and more limited than those at the Central Road premises. However, we persisted with both our political and formal education, and in the end I managed to pass my matric exams. It was not a good pass, but at least politically I had become more mature, more tempered in the struggle and, indeed, had made many political friends, both among teachers and students.

By all accounts, the CIHS can be regarded as a Congress Movement success story in that it created a better-developed and more conscious political cadre for the struggle. I and many other students who were products of the school bear eloquent testimony to this proud record. Many of the school's students later went on to become leading political, academic and professional leaders, both in South Africa and abroad. In between the regimen at CIHS, we found time for sport, especially soccer, since it would allow us to enter African and coloured townships without arousing suspicion. I was a founding member of our club Dynamos, named after the famous Prague Dynamos football club, which had visited South Africa. Our formal attire of blue blazers and blue soccer kit was adorned with a badge depicting a red globe encircled by a Sputnik, the first Soviet-launched lunar spacecraft – our attempt at conveying a message that the world was going to be socialist. I was the goalkeeper and was initially nicknamed 'Bones' because of my thin legs. I later acquired the nickname 'Dagga' (marijuana) because my droopy eyes gave the impression of always being under the drug's euphoric influence. Ironically, this nickname even found its way into my banning order! Dynamos was particularly popular in the Indian community and years later, with the recruitment of non-Indian players, the club became an important base for the development of non-racial professional soccer in South Africa.

University studies

After completing matric, I won a university scholarship from the Kholvad Madressa, named after the village in India from where my grandfather, father, mother and other leading members of our community had originated. As fate would have it, I happened to be among the last black students allowed to enrol and study at Wits, which was set to become a predominantly white institution.

The story of my studies at Wits exposes the absurdity of our society. On completing matric, some of my friends who were already at Wits reminded me that my education had been more political than academic, and hence they advised that it would be more realistic for me to choose Afrikaans over English as a major. I was told that the main reason for this choice was that a certain Professor PJ Nienaber, who taught first-year Afrikaans, was a racist. In order to have as little contact with black students as possible, he refrained from asking them any questions in class and simply passed everyone – irrespective of how well or poorly they performed. I took their advice and chose Afrikaans as my major and passed my first year without much effort.

My second year proved to be both a fantastic and challenging experience. Among others, I was taught by Professor NP van Wyk Louw, one of the most outstanding Afrikaner literary giants of our time. I learnt much about Afrikaans literature and history from him. (As a matter of fact, starting with the Afrikaner group in Dakar, Senegal, in July 1987, but also in other subsequent meetings, I used every opportunity to speak Afrikaans – admittedly poorly because I had had little need to speak much Afrikaans in exile.)

The racial divisions that characterised the larger society were replicated at Wits. Black students, for instance, could not use the university's sporting and other recreational facilities. And when we converged in one section of the canteen, the majority of white students – except for some Jewish students – ignored us. I was equally amused and angered that even at a 'liberal university' such as Wits, black students would find themselves confined to specific areas of the canteen and were prevented from participating in the myriad sporting, cultural and social activities. Wits had a beautiful and inviting swimming pool outside the main library but we were not permitted to use it. The best we could do was sit on the lawn and observe fellow students enjoying their swim. We did, nevertheless, attend multiracial parties in the white suburbs. The police were extremely hostile to these social gatherings because they were concerned that the Immorality Act forbidding relations across colour lines could be violated.

It was also at Wits that I came of age in appreciating the effects of indulging in alcohol. Illegal shebeens abounded near the famous 'Red Square' in the Indian area of Fordsburg. (This was where many Congress meetings and demonstrations took place and where, many years later, Indian traders were moved under the Group Areas Act. The historic square became an 'Indian Bazaar', and is known today as the Oriental Plaza.) One Friday night we made our way to one of the shebeens and ordered a bottle of Commando brandy, which we had seen in adverts. We naively filled our glasses to the brim, only to have the police arrive in an unexpected raid. In order to evade arrest, we downed our drinks – and I became so violently ill that I had to rush to the back yard in embarrassment. We later learnt that the police were not conducting a raid, but in fact collecting bribe money and that many problems with the police could be resolved 'under the table'. This was my initiation into the world of illegal drinking and police corruption, albeit unceremoniously.

At this time the supporters of the PAC at Wits were particularly vocal and active. PAC leader Robert Sobukwe was my Zulu lecturer, and it was interesting to experience how he used his lectures to convey subtle and nuanced political messages. With a sense of *déjà vu*, it felt as if my CIHS experiences were being repeated at Wits, and the campus became a terrain of struggle between Congress and the PAC. Fortunately, there was no physical violence, but lots of noisy arguments and debates.

At Wits, I was also one of the founding members of the Human Rights Committee along with Gerard Ludi. Besides being quite active in the Congress of Democrats, Ludi was part of our social circle and would often accompany us to multiracial parties in the suburbs, which came under the watchful attention of the Special Branch. Our committee activities, of course, also came under the scrutiny of the security police and our members were constantly harassed. As it turned out, Ludi was the Special Branch informer 007, recruited when he was at Wits. In this highly charged social and political environment and against the discriminatory odds, I completed my Bachelor of Arts degree at the age of 23, majoring in Sociology and Afrikaans.

The early 1960s – the tide turns

When it comes to the Sharpeville massacre of March 1960, it is important to recall essential facts that have not only been contested over the years, but may also be subject to specious interpretation. At its 1959 congress, the ANC decided to launch a massive anti-pass campaign. The PAC – in a rather opportunistic move and without much preparation, organisation or discussion – subsequently decided to launch its own anti-pass campaign in order to disrupt and pre-empt the better-organised ANC campaign. While the PAC turnouts in many parts of the country were less than impressive, there was a relatively big march to the police station in Sharpeville – a stand that was met with a murderous and brutal ending at the hands of the police.

The PAC did not fully appreciate the consequences of its precipitate action. Leader Robert Sobukwe was arrested and sentenced to three years' imprisonment, as were many other PAC cadres. Yet the PAC continued to build its movement on a narrow and sectarian Africanist approach to politics. The sad irony, as is well known, was that the PAC broke away from the ANC. Some of its leading figures thus had their roots in the Congress Movement, yet they articulated very anti-Congress positions in mobilising on behalf of the PAC.

Above all this, Sharpeville was a turning point, both nationally and internationally. It galvanised the anti-apartheid forces abroad and, at the same time, led the ANC to call for a nationwide pass-burning campaign led by leading figures, such as Luthuli in Durban and Mandela in Johannesburg. The pass was the most hated symbol of apartheid and the ANC campaign was successful insofar as it brought out thousands of people across the country in protest to publicly burn passes.

The response of the National Party was swift and fierce. It gave notice that non-violent mass-militant action would not be tolerated; a state of emergency was declared in the aftermath of the Sharpeville massacre and scores of leaders from across the country were arrested and detained for long periods of time. Most tellingly, both the ANC and PAC were banned on 30 March 1960.

In September, the ANC Executive met secretly and decided to continue the struggle underground. As a result, ANC structures had to be changed in order to meet these new realities and a number of unpopular moves had to be made, one of which was the disbanding of the Youth League and the Women's League. Quite critically, the organisation had not sufficiently prepared for its banning and had, therefore, not planned the underground phase in sufficient detail. Some embryonic structures had, however, been put in place, largely because leaders such as Nelson Mandela, Govan Mbeki, Walter Sisulu, Ahmed Kathrada and Joe Slovo had anticipated the banning and stressed the importance of preparing to work underground.

Mandela had been banned again and again under the Suppression of the Communism Act, but his banning order was set to expire in 1961. This coincided with the calling of an All-In African Conference in Pietermaritzburg on 25 March 1961, a conference attended by 1 400 delegates from all over the country and representing an estimated 150 political, social, professional, cultural, sporting and religious organisations. The aim was to plan for a national constitutional convention. Mandela was set to be the keynote speaker, his first public speech in five years, but delegates had not been informed. I learnt that when he entered the hall, all hell broke loose. His address was excellent and had a major impact on the delegates. It was clear from the speeches, including that of Mandela, that our leaders were openly coming to the conclusion that non-violent methods of struggle were being suppressed and that other forms of struggle would have to be considered.

The conference demanded the convening of a national convention of elected representatives to work out a non-racial democratic constitution. As an important initiative to form a united front, this gathering made a huge impact on political organisations and had a profound effect on political thinking in South Africa generally. A National Action Council was thus elected, with Mandela as secretary. The Conference resolved that if the regime refused to call such a convention, a three-day strike would be organised on 29 May 1961, the same day South Africa was to be declared a republic. Once again the PAC played a negative, counter-revolutionary role. The PAC's tactic was to sabotage this important initiative and at the last minute they withdrew from the convention.

The reaction of the Verwoerd regime to the call for a three-day strike was to mobilise the army; all meetings were banned and over 10 000 people were arrested. And yet, despite the unprecedented reign of terror, almost half of all workers in Johannesburg went on strike, although the response in the other major centres was not as encouraging.

Mandela, in a briefing to the foreign media, stated: 'If the government's reaction is to crush by naked force our non-violent struggle, we will have to reconsider our tactics. In my mind we are closing a chapter on this question of a non-violent policy.'

The decision to embark on an armed struggle was not an easy one, nor did it remain uncontested. The SACP, which had been operating underground for some time, had started discussing on the possibilities of an armed struggle as early as 1960. I learnt while in exile that Moses Kotane and Bram Fischer were opposed to the idea. However, once the decision had been made, a National High Command was created, consisting of Sisulu, Mandela, Slovo and Raymond Mhlaba. Regional High Commands were established in Port Elizabeth, Johannesburg, Durban and Cape Town, and to complement the High Command, Mandela and other leading members of the movement – including Govan Mbeki, Ahmed Kathrada, Walter Sisulu and Joe Slovo – formed an underground High-Command structure that set up headquarters on Lilliesleaf Farm in Rivonia, Johannesburg.

In 1961 the country was rocked by acts of sabotage and the ANC announced through leaflets and radio broadcasts that it had adopted armed struggle, which would be conducted by its armed wing Umkhonto weSizwe (MK). It called on Congress members to join this new manifestation of the struggle.

A manifesto declared: 'We, of Umkhonto we Sizwe have sought – as the liberation movement has sought – to achieve liberation without bloodshed and civil clashes. We hope, even at this late hour, that our first actions will awaken everyone to the realisation of the disastrous situation to which the Nationalist policy was leading the country ... Our actions are against the Nationalists' preparations for civil war and military rule ... We are working in the best interests of all the people of this country: black, brown and white, whose future and well-being cannot be attained without the overthrow of the Nationalists ... the people's patience is not endless. The time comes in the life of any nation when there remain only two choices: submit or fight. That time has now come to South Africa.'

When we in the TIYC received copies of the manifesto, we discussed its contents and implications and secretly distributed it within our communities. It was a sound explanation of why the armed struggle had been adopted, while also emphasising the non-racial aspect of this stage of our struggle.

In 1960 Oliver Tambo was instructed to leave South Africa and to set up ANC offices abroad. The first offices opened in London and Dar es Salaam with the objective of mobilising political, economic and military support. Dr Dadoo of the SACP also went into exile, his mandate being to win support from the Soviet Union, other socialist countries and the communist parties of Western Europe.

Mandela then left South Africa 'illegally' in 1962 to attend a summit in Addis Ababa of the Pan-African Freedom Movement of East, Central, and South Africa (PAFMECSA), the precursor of the OAU, which was founded in 1963. Mandela was accompanied by Oliver Tambo and Robert Resha and strongly urged African countries to isolate apartheid South Africa and to mobilise world opinion by imposing sanctions on the regime. For this purpose, Tambo was appointed to the Coordinating Freedom Council, the governing body of PAFMECSA. Mandela also called for support for the armed struggle, and after the summit he visited Algeria and Morocco where he received military training.

All these events were taking place in the heyday of decolonisation and an ascendant African nationalism. Against this backdrop, the PAC fully exploited the opportunity to distort the South African struggle, and the ANC delegation to PAFMECSA was confronted with the argument that the PAC was the only genuine African nationalist movement in South Africa, as opposed to the ANC, which was dominated by minorities and communists. This tension continued to bedevil any attempts to develop a working rapprochement between the two organisations, both at home and abroad.

By 1962, the ANC leadership conceded that the sabotage campaign had not been as effective as they had anticipated, largely because the military units did not have quality equipment to carry out such actions. Govan Mbeki and Joe Slovo were then asked to draw up a plan for the next phase of the armed struggle and, in terms of this mandate, they produced a six-page draft document for Operation Mayibuye, which provided a framework for launching guerrilla operations and sparking a mass uprising against the government. The High Command agreed to this ambitious blueprint and it was submitted to the joint leadership of the SACP and the ANC. But it was only in exile that I learnt that there were serious disagreements about whether the document was ever officially adopted by either.

In fact, Bram Fischer provided an acerbic opinion on this matter at his trial. He stated that Operation Mayibuye was 'a complete departure from the ideas on which Umkhonto had been founded. I was totally opposed to the whole idea ... It was a plan that was politically wholly incorrect and wholly unsuited to the situation in South Africa and was totally im-practicable ... It could have achieved nothing but disaster ... an entirely unrealistic brain child of some youthful and adventurous imagination. It was a plan which had not even been approved by Umkhonto ... and we as the CC certainly expressed our complete disapproval ...'

As the iron fist of apartheid-style terror took its toll, far too many people started visiting the Lilliesleaf underground headquarters and this had serious security implications. Many cadres were being tortured in detention and it was simply a matter of time before someone would crack and disclose the location of the underground headquarters. Indeed, short-ly before the raid on Lilliesleaf a decision had been taken to vacate the place – but the precaution proved too late, and the movement suffered one of its worst setbacks since the ANC was formed in 1912, when the police deftly raided the farm on 11 July 1963. In one fell swoop, they arrested six key ANC leaders, namely Govan Mbeki, Walter Sisulu, Raymond Mhlaba, Rusty Bernstein, Ahmed Kathrada and Bob Hepple. More arrests followed the raid, including that of Denis Goldberg, Harold Wolpe and Arthur Goldreich, as well as many other activists at different levels and from across the country. They included my friends Indres Naidoo, Shirish Nanabhay, Reggie Vandeyar, Isu Chiba, Abdulhay Jassat and Mosie Moolla – some of the first South Africans of Indian origin in the Transvaal to be arrested. As a result, the Congress Alliance structures were totally decimated and hundreds of our leaders and activists were imprisoned.

After 90 days in solitary confinement, the Rivonia trialists were finally charged on 6 October 1963, with Mandela joining them as co-accused. He had already been convicted for leaving the country illegally. Following a lengthy trial, on 11 July 1964 all the accused were sentenced to life imprisonment. However, by bribing prison officials at Marshall Square and through clever disguises, Wolpe, Goldreich, Jassat and Moolla made a daring escape and fled into exile.

The denouement of this chapter was the banning order of both my brother Essop and I under the Suppression of Communism Act in January 1964. The order was very restrictive. It meant that we could not be members of any political organisation; we could not enter any educational or industrial institution; we could not be in crowds of more than two; we could not communicate with each other; anything we wrote could not be communicated; and we could not participate in any political, educational, cultural, social or sporting activities. Of course, we used various methods to circumvent the banning orders, but for all intents and purposes – and given the total repression unleashed by the National Party – it was becoming increasingly difficult to sustain any meaningful political or any other activity. We were not even in a condition to earn a living.

One of the saddest moments of my life was when I heard of the death of Bram's wife, Molly Fischer, in a car accident near Ventersburg in the Free State. Essop and I applied for the easing of our banning restrictions so that we could attend her funeral, but this request was rejected.

And so, even in these early years, it was becoming clear that my life and that of so many others within the context of South Africa at the time was inextricably linked to the developments taking place around me – in my home, on the streets and within the broader political arena. With this realisation came a growing sense of frustration, a loathing of the increasingly apparent injustice of life here, in this country. The big question then was, what next?

Chapter 2

The exile years

All resistance was effectively destroyed in the wake of the outlawing of the ANC, the arrest of the Rivonia leaders and suppression of all other layers of the ANC underground structures. This state of affairs was exacerbated by the vicious onslaught against all opposition and forms of protest by the apartheid system. Given the ruthless restrictions of our banning orders, in 1964 Advocate Ismail Mohammed (who became the first Judge President after 1994) negotiated for Essop and I to leave South Africa on 'exit' permits. Helen Suzman, as the lone representative of the Progressive Party in Parliament, also brought pressure to bear on the regime to grant us exit permits so that we could join our father in London and complete our studies in the UK.

The night before we left, in late November 1964, we daringly defied our banning orders and decided to paint the town red with a few close friends. We made our way from one shebeen to the next – although the occasion was tinged with sadness since we were filled with trepidation, uncertainty and uneasiness. I had no idea when and if I would ever see my family again: my mother Amina and three brothers Ismail, Nassim and Juned; but also all my friends and, indeed, the country. But the decision had been made and Essop and I were on our way into the unknown world of exile.

So, with the slogan 'Freedom in our lifetime' ringing in my ears, I left South Africa, convincing myself that it would be just a matter of time before I returned to continue the struggle. Did I really believe this or was I merely rationalising my passage into exile? Even while waiting for the plane to take off, I agonised about our decision to leave and whether we were deserting the people and the struggle at such a crucial moment in our history. But given the harsh political realities that existed then, I took some comfort in the thought that this was a temporary departure and that, after completing my studies, I would return to the country to continue the struggle.

I had never before been out of South Africa, or on an airplane for that matter. I was anxious, frightened, relieved and excited at the same time. In those days, black passengers had to sit at the back of the plane, and as I took my seat I recalled the words of the Afro-American civil rights song 'Back of the Bus'. When we landed in London, it was miserably wet and cold. Later we learnt that it was the worst weather experienced in decades in the UK. As we disembarked, reluctantly carrying the blankets my mother had insisted that we take to protect us from the cold weather, I still wrestled ambivalently with my decision to leave and whether it was the right move. Moreover, I began to wonder how I would survive in such intemperate weather conditions.

As we passed through immigration, I was relieved to see my father. It was a strange experience to be travelling on the London tube with whites and blacks together. We went to a flat in Clapham Common, which was to be our home for a few months and one we shared with our relatives, the Bhyats (Hamid, Zaibie and their three children, Farouk, Zaheer and Shameem), and their friend Iqbal Moola. Imagine nine of us squeezed into one flat! Later we were joined by Dasoo and Salie Joseph, old friends and Indian Congress activists, who stayed in the flat below. Bennie Bunsee, who had left the congress to join the PAC, lived in the flat above. Being a 'political house' seemed to make exile more tolerable.

Over the next few days we met with Dr Dadoo and Barney Desai, old family friends and leaders of the TIC and SAIC. It was great to see familiar faces, reminisce about old times and discuss future plans. I was, however, disappointed that in exile 'Uncle' Barney had decided to join the PAC, of whose record in the struggle I was extremely critical.

University College of London

Dr Dadoo arranged for us to meet Michael Harmel, who had been our principal at CIHS and a leader of the SACP. Harmel introduced Essop and me to his contacts, who graciously assisted us with enrolling at university and securing scholarships. Essop went on to do a course in International Relations at the University College of London (UCL) before joining Thabo Mbeki at Sussex University, where he completed his Master's and PhD degrees. I decided to study law and was fortunate to be accepted at UCL months after the course had commenced.

My choice of law needs some explaining. When I was growing up, my parents, like many other parents in our community, insisted that our first priority should be to become doctors; if that failed, then lawyers and, lastly, teachers. With hindsight, my decision to study law was a mistake. I soon discovered that I was not suited to the discipline and rote learning required for a law degree. So it was that in 1966 I decided to give up my attempted career in law, enrolled for the UCL diploma course in International Relations, which I thoroughly enjoyed, and passed, excelling even. The course further enhanced my understanding of international political, economic and social developments that were having such a profound impact on the 1960s environment. UCL was also a good platform from which to participate in the protest activities of that period. I addressed many student meetings and helped form anti-apartheid groups on several campuses. The London School of Economics, where my friend and comrade Ronnie Kasrils was a student activist, was seen as a 'hotbed' of revolution.

Sussex University

In 1967, after completing my diploma course at UCL, I went to Sussex University to read for a Master's degree in International Relations. By that time Thabo Mbeki and other South Africans who had been politically active at Sussex University had left, but the university continued to be a terrain of political activity, albeit not to the same degree as before. I took an active part in political activities on campus and travelled to London on weekends to attend ANC YSS meetings. Rallies and demonstrations took place on issues concerning a broad spectrum of African countries, among them South Africa, Namibia, Zimbabwe, Angola, Mozambique, Guinea Bissau, Cape Verde and further afield. I also became involved in demonstrations and meetings in solidarity with struggles in Vietnam, Brazil, Argentina, Chile, Palestine, Iran and Iraq. This heady exposure made for an exciting period of political activism and learning while I was also trying to complete my studies. I did, however, manage to complete my Master's degree in 1968, with a thesis on the Non-Aligned Movement (NAM).

During my time at Sussex, I shared a large flat on the Brighton beachfront with Essop, Philippa Ingram and Peter Lawrence, all of whom were active in the politics of the time and had been close friends with Thabo Mbeki when he was at Sussex. I was familiar with many of the Sussex crowd but always felt that, as a latecomer, I had missed the 'seminal moment' and was not part of the 'in-crowd'.

Sussex was a new 'pink-brick' university that was seen as an alternative to the more elite universities of Oxford and Cambridge (as opposed to the old established 'red-brick' alternatives like Manchester and Bristol). Trends in Marxism, Leninism and Trotskyism exercised a strong influence at Sussex. In particular, groups representing various versions of Trotskyism and anarchism were very active on campus and we were constantly having heated arguments with them. The ultra-left, most notably the Trotskyites and the Maoists, rejected the concept of a National Democratic Revolution

(NDR). They were intellectually well prepared and constantly admonished us for our conduct within the struggle, and we were often referred to as 'the black bourgeoisie'. This was rather ironic, because I hardly came from a middle class or bourgeois background – while many of them came from very rich families. I suppose they could claim that they were committing 'class suicide'.

I often asked why they continued to lecture and admonish us about the maturing socialist revolution in South Africa and elsewhere in Africa – which they accused us of betraying – and yet I saw no signs of them creating conditions for a socialist revolution in the advanced industrial countries, including the UK. We were living in an era when capitalism in many industrialised countries was in a serious crisis, and reaction and counter-revolution were gathering apace in the UK and other Western countries. It amused me that, while many 'leftists' had good textbook and theoretical knowledge of 'left' politics, they were unable to relate theory to practice; they were content to 'export revolution' and to engage in debates, but were lacking in praxis. I was fond of referring to this phenomenon as 'left intellectual imperialism'.

We also had several discussions on the 'betrayal of socialism' in the Soviet Union and the other socialist countries. At the age of 27 I was a confirmed and uncritical supporter of socialist countries without any real grounding in the distortions and serious problems that had emerged in them. Moreover, socialist countries were supporting national independence struggles in Africa and elsewhere. It was only after Leonid Brezhnev's denunciation of Stalinism and the impact this had on socialist discourse that some concerns were raised about developments in the socialist countries. However, I continue to believe that tremendous progress had been made in Russia after the 1917 revolution, as manifested in fields such as housing, health, education, culture and job creation. The Soviet Union and other socialist countries were also an important counter-weight to the political and economic global dominance of the United States and North Atlantic Treaty Organisation (NATO).

I remain convinced that the imperialist invasion of Russia after the 1917 revolution, together with the 'containment' and 'rolling back of communism', both contributed to and exacerbated the negative aspects of Stalinism, thereby aggravating the contradictions of the Soviet Union and other socialist countries. These perspectives helped to hone my own intellectual development during those years. I learnt the importance of rejecting dogmatism, avoiding absolute positions and to be constructively critical and to always look for alternative information to that presented by the mass media. Already then, I came to appreciate the reality that the media are not neutral, objective or above class contradictions.

Another important event in my political development was the World Youth Festival held in Sofia, Bulgaria, in 1968. I was thrilled that I was nominated to be part of the ANC Youth delegation, but to qualify one had to participate in the choir. This was a traumatic experience for me, largely because I could neither sing nor remember lyrics. After weeks of rehearsals, the choir master refused to continue unless Abdul Bham, another delegate, and I were removed. This summary dismissal took me by surprise because I had always mimed my way through rehearsals – but, belatedly, I realised that I had made the terrible mistake of standing next to Abdul, who was an even worse chorister than me. Eventually it was decided that we both could stay in the delegation provided that we were not in the choir, but contributed to political preparations instead.

It was an exciting and happy moment for all when the London contingent met with the rest of the ANC Youth delegation in Bulgaria. Old friendships were renewed and new friendships forged. This was my first experience of meeting ANC Youth and youth of other nationalities from so many other countries. Our excitement, however, was shattered at our first delegation meeting when members of the ANC Youth delegation from the Soviet Union challenged the leadership of Johnny Makhathini as head of the delegation because, they argued, he had not been democratically elected and they did not consider him to be 'left'. After hours of intense and heated discussions, mediated by Thabo Mbeki, they finally accepted Makhathini's leadership. Our delegation participated actively in many of the political commissions, including – as I recall – one of our comrades explaining the importance of the armed struggle and the AK-47 to a commission on science and technology. The best moments, however, were when the South Africans gathered in their rooms in the evenings, drinking and vociferously singing freedom songs and loudly exchanging stories about home and exile.

A few days into the conference each delegation had to choose a few people to go on an excursion. To get out of the conference room, I volunteered enthusiastically. We were taken by buses to a mountain and informed that we would have 'great fun' walking to the top! This was not what my comrades and I had bargained for, but there was nothing we could do. We started drinking, only to be approached by Bulgarians who advised us of the dangers of drinking on a mountain walk. I was also confused that one of our comrades had brought an ANC flag, which we had to carry to the top of the mountain. I do not know what the other delegates thought of this spectacle, but after several arduous and tortuous hours we finally reached the summit – only to be confronted by a storm that seemed to come from nowhere and we had to scramble back down the mountain to find shelter.

To this day, it remains a mystery how we all managed to reach the foothills safely. Needless to say, that was the end of my mountaineering days.

Evolving in 'leftist' politics

Questions persisted about the most appropriate relationship between the ANC, the SACP and other parts of the Congress Alliance. There were also issues, raised by Chris Hani and other members of MK, about the nature and effectiveness of the leadership of the ANC in exile. In the early 1960s there was a growing chorus of criticism levelled at the leadership, its style of living and its failure to advance the armed struggle. But one of the most controversial matters was opening ANC membership to minorities of whites, Indians and coloureds who were allowed to join MK but not the ANC itself. This went to the heart of the cleavages between those who espoused a narrow African nationalism – including some members of the SACP – and those who were more committed to the non-racial ethos of the ANC as the mortar that held the Congress Movement together.

The urgency of addressing these matters led squarely to the ANC's Morogoro Conference in Tanzania in April 1969. The conference made an important strategic decision that all the ANC's structures below its NEC should be open to all South Africans, irrespective of race, ethnicity or religion. Henceforth, and for the first time in the organisation's history, we could now be members not only of the ANC YSS but of other structures as well, despite opposition from chauvinist Africanists led by the 'Gang of Eight', who later resigned from the ANC. They objected to the 1969 Morogoro decisions and maintained that the ANC had been hijacked by communists, Indians and whites. It was difficult for me to understand and accept that prominent and respected leaders such as Robert Resha and the cousins Ambrose and Tennyson Makiwane could be such opportunists and take such reactionary political positions. For me, the Morogoro decision was an affirmation of my earlier experiences of the ANC as a genuinely non-racial organisation that had mobilised and united all racial, ethnic and religious groupings.

This affirmation had strong roots in the London ANC YSS, where we always ensured that the perspective and philosophy of non-racialism taught to us by the ANC since its formation in 1912 was the vision that drove and underpinned all our activities. I believe this explains why the PAC and its 'narrow African nationalism' failed to garner much support in exile. Indeed, after 1990 when we returned to South Africa, the PAC never gained a foothold among the majority of South Africans. Historically, the ANC had managed to defeat all attempts to split the movement against what seemed insurmountable odds. We were able to defeat such tactics and remain united because of the solid political and ideological foundations built on the consistent non-racial policy frameworks of the ANC and SACP.

In Europe generally and the UK specifically, the 1960s and '70s were decades of unprecedented challenges to authority – typically represented by massive protests against government policies. These challenges manifested in many ways, especially in spawning a subculture of drugs, free sex, gay and lesbian rights, and protest music. More significantly, this was a period of virulent protests throughout Europe against American aggression in Vietnam and South-East Asia. There were also robust campaigns against weapons of mass destruction (organised by the Campaign for Nuclear Disarmament [CND]), as well as a groundswell of protests against South Africa's apartheid regime, the Ian Smith coup in Rhodesia and Portuguese colonialism in Africa.

After my formative and relatively cloistered years in Ferreirastown, I was now caught up in a whirlwind of an entirely different and tumultuous lifestyle. Fortunately for me and my peers, our involvement in the struggle and the discipline imposed on us by the movement saved us from becoming part of the lost exile generation. The experiences of being in Europe over a span of three decades were invaluable in helping to mould me into an activist who was able to deal with the many challenges and adversities of life and, even more crucially, those that arose during the consolidation of democracy in South Africa after 1994.

I met many student activists from Europe, North America, Africa, Asia, the Middle East and Latin America. We had insightful and informative exchanges about our respective struggles for justice and freedom, and these helped me develop a better understanding of how closely our struggles were connected in a normative and political sense. The common 'enemy' binding all of us was imperialism, which ruthlessly exploited the tensions of the Cold War to subvert genuine struggles for national liberation and democracy. The ANC, Mozambique Liberation Front (FRELIMO), South West African People's Organisation (SWAPO), the People's Movement for the Liberation of Angola (MPLA), and Zimbabwe African People's Union (ZAPU) were egregiously labelled as 'pro-Soviet communist fronts' that had to be defeated. On the other hand, the apartheid regime, Portuguese colonialism, reactionary African governments, the military juntas in Latin America and client regimes in the Middle East, such as the Shah of Iran, were regarded as 'anti-communist democratic forces' that had to be protected and supported at all cost. Even at that time, the major powers – the USA, UK and France – were blatantly involved in regime-change activities. My experience overseas had a tremendous influence on me during our democratic transition when we had to deal with country-specific problems. We were criticised, for example, for pursuing 'quiet diplomacy' in Zimbabwe, but the reality was that we were opposing externally defined regime change and seeking a negotiated solution.

The 1960s and '70s saw not only the intensification of anti-apartheid and anti-colonial struggles in Africa, but also the intensification of American aggression in Vietnam. The brutality and inhumanity that were hallmarks of this aggression shocked us all and served as a mobilising tool for a vast majority of people in Europe. This made the Vietnam Solidarity Campaign one of the strongest and most representative solidarity movements at that time. Thabo Mbeki, leader of the ANC YSS in the UK, and my brother Essop represented the YSS on the Vietnam Solidarity Campaign. It managed to mobilise representatives of all political parties into its ranks, including the Labour Party, the Communist Party, Trotskyites, a section of the Liberal Party and even a few members of the Conservative Party (CP). Also joining the campaign were trade unionists, religious leaders, and students, sports and cultural activists.

But contradictions did not bubble far below the surface. The Trotskyites and Maoists, as representative of the ultra-leftist strain of thinking, attacked American imperialism while also attacking the Vietnamese National Liberation Front (NLF). They did so in committee meetings and demonstrations, as well as through their posters and leaflets. One of their slogans was *Hey, hey Ho Chi Minh, how many kids did you kill today?* This was a play on the more popular slogan, *Hey, hey, LBJ* [US president at the time] *how many kids did you kill today?* Their dogmatic emphasis on class struggle meant a total rejection of the relevance of the national liberation struggle.

There was constant wrangling and rivalry between the Trotskyites and Maoists, as well as other supporters of the Vietnamese struggle. The fact that Trotskyites and their ultra-leftist ilk organised on the basis of anti-Sovietism compounded the tensions. We consistently argued that we should be united in our commitment to mobilise international solidarity against American aggression and should not attempt to impose solutions on the Vietnamese people. The ANC YSS played an important role in ensuring that there was a more nuanced approach to the anti-imperialist content of the Vietnam Solidarity Campaign.

We spent many days demonstrating outside the American embassy in Grosvenor Square and, as American aggression intensified, hundreds if not thousands marched from Hyde Park to Grosvenor Square. A significant lesson for me was how the ultra-left operated, especially the International Socialist Party. They were small in membership, but because of their organisational capacity in producing banners, posters and leaflets, they were better able to give an impression of a strong organisation with substantial support.

I will never forget one huge anti-American demonstration. The ANC YSS and other South African exiles were marching behind the ANC flag when the police attacked the demonstrators and tried to grab the ANC flag. Thabo Mbeki, who was holding onto the flag, refused to let go and a policeman punched him, breaking his tooth. He never replaced it. We always joked that his broken tooth remained a symbol of our fight against imperialism, and the unity of the Vietnamese and the South African struggles.

The worst and most blatant example of imperialism at the time was the American-organised coup in Chile in 1973, when the democratically elected government of Salvador Allende was overthrown and the military junta of Augusto Pinochet was installed. We heard of opponents of the junta being systematically kidnapped, rounded up in stadiums, tortured and then just 'disappearing'. Demonstrations by mothers with signs reading 'Where are our children?' were both moving and shocking. There were large numbers of Chilean exiles in Europe and we built strong relations with them. Their music, posters and slogans made a huge impact on South Africans in exile.

One complex and difficult issue was the Irish struggle. The British occupation of Ireland had become more aggressive and ironfisted, and it was clear that continuing repression was leading to even greater violence. While we did not necessarily agree with some of the tactics adopted by the Irish Republican Army (IRA), we were publicly critical of 'state terrorism' meted out by British authorities. The arrests, hunger strikes and deaths in detention of activists motivated me in support of the Irish struggle – so much so that I participated in many demonstrations against the British occupation of Ireland. We were aware that such participation brought us more attention from British security forces, which probably resulted in greater surveillance of our activities, but we were not deterred.

Another important issue that ignited great concern during these volatile decades was the proliferation of weapons of mass destruction and the growing threat of a nuclear war. Hundreds of thousands of people across political, class, academic and national lines protested against increasing nuclear militarism, especially by the US. I participated in many marches organised by the CND. The atmosphere in these marches and demonstrations was, however, very different from the Vietnam solidarity marches. In general, the crowd was older and the atmosphere more 'relaxed' in the sense that there was less physical confrontation with the police. The slogans were mostly ideologically compatible and there was a lot of music and singing, with the lyrics of Pete and Peggy Seeger, Joan Baez and Bob Dylan the order of the day.

When I was still in South Africa, I had been taught about how the confluence of military and industrial power in the US had influenced its policies, as well as those of other major Western powers. Since the early days of the formation of the ANC and the then CPSA, especially during and after World War II, Alliance literature was filled with the importance of world peace and its relationship to anti-imperialist and liberation struggles. Now in action, I had a better appreciation of the correctness of this analysis. The CND campaign helped me to understand the power of the military-industrial complex and the links between world peace and the struggle for national liberation and democracy.

My broader world view, and the intellectual germination that went with it, was shaped by this deeper understanding of the nature of imperialism and neo-colonialism, and how the Cold War was used by Western powers to subvert genuine liberation struggles in Africa, Asia and Latin America. I developed a deep antipathy towards Western collaboration with reactionary forces throughout the world. The Americans carried out their aggression in Latin America quite openly and blatantly, while the British, French, Germans and others were more subtle. However, they shared similar long-term objectives, undermining genuine liberation movements and propping up reactionary regimes and military juntas.

The Anti-Apartheid Movement

The Anti-Apartheid Movement (AAM) in the UK developed into a global force and provided the impetus for replicating its letter and spirit in Western Europe, the socialist countries and North America. We must, however, also recognise the outstanding role of African countries, the OAU, the UN and the NAM in making the broader anti-apartheid movement a truly international phenomenon without parallel in history.

It is a truism that without the economic, military and other forms of support of Western states, the South African regime could not have continued its repressive policies with such impunity and for so long. As a worldwide phenomenon unprecedented in its geographic scope and operational reach, the AAM had its roots in the Treason Trial of 1956, and the wave of repression unleashed by the apartheid regime in the 1950s and 1960s. Key South African student activists studying in the UK, such as Vella Pillay, Tony Seedat, Mac Maharaj, Steve Naidoo, Abdul Minty and Kader Asmal, with the support of British activists, started the boycott movement. This was to be the beginning of decades of demonstrations, marches, pickets and meetings against the apartheid regime.

The sanctions campaign

In response to a wave of repression that was seeing no respite, in 1959 Chief Luthuli called for international sanctions against apartheid South Africa. The sanctions campaign resonated strongly among some sections of the British public, in large part because it exposed the excesses of British vested economic interests in South Africa, as well as the British government's support for white minority rule. The seeds of the campaign were thus being sown on fertile ground, with growing anti-colonial sentiment settling among the British people. When the British prime minister Harold Macmillan addressed the South African Parliament in February 1960, he spoke of the 'wind of change' sweeping over Africa. After the Sharpeville massacres in March that year, the sanctions campaign was intensified and March 1961 was declared Boycott Month; demonstrations, pickets and meetings were organised in almost all the big cities across the UK. The demonstration to launch the Boycott Month in Trafalgar Square attracted over 15 000 people, providing the impetus for the Boycott Movement to evolve into the AAM.

When Nelson Mandela 'illegally' left South Africa and travelled to Ethiopia in 1962 to attend the PAFMECSA conference, he called for the expulsion of the apartheid regime from the Commonwealth and the International Labour Organisation, and for mandatory UN sanctions. The ANC delegation strongly argued that international solidarity and sanctions were important pillars of our overall strategic approach, but warned against any illusion that this would dilute the intensity of the political and armed struggles in South Africa. This was the basic normative principle and strategic approach on which the anti-apartheid movements were built.

The Treason Trial, the execution of trade unionist Vuyisile Mini, and the deaths in detention of Looksmart Solwandle Ngudle in 1963 and Babla Saloojee in 1964, as well as increasing reports of widespread arrests and torture of political detainees, helped to further inflame British public sentiment. Thousands of British citizens participated in anti-apartheid activities, representing all sectors of the political, labour, religious, academic, student and sporting fraternities.

Following the Rivonia arrests on 11 July 1963, the UN General Assembly passed a resolution in October that called on all member states to pressurise the South African government to stop all political trials. In response, the international AAM launched the World Campaign for the Release of South African Political Prisoners. A petition was signed by over 194 000 people and aroused support throughout the world. Given public pressure, the British government voted in favour of Security Council Resolution 191, which called on the South African government to release all political prisoners.

In 1964 Ronald Segal and Ruth First (an economist by training, the wife of Joe Slovo and later assassinated at Maputo University with an apartheid parcel bomb) organised a major London conference on economic sanctions, following discussions with Oliver Tambo. The conference documents effectively became the basis of an economic sanctions campaign. Then, in the wake of Britain's decision to sell 16 Buccaneer aircraft to the South African regime in November 1964, the ANC and the AAM organised a major conference on arms sales to South Africa. This, in turn, was the beginning of the arms embargo campaign, and when the Labour government came to power in the UK in October 1964, its first policy decision was to stop British arms exports to South Africa. This, however, excluded the Buccaneers contract. A government committee warned Harold Wilson, British prime minister at the time, that 'we have considerable interests in South Africa which would be at risk if our actions over arms exports are so sharp as to provoke an emotional reaction by the South African government'.

Defence Minister Denis Healey sought to give the decision the narrowest of interpretations, thus leaving many loopholes for continuing arms sales to South Africa. Some of Wilson's cabinet members argued that sanctions would not ensure a transition to majority rule and would likely produce chaos, leading to communist domination. I was aware of the 'Cold War' mentality in the UK, but was surprised at how strongly some key Labour Party leaders subscribed to this perspective.

Following the Unilateral Declaration of Independence (UDI) on 11 November 1965 by the then Rhodesian prime minister Ian Smith, Rhodesia became a key element of the Labour government's southern African policy, and the ANC called on the international AAM to campaign against Smith's UDI. From that point, the Rhodesian issue became an important component of the anti-apartheid struggle. The AAM called on the Labour government to take a clear stand against the UDI and argued that any sanctions would be ineffective if they were not also imposed against South Africa. The economic sanctions campaign against South Africa and the campaign against the Rhodesian UDI thus resulted in tensions between the ANC, the AAM and the Labour government.

In order to avoid sectarianism, the AAM worked closely with and brought together a broad spectrum of organisations. Having learnt about the importance of the unity of forces in support of Vietnam, Africa, Latin America and elsewhere, the AAM sought to build a broad-based solidarity movement in support of the struggle of the South African people against apartheid. By the end of 1967, the AAM decided to shift its emphasis from parliamentary lobbying to building a powerful political base, centred not only on political parties but also on the trade union movement, youth and student groups and other militant organisations. This shift reflected the general militant tendency and radicalisation of youth and student organisations throughout Europe in the 1960s. The AAM national committee was greatly strengthened when the Radical Student Alliance, the UN Student Association and the Union of Liberal Students joined. However, while controversial and contentious, after 1967 and in response to a call from the ANC, the AAM was requested to lay the groundwork for supporting the armed struggle under the slogan 'Oppose Apartheid – Support SA Freedom Fighters', but the net effect of the AAM's support of this call was that it alienated some of its traditional supporters.

In 1969 the South African regime arrested many ANC and other activists under the Terrorism Act. This new wave of repression and terror back home led to the formation of 'South Africa – The Imprisoned Society' (SATIS), which organised daily demonstrations and pickets outside South Africa House in Trafalgar Square in which I was a regular participant.

The ANC managed to build a very close and strong relationship with the AAM because of the quality and relatively large presence of our leaders and members in London and elsewhere in Europe. The PAC, on the other hand, was not a serious actor. They paid lip service to the struggle although, as time progressed, they did indeed find support among some genuinely committed people. This was especially so among international solidarity groups that emerged after the Cultural Revolution in China and tended to support the PAC as a countervailing act against the ANC. Moreover, the respective governments of Britain, Germany, France, Italy, and America were all hostile to the ANC because of our anti-imperialist positions and the erroneous perception that the ANC was a 'communist organisation'. This provided the rationale intended to weaken and isolate us.

When the CP won the elections in 1970, UK Prime Minister Edward Heath announced the resumption of arms sales to South Africa. In October of that year, over 10 000 demonstrators marched from Hyde Park to Trafalgar Square and the AAM petition opposing the lifting of the arms embargo was signed by 100 000 people. These significant public protests and the strong opposition expressed at the Singapore Commonwealth Conference forced the Conservative government to reconsider its arms policy.

After 1970, the AAM made an important tactical shift in its role, which henceforth would be to isolate the apartheid regime in order to weaken its capacity to resist democracy and avoid a race war in southern Africa. The linking of the anti-apartheid struggle with the anti-racism and anti-fascism struggles in the UK went some way to countering the negative reaction to our armed struggle.

By a confluence of fortunate circumstances, before and after World War II the World Council of Churches (WCC) had consistently taken strong positions against anti-semitism and racism, so it was inevitable that it would become involved in the anti-apartheid struggle. In 1960, the WCC participated in a conference in South Africa where it expressed serious concern and registered its opposition to apartheid policies on theological and pastoral grounds. In 1968, the WCC conference in Uppsala, Sweden, fully supported the call for economic sanctions. It called on its affiliates and associated individuals to withdraw all investments from institutions that helped to promote racism in whichever form or fashion.

In 1969, the WCC officially adopted a programme against racism and, with South Africa's racial order manifesting the worst forms of institutionalised racism, the country inevitably became a primary target. The WCC also took a very important resolution that recommended that 'if everything else failed' (meaning peaceful and non-violent struggle), churches should support the liberation movements, including those involved in armed struggle aimed at the elimination of the political or economic tyranny that made racism possible in principle and practice.

This resolution was significant because, in the wake of the ANC announcing publicly its commitment to the armed struggle, many anti-apartheid supporters were concerned about the consequences of such a decision. I and other comrades spent considerable time explaining the concept of a 'just war', which in our case was a normative concept that privileged legitimate opposition against improper state conduct where the means employed by the state were disproportional to the ends sought. This included abrogating all restraints on the use of violence and resorting to immoral and unjust methods, which were indiscriminate and caused needless suffering in the pursuit of particular state objectives. The support of the WCC was a major victory that helped us to convince more and more people about the legitimacy of the 'just war' concept and the moral imperative behind supporting the armed struggle in southern Africa.

In Europe, it was less of a challenge convincing people of a 'just armed struggle' against a system that the UN had declared a Crime Against Humanity, because they had experienced the dark years of fascism and many had been involved in the struggle against Nazism. In a much more empathetic way, they found common cause and an understanding of why the South African people had adopted the armed struggle.

In 1970 the British National Union of Students (NUS) Conference passed a resolution supporting the armed struggle in southern Africa. It also called for a total educational, cultural and sporting boycott of South Africa, thereby reflecting NUS's 'left-ward' trend. The NUS-AAM nexus thus became a strong foundation on which anti-apartheid activities were organised.

In order to enhance support for economic sanctions and to counter the argument that sanctions would have a negative impact on British workers, in 1973 the AAM exposed 23 major British companies who, while retrenching their workers, were increasing their investments in South Africa. This was a creative way of connecting British workers' interests with the struggle against apartheid South Africa. The campaign against the involvement of British companies in South Africa intensified and trade unions, student organisations, churches and individuals started withdrawing their investments or support for companies and banks. Students at more than half of Britain's universities called on their institutions to disinvest from companies with South African connections. This, too, had a considerable impact on the collective public mind.

The Soweto student uprisings on 16 June 1976 and the massacre of protesting school children also exercised a profound influence on public opinion in the UK and Europe, which became stronger and more vociferous in opposition to apartheid. And after the murder of Black Consciousness leader Steve Biko on 12 September 1977, student solidarity activities intensified even further and students increased pressure on academic institutions to withdraw their investments in South Africa. They energetically embarked on a campaign of picketing, demonstrating and disrupting board meetings, and also launched an impressive media offensive.

In September 1977, the apartheid regime under BJ Vorster, Verwoerd's successor, banned 19 anti-apartheid organisations in South Africa, including the Christian Institute. This so inflamed the British Council of Churches that they and others became more active in the anti-apartheid campaign.

The popular mood in the country certainly caused sound waves in government, such that in November 1977 Britain dropped its Security Council veto and voted for a mandatory arms embargo against South Africa under Chapter VII of the UN Charter. This period also saw some change in the Labour government's policies towards economic sanctions – the result of a groundswell of public opinion against apartheid and increasing pressure from the Labour Party's Executive Committee and the labour movement. As if rising to the ethical challenges, in 1978 the party conference adopted a NEC statement in support of a UN mandatory oil embargo and trade sanctions against South Africa.

The AAM's tactical objective to incrementally extend the scope of sanctions was thus succeeding. It started with the political prisoners' campaign, then the economic sanctions, extended to the arms embargo, and finally went on to include academic, cultural and sporting boycotts.

Because of the historical and colonial links between the UK and South Africa and robust institutional connections in these latter fields, powerful forces tried to oppose the growing campaign, and apartheid South Africa ingeniously used sporting, cultural, religious and academic links with Britain as important weapons of their 'outward-policy' campaigns.

The disinvestment campaign accelerated when Barclays Bank's involvement in the Cahora Bassa dam project in Mozambique was exposed and, as a consequence, the push against British companies investing in South Africa, Rhodesia and the Portuguese colonial territories grew further in intensity. Barclays Bank had a strong presence on university campuses, and students throughout the UK launched an impressive anti-Barclays Bank campaign. Many universities were pressured to disinvest from Barclays and thousands of individual students closed their accounts there. The campaign against Barclays had an important knock-on effect, too, as it encouraged the targeting of other major companies, such as British Leyland, General Electric, the British Steel Corporation and Rio Tinto-Zinc, which were involved in important sectors of the South African economy.

The sports boycott

The most visible and widely reported successes against the system of apartheid were scored on the sports fields. In 1962, the South African Non-Racial Olympic Committee (SANROC) and the AAM registered a major victory when South Africa was expelled from the Olympic Games.

In 1965, the South African cricket team's tour to the UK took place despite protests objecting to the event. But the AAM once again used the tour to bring thousands of protesters to the streets, which affected the playing and atmosphere of the games. I participated in several demonstrations outside the hallowed Lords cricket ground in London and other venues throughout the UK. However, as the sports protests became more fervent, so the British sporting establishment became more intransigent; in 1969–70, both the South African rugby and cricket teams were invited to tour the UK.

This once again provided the AAM with an opportunity to raise the profile of protest against apartheid. The South African rugby team was scheduled to play 23 matches and the cricketers 22 matches throughout the UK. A 'Stop the Seventy Tour' (STST) committee was established, with thousands of demonstrators responding to the call. Under the joint STST-AAM umbrella, mass protests and direct action continued for over three months against the rugby tour. The first game at Oxford had to be moved to Twickenham and only took place because of the heavy police presence, but this did not deter more than 50 000 people from participating in demonstrations.

During this time, I travelled to many parts of the UK to participate in these momentous demonstrations against the Springboks. The tactic of entering the grounds as spectators and then disrupting the game was both popular and effective, but also meant that the police began to deal violently with demonstrators. At one demonstration in Birmingham I was dragged from the stands and pushed down a tunnel until I hit a wall. Fortunately, I was not badly hurt and it was difficult to lay charges. I was, of course, evicted from the grounds, and we travelled back to London bruised but happy that we had made our point.

The rugby protests, in turn, laid the foundation for protests against the cricket tour, and organisations representing most of the major sectors of society and a broad spectrum of people participated – with the result that the Cricketing Council was forced to reduce the tour to 12 matches. The Supreme Council of Sport in Africa warned, however, that if the cricket tour was not cancelled African countries would not participate in the 1970 Edinburgh Commonwealth Games. And so, given the unprecedented mass protests and the impending elections, the British government urged the Cricketing Council to cancel the tour. This was the AAM's most significant victory since its formation. The South African issue had penetrated thousands of British homes and the nefarious racial nature of the apartheid system had been exposed by unparalleled publicity. Individuals who I met regularly, such as Peter Hain, Sam Ramsamy, Dennis Brutus, Chris de Broglio and Steve Tobias, played a leading role in the sports boycott campaign.

The ANC and the Lusaka Manifesto

The AAM found itself on the horns of a dilemma when the Lusaka Manifesto was adopted in April 1969 by 14 Eastern and Central African states at a summit in Lusaka, Zambia. The manifesto, while reiterating a commitment to the liberation struggle, erroneously suggested that the country signatories were willing to normalise relations with the apartheid and Portuguese colonial regimes *if* these regimes recognised the principle of human equality and the right to self-determination. The manifesto concluded that if the regimes in question responded positively to this overture, then the concerned African states would recommend that liberation movements desist from waging armed struggles.

The ominous message in this thinly veiled attempt at appeasement was that the ANC and other liberation movements would be urged to discontinue their armed liberation campaigns. Failing this, support would be withdrawn and, most critically, we would not be able to conduct our struggles from African territories.

When the Lusaka Manifesto was adopted by the OAU and the UN, major Western supporters of the apartheid regime were emboldened and found a convenient political instrument with which to mobilise support against the ANC and PAC. This, of course, had a far-reaching impact on the work of anti-apartheid movements throughout the world.

The Lusaka Manifesto was heatedly debated in both the ANC YSS and other ANC structures in London and elsewhere. The consensus was that political and economic interests and opportunism emanating in the West had conspired with anti-communist and narrow Africanist positions to create fertile ground for powerful Western governments. This would help to exert pressure on some countries in Africa to seek a compromise solution with the apartheid regime and Portuguese colonialism.

The Lusaka Manifesto was an aberration at a time when the apartheid government was intensifying its 'total onslaught' strategy against all opposition inside South Africa, and using its military and economic might to destabilise countries in southern Africa. I was perplexed that some African states believed that the South African and Portuguese regimes would willingly accept the principle of human equality and the right to self-determination. More significantly, the adoption of such a manifesto without consulting the liberation movements was a worrisome portent that some African countries were willing to sacrifice the liberation struggles in southern Africa on the altar of undefined short-term gains or naively believed that the regime was seeking a genuine solution.

Some ANC structures, including our YSS in London, vociferously argued that the ANC should launch a campaign against the signatories of the Lusaka Manifesto, and that we should organise protests and demonstrations outside their embassies. But the ANC leadership, led by Oliver Tambo, cautioned that it would be dangerous to respond angrily or impulsively and that we ought to consider long-term realities. In their wise counsel, the leadership explained that if we were to succeed in our struggle we needed the full support of African states, even if they temporarily went off course. Also, it was important to distinguish between those African states that came to wrong conclusions – not because of opportunist reasons, but because they were genuinely seeking a solution, albeit a wrong one – from other African states, such as Hastings Banda's Malawi and Mobutu Sese Seko's Zaire. These were simply caught up in neo-colonial machinations and found themselves under extreme pressure from the regime and their former colonial masters. Our leaders cautioned that any public attack against the Lusaka Manifesto would only create more fertile ground for the Vorster regime's 'outward' policy and would antagonise those genuinely committed to our struggle.

For many of us in London and in the AAM, this guidance was not easy to accept. We were going through a dangerous and difficult period where, for example, ANC cadres had been expelled from Swaziland and Lesotho and some of our cadres operating in Botswana were arrested. In 1969 the ANC camps in Tanzania were closed down and cadres had to be airlifted to the Soviet Union immediately. As it transpired, our leadership's perspective proved to be both wise and accurate. As they predicted, the regime did not respond positively to the Lusaka Manifesto. On the contrary, it increased its destabilisation activities against neighbouring states, which made it possible for us to convince the OAU and the International Solidarity Movement that the South African and Portuguese regimes were, in fact, not committed to finding genuine political solutions. The message of the ANC and AAM had certainly found a more receptive audience. We averred that in order to achieve democracy, peace and stability in southern Africa, the proper strategic approach would be to rally support for the liberation struggles and to bolster the international campaign for isolating the regime.

Work, marriage and fatherhood

After completing my Master's degree at Sussex University, I returned to London. By the mid-1960s, my family had moved to North-End House in West Kensington. Similar to our Orient House flat in South Africa, it was a meeting hub for senior Congress leaders and many leaders and activists of the ANC YSS who would visit on the weekends to take part in discussions or simply to socialise. In many ways North-End House was my 'home away from home', and this more comfortable flat made my adjustment to London that much easier.

I found employment with the help of people like Paul Joseph and Billy Nannan, who were working at Abbey Life, an insurance company established by two South Africans: Joel Joffe, who was a Treason Trial lawyer, and Mark Weinberg. They deliberately employed exiled South Africans, and for a brief period I did my 'stint' as an Abbey Life employee. It could be said that this was my first experience as a white-collar worker.

In the UK, pubs are the places one goes to meet friends, make new friends and listen to protest songs. On Sunday nights, especially after demonstrations, we would go to a pub in King's Cross frequented by members of the Young Communist League, or The Cedars in West Kensington. Here we merrily sang protest songs from throughout the world. It was a great atmosphere and I developed many friendships there.

In 1971 I took the bold step of marrying Gloria Wilkinson – in a double wedding at which Essop married Meg Shorrock. The registrar appeared to be stunned by the fact that all four of us lived in the same flat in North-End House. In fact, it so confused him that he tried to marry me to Meg. Elderly relatives warned that double weddings are bad luck and that one of the marriages would fail. As it turned out, they were right, and my union with Gloria did not last long, though we remain on friendly terms.

The offices of the ANC, the SACP and the AAM were all close to Goodge Street tube station, and we also used to meet up socially in that area. During this time I also developed a relationship with Christabel Gurney, a member of the Anti-Apartheid National Executive Committee and the editor of *Anti-Apartheid News*, who received an OBE in June 2014 for 'political service particularly to Human Rights'. Christabel and I have a son, Sam, who was raised by his mother in a left-wing, loving and independent way to become a chip off both the old blocks. Sam studied International Relations at Sussex University, where he became president of the Student Union, and he is now a trade unionist and Labour Party activist, working in the British Trade Union Congress's International Relations Department. I regret that I was not able to spend more time with him when he was growing up, but I remain proud of him and happy that he is on very good terms with our family and close to many of his South African cousins.

Revolutionary Council

After my short stint at Abbey Life, I was deployed to work full-time for the ANC office in London, where Reg September was the Chief Representative, having succeeded Mazisi Kunene. Shortly thereafter, I was redeployed to work with the RC in London. The RC was a strategic body established at the Morogoro Conference in April 1969, and its primary function was to give shape and substance to the internal political and armed struggle.

Now I was involved in a two-pronged terrain of struggle. While I continued with some solidarity activity, I was now fully involved in 'internal reconstruction' work under the leadership and guidance of Dr Dadoo and Joe Slovo. Other comrades involved in the work of the RC included Ronnie Kasrils, Jack Hodgson, Ronnie Press, Mannie Brown, Barry Feinberg and Stephanie Sachs, and we were engaged in multiple tasks: we created a library of topographical maps of South Africa; we gave extensive political lessons, which included Alliance politics and the situation that prevailed in Africa and globally, to new arrivals from South Africa; we recruited cadres to return to South Africa where they would either work in underground political structures or join MK; and we recruited international supporters to help us with our underground activities both in South Africa and in the Frontline States of Angola, Botswana, Mozambique, Tanzania, Zambia and Zimbabwe.

Those were dynamic times because many South Africans, especially our young white compatriots, were coming abroad to avoid conscription. It was in this spirit that I, Bill Anderson, Gavin Cawthra and others formed the Committe on South African War Resistance (COSAWR). We had to determine whether we should recruit the young white war resisters to remain in exile, train them to return to South Africa to do underground work, convince them to become involved in open political work among the white constituency back home, or to join MK. In London, we opted to concentrate more on recruitment for underground political work, especially propaganda activity. In cases where this was not feasible, we did encourage white youth to work above ground, especially at universities where they could develop the consciousness of their counterparts in opposing apartheid and, at the same time, better understand ANC policies. However, some of our colleagues in the frontline areas of southern Africa placed greater emphasis on recruiting for the armed struggle.

We, of course, had no facilities to offer military training in the UK, but taught carefully selected recruits the art of sabotage techniques, surveillance, counter-surveillance, secret writing, setting up underground propaganda structures, producing leaflet bombs, recruiting methods and protection against infiltration. At the Kasrils' home in Golders Green, we created a secret room where we stored an excellent collection of South African topographical maps, which we had purchased from specialty shops across London. We also used the room to make secret containers in which we would smuggle propaganda and other material into South Africa. The Kasrils' sons, Andrew and Christopher, were young at the time and I always had to bribe them with sweets to keep them away from the 'operations' room. I spent a considerable amount of time at the Kasrils home, and Eleanor, Ronnie's late wife, was especially tolerant of our constant coming and going and never hesitated to provide us with food and refreshments. She was indeed a friend and a tower of strength.

We had a similar operations room in Barry Feinberg's art studio. Years later the Kasrils and Feinberg children told us that we had not fooled them. They were all too aware of our operations rooms. Andrew Kasrils relates the story of a day when he opened the door to the secret room and was shocked to find a 'tall black man' standing in the room. He had actually stumbled onto Chris Hani who had come to look at the maps. We were fortunate that the children never spoke to others about the secret rooms. Oliver Tambo, who always took a keen interest in the work of the RC, was directly involved with this project and often met with us in the secret room at Ronnie's home or at Jack Hodgson's flat in order to assess the work we were doing and to encourage us.

Jack Hodgson had seen action in World War II and, during the formation of MK, worked on the development of homemade weapons and bombs. He now worked with Ronnie Kasrils, Barry Feinberg, Ronnie Press and me in creating 'leaflet bombs' and radio broadcasts to be used in the country. One of our key activities was our propaganda efforts, at a time when the ANC structures were decimated and the apartheid juggernaut was moving triumphantly throughout the country. We paid special attention to the increased distribution of ANC educational literature, leaflets and radio broadcasts in South Africa. The leaflet bomb technique was an important innovation. We learnt much about agitprop work from, among others, Soviet partisan activities during World War II, as well as the Cuban and Vietnamese experiences.

Considerable time was spent experimenting with leaflet bombs, and there were some very amusing incidents. Ronnie Kasrils and I had once gone to Hampstead Heath to test a new version of a leaflet bomb. We set up the device and I took up position to witness the results while Ronnie prepared to set it off. I was still positioning myself when the rocket flew past me and hit a tree. I ended up in a state of shock because, if the trajectory of the projectile had been two or three centimetres in the wrong direction, I would certainly have been decapitated. Ronnie was equally shocked and, to help regain our composure, we popped into the nearest pub and downed a good few pints before we proceeded to Jack's flat to complain about the leaflet bomb malfunctioning and nearly decapitating me.

Another incident occurred when we were experimenting with a leaflet bomb in Jack's flat in Chalk Farm. His wife, Rica Hodgson, was working for the International Defence and Aid Fund and 'tolerated' our work in their flat, but Jack was always meticulous in ensuring that everything was 'clean' before she returned. One day as we were experimenting, the leaflet bomb went off and the rocket hit the ceiling, badly damaging it and the table on which we were working. There was great consternation as we desperately tried to clear up the mess. Not having much success, Ronnie and I absconded and left Jack to deal with Rica's agitation. I am sure Jack was persuasive enough to have convinced Rica that Ronnie and I were to blame.

We also created secret compartments in suitcases for delivering leaflets, and on several occasions packaged these and other propaganda material in gift containers, which we sent back to South Africa. We used gifts, mainly from Fortnum & Mason, an upmarket store in Knightsbridge. We were advised that customs officials in South Africa would hardly be suspicious of containers from such an exclusive shop and therefore not realise that these were replete with leaflets and other propaganda material. Whenever I went to the shop I was very nervous because it was frequented by wealthy customers from all over the world and, given my attire and obvious discomfort, I was scared I might be suspected of being a shoplifter. Fortunately, my concerns were never put to the test.

Ronnie Kasrils, others and I recruited cadres to go to South Africa and the surrounding region to establish safe bases for our underground operatives or to disseminate illegal ANC and SACP propaganda material. These internationalists, many of whom remain unknown, made a major contribution at a very difficult time in our efforts to re-establish the ANC presence inside South Africa. Given the 'need-to-know' rule of our underground work, I was not aware that Ronnie had recruited Sean Hosey and Alex Moumbaris and his wife to carry out underground activities in South Africa. I only became aware when they were eventually arrested. Following their arrest, I had to canvass for their release as well as maintain contact with their family members. I was also not aware that in the mid-1960s Ronnie had recruited David and Sue Rabkin and Jeremy Cronin to return to South Africa to form a propaganda unit. The Rabkin-Cronin-Halliday team and the Jenkin-Lee team, another team of recruits, were responsible for the distribution of a large amount of ANC and SACP propaganda material that helped us break through the 'curtain of silence' surrounding the Alliance. I have no doubt that leaflets and publications such as *January the 8th*, *Sechaba*, *Mayibuye*, *African Communist* and *Search Light* all had a formative influence on the political consciousness of our people at the time.

Tim Jenkin and Stephen Lee were South African students who had been on holiday in Europe and walked into the ANC offices in London one day. Our Chief Representative there, Reg September, knew that when South African passport holders came into the ANC office he should immediately ask them to leave and then arrange for Ronnie Kasrils and myself to meet them secretly for an assessment, which we duly did. The two were anxious to return to South Africa, but in the end had to stay in London for at least one year. They were 'walk-ins' and, as such, we had to 'check them out' thoroughly before recruitment proper. Once we were satisfied that they were not infiltrators, we put them through an extensive training course that concentrated on underground methods. Upon their return to South Africa, they established an outstanding and very effective propaganda unit.

The Jenkin-Lee team proved extremely effective because there were times when they would set off eight or more leaflet bombs simultaneously, thereby giving the impression that there were many units functioning in South Africa. This was a very exciting period, and when the Soweto uprisings occurred in June 1976, our propaganda units were in place to set off many leaflet bombs and banners throughout the country.

We did, however, suffer a major setback in July 1976 when the Rabkin-

Cronin team was arrested; David was sentenced to 10 years and Jeremy Cronin to seven years' imprisonment. Sue was pregnant and, after pressure exerted via the British government, she was deported from South Africa.

Then, in March 1978, the Jenkin-Lee team was also arrested and charged with distributing as many as 17 sets of pamphlets and detonating more than 50 leaflet bombs over two years. They were also charged with making several street broadcasts. Tim was sentenced to 12 years in prison and Steve to eight years. The arrests of these two teams proved a serious setback for our propaganda endeavour in South Africa.

I had built an excellent relationship with Tim and Steve when they were in London and their arrest came as a huge blow. Tim was a highly skilled technical expert and I was excited to learn that at the end of 1979 he had managed to make duplicate keys of at least 17 doors in Pretoria's top-security prison. It was this expertise that enabled him, Steve and Alex Moumbaris to escape from prison. Tim's ingenuity not only caught the security apparatus but our entire movement by total surprise. Their daring escape created a sensation in South Africa and was a publicity coup for the ANC. Both Tim and Steve returned to London, after which Tim became involved with the work of the Regional Politico-Military Council (RPMC). In later years, he played a major role in helping the Vula operatives (our exile leaders who had returned to the country to strengthen the internal structures) to establish the secret communication systems between the exile leadership and Nelson Mandela when he was imprisoned at Victor Verster. However, given the rules of our underground system, I was never aware of the full scope of his work.

The Ahmed Timol unit

Before my exile, Ahmed Timol was a teacher living in Roodepoort, and every Friday he and Yusuf (JoJo) Saloojee – who was a teacher at the same school – would drive to Johannesburg to spend weekends with us. We were close friends from the days of Ferreirastown and the TIYC. Schooled in the struggle, Ahmed and Yusuf used every opportunity, including the school platform, to propagate the movement's message and to challenge the authorities. However, they were also responsible for my brief stint as a teacher when I was serving my banning order. This stint literally lasted a few hours in commerce, a subject that I knew nothing about, although Ahmed and Yusuf had assured me that they would help me to prepare the lessons. No sooner had I entered the school than I was alerted that the Special Branch had arrived and I had to beat a hasty exit. My foray into the working class thus ended very abruptly. Ahmed and Yusuf were among the last people with whom Essop and I interacted before going into exile.

Yusuf Saloojee went on to teach in Zambia and later proceeded to Canada where he became an ANC representative. He played an important role in building the Canadian AAM, and recruited many Canadians to relocate to South Africa or the Frontline States to assist us with underground activities. In 1966 Ahmed Timol went to Saudi Arabia to make the Haj pilgrimage and while there, he met with Dr Dadoo and Molvi Cachalia. After several intensive political discussions, he proceeded to London for further dialogue. Thus in April 1967, I was overjoyed when he unexpectedly arrived at our flat in North-End House; it was indeed a joyous reunion and celebration. Ahmed was resourceful and took up a teaching post at a school that catered for immigrants in Slough, Berkshire. He became an active member of the National Union of Teachers but also took part in many campaigns, including those relating to Vietnam, Chile, Palestine and South Africa, as well as issue-specific ones such as nuclear non-proliferation.

It was during a march in Aldermaston, organised by the CND in Easter 1967, that Ahmed met his partner, Ruth Longoni. She was a member of the British Communist Party and worked for the left-wing journal *Labour Monthly*. Ruth soon became our good comrade and dear friend.

After two years in London, the leadership decided that Ahmed should return to South Africa to assist with setting up our SACP and ANC under-ground network. He first went to the Lenin School in Moscow, accompanied by Thabo Mbeki and Ann Nicholson, in preparation for his return to South Africa. Other than studying Marxism-Leninism, he was given training in Military Combat Work (MCW), which included establishing underground structures, recruitment tactics, secret communications, and propaganda preparations and dissemination. When Ahmed returned to North-End House, nobody openly talked about his eight-month absence because there was an unwritten code that the coming and going of South African passport holders should never be discussed. However, privately he shared his Soviet experiences and discussed his return to South Africa quite extensively with Essop and me. In London, he received further training from Jack Hodgson and Stephanie Sachs who handled secret communications from the country.

Ahmed departed for South Africa in February 1970 and his separation from Ruth was undoubtedly difficult. At that time, she could not accompany him because she was white and, under apartheid laws, risked falling foul of the Immorality Act.

Ahmed resumed his teaching at Roodepoort Indian High School in April 1970, and within three months reported back to London that 'my experience in London was invaluable ... I realised that sincerity alone is not enough. One must either understand the social forces which move society onwards or become the blind fool of forces which one cannot understand

and therefore cannot control or bend to our will … I am convinced that our strategy of protracted struggle will be met with growing response from the urban proletariat and that regular coordinated sparks in our cities will cause real panic and put pressure on our enemies'. He sent a mailing list of people who should receive SACP and ANC material and other types of propaganda, as well as the names of potential recruits for internal underground work. In subsequent reports, he provided insightful and useful analyses of the deteriorating political, social and economic situation, and the detrimental effects this had particularly on the impoverishment of Africans and coloureds.

In August 1972, Ahmed and one of his recruits, Salim Essop, were arrested after the police alleged that they had found illegal literature in the boot of his car. Many others who had worked with Ahmed were also arrested and held at John Vorster Square. On 27 October the security police informed Ahmed's mother at their family home that he had tried to escape by jumping out of the tenth-floor window of John Vorster Square and that his body was at the government mortuary in Hillbrow. I was informed early that morning and was devastated. I anxiously phoned one of my senior leaders, who sternly informed me that I was breaking the rules of underground work, which was not to discuss sensitive matters over the telephone. We subsequently learnt that the Special Branch version of events was a gross travesty of the truth because Ahmed was murdered in cold blood. The testimonies of the other detainees indicate that some of them, including Ahmed, were severely tortured. Thousands of people representing all sections of South African society attended Ahmed's funeral and the movement called on the community to observe a national day of protest and mourning.

At an international level, there was a general outcry and palpable rancour towards apartheid's security agents. We organised petitions, demonstrations and memorial services in Ahmed's memory, and Amnesty International called for an impartial commission of inquiry, urging people to protest against detention without trial. The organisation demanded the release of detainees and asked the UN Secretary-General to investigate Ahmed's death. India used the UN General Assembly to denounce the deaths of Asians and others in detention and to declare as 'criminals' those responsible for this heinous deed. The UN Special Committee on Apartheid was further asked to prepare a report on all known cases relating to the maltreatment and torture of prisoners in South Africa, since Ahmed was the 22nd comrade to have died in police custody – and many more were to die in custody in later years. President Mandela, in a speech on the occasion of the renaming of a school after Ahmed, stated that:

Ahmed Timol will help you understand the courage of those who opened up the way for all of us who are free today ... It is a great privilege to have the task of unveiling the plaque that bears the new name of the school. Let us remember Ahmed Timol in our striving.

The start of military training

In the early 1970s, the CC of the SACP sent a request to its counterpart in the German Democratic Republic (GDR) to train small groups of ANC members in counter-intelligence. This was mainly because the South African regime had managed to infiltrate our ranks so we needed to improve and extend our basic counter-espionage skills in order to neutralise this threat. The General-Secretary of GDR's Socialist Unity Party and the Chairman of the State Council, Erich Honecker, had personally agreed to the SACP request and, on the basis of this agreement, a former Wits student and member of the ANC and SACP, Billy Nannan, and I undertook a three-week training programme in the GDR. It was an excellent course where we enjoyed the undivided attention of our instructors. We were trained in MCW, including building underground structures, surveillance and counter-surveillance, intelligence and counter-intelligence, secret communication, photography, preparing forged documentation and lock-picking, which I could never master. I concentrated quite intensively on photography and forged documentation since this would be a primary focus on my return to London. We also received some basic military training, during which we were taught to use weapons, the most popular being the AK-47.

Although there were only two of us and we were not based in a military camp, the discipline required was no less demanding: we had to get up at the crack of dawn, do homework and prepare for our MCW courses and shooting exercises. Practising shooting in the snow was one of the toughest things I have experienced and the purpose of which I never really understood. I complained that in South Africa we would never have such extremes of winter, but our interlocutors were not interested in my entreaties and insisted that I needed to adjust to 'conditions'. After three weeks, we left confident and emboldened that we would be better able to do our work for the RC.

My second training in MCW in the GDR took place with a group of four comrades. There was the commander of our group, his deputy and two other younger participants. The commander and his deputy had their own rooms, while I shared a room with the two younger comrades who were called 'Stalin' and 'Collins'. Collins was a bright young activist who, sadly, died in a mysterious motorcycle accident in Zimbabwe a short while after he returned to Africa. Suspicions were raised about the accident, but we were not able to prove any foul play.

Given the 'need-to-know' rule of our operations, the others were not familiar with my work in London. I found our training on interrogation techniques and combat work to be very interesting. I was surprised that our two younger comrades, especially Stalin, insisted that torture was a legitimate practice in a revolutionary situation. Thankfully, our German instructors subtly tried to discourage torture as a means of extracting information, but Stalin could not be convinced and we finally agreed to disagree. The intelligence courses lasted three to five months, but it was the physical training that I found particularly punishing. I have always been scared of heights and was simply irredeemable when it came to the obstacle courses. Moreover, our instructor was a difficult task master and put a lot of pressure on me. I sometimes suspected that he had decided that I was one of those 'softies' who had to be taught a lesson. The truth was that I was not a suitable candidate for rigorous military training.

Before departing from the GDR I informed my comrades that ours was a revolutionary army and we, therefore, could not deal with comrades in a conventional and hierarchical military system. While ANC cadres needed a modicum of discipline and respect for authority, their manifestations could not be in a pure militaristic sense and hence 'revolutionary discipline' should be at a premium. As such, all structures of the movement, especially MK and Intelligence, had to be driven by the political vision and the strategy and tactics that underpinned the struggle objectives of the ANC. I advised them that once they returned to Lusaka and their respective deployment areas, they should seriously reflect on their training experiences, but more crucially on the dangers of an overly militaristic orientation to our work. There was more of a political imperative to create a new and different type of cadre that would require interacting with comrades in a disciplined but fraternal manner. I jokingly told them, 'See you soon in Lusaka.' I subsequently met two of them on a visit there.

In May 1973 I was informed that I would travel to Moscow for an eight-month training course but, sadly, on the eve of my departure, 26 May 1973, I received news that my mother had been killed in a car accident in Mumbai, India. I immediately phoned Dr Dadoo to ask whether my trip could be postponed. Dr Dadoo expressed his condolences, but politely informed me that 'all the necessary arrangements had been made' and I should therefore proceed to Moscow as planned, which I did. In hindsight, Dr Dadoo's decision was correct. For one, I did not have money to fly to India and, secondly, in terms of Muslim tradition my mother would already have been buried. As tragic as this moment was, I understood that 'the struggle was the family'.

I stayed in a flat just outside Moscow and for eight difficult, challenging and isolated months my only contact was with my trainers, who could only communicate with me through a translator. At the end of each day, I studied my notes and completed the prescribed 'homework'. Russian television was my main form of recreation and I spent a lot of time watching sports and cultural channels. This is when I first developed some appreciation for classical music and ballet. Needless to say, Russian vodka also provided a welcome diversion. On occasions, I would be given a ticket to the Bolshoi theatre and the hockey stadium, which I enjoyed thoroughly.

Some Saturdays I was able to take the subway into the centre of Moscow where I met my brother Essop, who at the time was studying at the Lenin Party School in Moscow, and we were able to talk about my mother's death, which provided me with some comfort and closure. I recall, however, on the days we met we would struggle to find a restaurant where we could have a meal since it seemed that every Muscovite wanted to eat out on a Saturday night. I was surprised that many buildings were called *pectopaht* and asked Essop whether even in the Soviet Union there was monopoly ownership. He was highly amused and explained that *pectopaht* meant 'restaurant'.

Essop and I could not meet every weekend because of the weather conditions and the regulations, but our occasional meetings and the political and social discussions we had helped me to adjust to my eight months of loneliness and isolation in the Soviet Union. Of course, I was bound by the rules of strict secrecy and could not divulge any details of my training to him. He, on the other hand, gave me a good sense of his Marxist-Leninist training, which made for interesting discussions.

The specialised training I received was similar to that of the GDR but more extensive in scope and more intensive in content. I improved my practical knowledge about combat work, especially in disciplines such as the production of false documentation, surveillance and counter-surveillance. I enjoyed the field exercises when I was taken by bus to the suburbs of Moscow. Here I had to 'stroll' round a designated area for hours, using the various techniques I had been taught to spot the 'enemy'. When I returned to the flat, I had to identify all surveillance subjects either on the bus or during my walks and my ability to do this improved as we went along. The dead-letter drop exercises were also very interesting. I was not exposed to field work in recruitment techniques and identifying and interrogating infiltrators, but had extensive lectures on these matters. Unfortunately, as with my training in the GDR, I continued to struggle with picking locks.

On occasion and weather permitting, I walked in the park close to my flat but could not adjust to the idea of walking for no purpose. I had naively believed that one only walked in order to get from one place to another and for a specific objective. Walking for leisure or exercise was something I had not internalised. I was initially confused when I saw people standing around raising their fingers. On enquiring, I learnt that these were groups of people trying to form a syndicate for buying vodka to share. The number of fingers indicated how many people were required. I adventurously joined in this activity and we all drank from the same plastic cup in big gulps. It may not have been the most 'civilised' thing to do, but was a great way of socialising with the common folk of Russian society.

During the course of my training I went to Sochi for a short break. My cover was that I was from India, but problems arose when I met people who were actually from India. When socialising it was especially difficult to maintain this cover, and I then had to pretend that I was from East Africa. In my training it was stressed that important and popular public places should be avoided because they were frequented by 'enemy agents'. I do not know whether the Soviet trainers ever solved this dilemma, but I concluded that there must have been different levels of training courses and exposure, which explained why some trainees and I were allowed to visit the Bolshoi theatre, museums, hockey games and so on.

As I left Moscow, I began to appreciate that while my time in London had been instrumental in my intellectual growth, increasing activism and integration into ANC structures, I also found Marxist-Leninist thinking to be a particularly useful prism through which various activist struggles for freedom and justice could be viewed, whether in South Africa or elsewhere. My new training added another layer to my political and ideological maturation and would stand me in good stead in later years. However, no sooner had I returned to London than I had to put my training into practice.

Ann Nicholson, a comrade in exile whom I had met in South Africa, was a member of the Congress of Democrats. After Ann left for Canada, I took over her work in preparing documentation, the most critical being pass books and passports for cadres who would be infiltrated into the country. It was an exciting challenge as well as a good learning experience. We would receive photographs from headquarters in Lusaka with false names, and based on this information I would create the necessary pass books and passports. The Soviet Union provided us with authentic-looking and excellent specimens of South African travel documents, replete with the immigration stamps from the countries to which South Africans were allowed to travel at the time. Soon I was able to produce our own immigration stamps. I felt rewarded when the ANC leadership regarded my forged documents as meeting standards of 'high quality' because these documents enabled cadres to enter South Africa legally and move through passport control points.

I spent six months in Luanda in 1977, sharing my experiences with comrades also producing false documents and smuggling propaganda and other material into South Africa. When I arrived in Luanda I shared a room in Residence 1 with Joe Modise and Joe Slovo. (Residence 1 had been the apartheid regime's embassy during the time of Portuguese colonialism.) I later moved to Residence 2. I recall Comrade Duma Nokwe, a senior ANC and SACP leader, visiting Luanda on his birthday and, not wanting to miss an opportunity to celebrate, I was mandated by my comrades to convince the logistics manager, Wolfie Kodesh, to give us some wine. Wolfie initially refused, but then agreed on condition that we cut down overgrown trees around our residences. The wine would be our 'reward'. After hours of strenuous gardening, we settled down to enjoy our reward – only to discover when we opened the wine bottles that the bottles were filled with water. Clearly some of the comrades in the logistics section had drunk the wine and refilled the bottles with water. Wolfie was furious, but could do nothing. On another occasion Yusuf (JoJo) Saloojee, who was then our representative in Canada, visited Luanda and we spent hours walking the streets of the city looking for curry powder to improve the taste of our regular diet of tinned food. Eventually, after many hours and several beers, we found Heinz curry powder. Delighted, we returned to the residence and waited expectantly for JoJo to cook the curry only to find, much to our dismay, that no amount of Heinz curry powder could turn tinned food into a Durban curry.

From Luanda I was despatched to Maputo to train comrades in secret communications, in particular the art of secret writing and deciphering coded messages on paper. The training went well until we had to put it into practice. Much to my horror, I discovered that some of the material required for developing secret communications – such as the paper and ink, which I had carried with me to Maputo – had been sabotaged. We spent endless hours scouring shops in Maputo looking for the 'right' paper. Unfortunately, our efforts were fruitless and I returned to Luanda very frustrated.

One night we were awakened by sounds of gunfire and rockets and saw tanks driving towards the State Broadcasting Centre. We were edgy and nervous, convinced it was a National Union for the Total Independence of Angola (UNITA) counter-revolutionary coup. We quickly removed all posters of Marx, Lenin and Castro and hid all the political literature. It was an hour later that we learnt that it was a 'left' coup attempt by the Nito Alves group. The coup failed, but leading MPLA comrades had been killed.

The Hinterland Project

Of particular interest during this period was the Africa Hinterland Project in the mid-1980s. This involved setting up an overland travel company in the UK for the express purpose of smuggling arms into South Africa and thereby helping to reinforce the armed struggle. The company was set up in Greenwich and managed to make over 40 journeys into South Africa in a purposefully designed truck where weapons could be hidden in secret compartments under the truck's seats. The truck was designed by Rodney Wilkinson who had in December 1982 planted two limpet mines at the Koeberg nuclear power station where he worked as a designing contractor years earlier. Following this mission the movement decided that Rodney and his partner, Heather Gray, should go to London and that is when I met Rodney. He was full of ideas, one of which was to smuggle weapons overland into South Africa. His idea was accepted by the MK Special Operations section, headed at the time by Joe Slovo. Mannie Brown and I were tasked to work with Rodney in executing the project.

With the help of British comrades, we set up Hinterland, a company that would organise and manage the overland African tours. Adverts for a six to seven week overland safari to South Africa beginning in Mombasa, Kenya, were placed in travel magazines. To our surprise, the response was very encouraging: many young people, initially from Europe and the US, but later from New Zealand and Australia, signed up and, by all accounts, they proceeded to have a great time.

Rodney was able to convert an old Bedford truck for this dual purpose of transporting tourists and weapons. Once the truck had been appropriately modified, it was shipped to Kenya. The tourists were then flown from the UK to Mombasa and on arrival picked up by the driver of the truck and backup persons who were recruited in the main from the UK and the Netherlands and who proved very able in carrying out the exacting assignments associated with the project. The truck then travelled to one of the Frontline States where, without the knowledge of the tourists, it was loaded with heavy weapons. When the truck finally crossed the South African border post, the drivers offloaded the weapons onto another prearranged vehicle, which they then left at a predetermined safe spot. Thereafter, our operatives would collect the weapons and distribute or bury them in strategic locations. Given the 'need-to-know' rule, I was not aware of details of the operations, such as who loaded the truck with weapons and who collected them in South Africa.

In any event, the Hinterland Project was a huge success – so much so that significant caches were dug up and handed over to the new ANC government in 1995. After my return from exile I was surprised to learn that the project had continued to function from Johannesburg. Even though the drivers were still mainly recruits from the UK and the Netherlands, the tour now included South African passengers for trips to the Okavango in Namibia, returning via Bulawayo in Zimbabwe, where the weapons were collected. The project enjoyed the highest levels of secrecy and continued to operate until 1993.

Since 1975, many among the internal leadership and activists from all sectors of society continued to meet with the ANC across the Frontline States, and I was acutely aware that we were entering a decisive stage of our struggle. In the late 1970s and '80s an increasing number of South African passport holders were arriving in the UK, Europe, the USA and Canada, and the volume of our work thus increased exponentially. It was recognised that London was an important 'forward area' and we were encouraged to involve more London-based folk in the work of the PMC. I recommended that Essop, Billy Masetlha, Wally Serote and Paluka Nkobi join the RPMC, and we also used the experience and expertise of other comrades, such as Tito Mboweni, Harold Wolpe, Brian Bunting, Ronnie Press, Bill Anderson and Gavin Cawthra to assist us in our work.

We recruited 'passport holders' for political underground work and propaganda units, and for establishing safe havens for trained cadres and leaders who were increasingly returning to South Africa; some were expressly recruited for MK activities, while others were given crash political courses and sent back to South Africa to do legal-political work with no immediate involvement with the underground.

Our propaganda activities inside South Africa increased quite considerably during this time. The *African Communist* was becoming very popular and was in great demand. A special magazine, *Search Light*, was produced in London to target South Africans of Indian origin. Frene Ginwala was the first editor and she had the irritating habit of using a red pen to correct our drafts. Perhaps it was a good thing that we had been forged in struggle, because the amount of changes she made with a red pen would have destroyed the confidence of anyone trying their hand at writing political articles for the magazine.

However – and from the distance of my new life in London – I could never have anticipated the extent to which the contours of our struggle would change in response to significant developments taking place in South Africa, particularly with regard to the cracking edifice of apartheid rule. The political ferment generated by the June 1976 student revolt would prove to be a decisive turning point, not only in my own life in exile but also in the annals of our struggle.

Chapter 3

The changing dynamics of struggle

As the apartheid regime became more desperate to shore up an increasingly shaky status quo, it resorted to greater coercive measures and state violence. Internal struggles were also starting to surface in the ruling National Party and the machinery of control became subject to growing concerns about how to protect white privilege in the face of mounting black resistance. The limitations of apartheid power continued to be exposed by a growing ensemble of international voices that questioned the moral propriety and political sustainability of the racist system. Of course, the pressures and calls for fundamental structural change in South Africa at home and abroad also had to battle with the powerful interests of the US and Western Europe, which preferred the status quo – which tended to exaggerate the communist threat – in terms of their Cold War perspectives. Underlying their posture was the mistaken belief that Western interests in South Africa could be the catalysts for incremental reform and the gradual erosion of apartheid. However, this did not take account of the growing vulnerability of the regime and the extent to which collective resistance to apartheid would alter the country's political dynamics by increasingly challenging the legitimacy of maintaining apartheid rule and white minority domination. It was particularly in the ANC's exile structures where adaptations had to be made in view of these dynamics. This related both to our strategic thinking and tactical operations.

The struggle intensifies

Because of its own structural, institutional and operational shortcomings, the ANC was unable to fully exploit developments in South Africa, especially after the 1973 workers' strike and the 1976 students' revolt. The revolt changed the political atmosphere in South Africa because it reverberated among Indian students in Durban, coloured students in the Western

61

Cape and all other African campuses across the country. This period also coincided with the rise of the Black Consciousness Movement (BCM) personified by Steve Biko and his comrades, who tried to instil an ideology that stressed pride and awareness of black values and culture as a means of emancipation from white racism.

Contradictions related to tribal and ethnic engineering were also becoming evident in the Bantustans of Transkei, Bophuthatswana, Venda, Ciskei and KwaZulu. However, although this artificial balkanisation of the country was exposing serious cracks in the monolith of Afrikaner power and control, and opened up space for political mobilisation, we in the ANC simply did not have the operational machinery or strategic approach to fully exploit the contradictions that had emerged in these homelands.

The resurgence of the struggle in the 1970s – and the regime's vicious response – had resulted in many youth taking refuge in exile. The propaganda activities of the ANC underground units, increasing sabotage activities and the spectacular political trials had popularised the ANC in the country. Some youth leaders had already made contact with ANC structures in the Frontline States and since the ANC was also better organised than the PAC in exile, large numbers of the 1976 youth cohort joined the ANC in exile. However, because of the weaknesses in our underground structures, many of the recruits were 'walk-ins' who had entered our ranks without coming through any of our formal structures and had thus not been tempered in the trenches of ANC struggle politics. This inevitably had an impact on their commitment, dedication and discipline. The new young cadres had come from a generation that was extremely militant, but also very impatient. They wanted to complete their military training and then hurry home with arms in order to confront the enemy. They took readily to the concept of liberation through 'the barrel of a gun', but were less sophisticated when it came to the importance of politics as the foundation of our armed struggle. Also, most of our recruits were from urban areas and the leadership was concerned about their social composition.

From around 1976 onwards the GDR had started to provide military training for ANC cadres in groups of 40 or 50. Training took place under the auspices of the GDR's Military Intelligence Department, which operated separately from its Foreign Intelligence Service. And so it was decided, based on our firm conviction about the importance of political education, that some comrades based in London would form a committee to prepare lectures about the ANC, the SACP and the South African Congress of Trade Unions (SACTU), which had also played a vital role in Kliptown's Congress of the People. A team consisting of Brian Bunting, Ronnie Kasrils, Pallo Jordan and I was tasked with developing lecture modules and visiting the camps in the GDR twice a year to deliver the lectures.

We had to strictly adhere to military regulations and a demanding regime. In the evenings we, as visiting lecturers, socialised with the German instructors and spent hours discussing the training programme as well as international affairs and African politics, and the atmosphere was always relaxed and friendly. During one of my visits, I awoke to a very tense atmosphere in the camp. The German comrades were extremely angry and informed me that some of our cadres, after arguments during the training session, had 'painted' slogans on their cars accusing them of being Nazis. This was a crisis that had to be defused immediately and so, after intervening with our cadres, I succeeded in getting them to apologise to our German comrades – although I am not sure whether relations between the instructors and that group of trainees were ever really normalised.

From my interactions with this new generation of ANC cadres, I realised that many had serious political knowledge deficits and shortcomings. This included any sound understanding of the history of the ANC, our strategic and tactical approaches, and the relationships between the armed and political struggle and between the national and class struggle – in short, all the fundamental issues that had shaped me in the struggle. The net effect of our political lectures was to contribute to the creation of a nucleus of political cadres who later became key ANC commissars and political activists in the MK camps. Some of them, at a very early age, also became leading lights of various ANC and SACP structures and, post 1994, played important roles in various structures of government, public administration and the private sector.

Internal reconstruction

At a political-military level, it was decided to address the weaknesses of our underground structures at a time when there was a changing balance of forces and a more propitious revolutionary environment. Not since the 1950s were conditions so suitable for the intensification of the political and, therefore, the armed struggle. This required us to double our efforts in infiltrating more trained cadres and leaders into South Africa. Also, many in the ranks of the leadership and activists were advised, notwithstanding the intensified repression, to remain in the country in order to strengthen or help establish underground ANC and SACP structures. They were further advised to selectively recruit cadres in order to strengthen and support the leadership hierarchy emerging from Robben Island.

There were sharp debates about the reality that, while we had in principle accepted the supremacy of the political struggle, we continued to send back some of our best and well-trained cadres to carry out armed propaganda activities. Some argued that while spectacular armed propaganda actions were carried out, these were not linked in any form or fashion to building strong and viable underground political structures. In the process, we suffered heavy casualties because some of our best cadres were either killed or arrested. Therefore, in order to ensure the survival of MK operatives, we had to build strong and effective underground political structures that were capable of mobilising the population in struggle. At the same time, however, we were mindful that armed propaganda activities were beneficial for popularising the ANC, enhancing the spirit of resistance and creating better possibilities for strengthening our underground structures.

Following deep and wide-ranging analysis of the ANC's organisational strengths and weaknesses, the NEC created the Internal Political and Reconstruction Department (IPRD). Its main task would be to concentrate on building robust underground political machinery and, with this as a foundation, we could then initiate a series of political and military actions. This would go a long way to ensuring the survival of our cadres and structures, as well as systematically propagating ANC, SACP and SACTU policies, strategies and tactics to the masses. The overriding concern in establishing the IPRD was that the ANC should be a more visible and living reality in the country. The situation also demanded an elaboration of our non-armed propaganda activities, which included written propaganda, street broadcasts and Radio Freedom. The IPRD, however, did not function as effectively as initially envisaged.

In 1978, this operational and philosophical reorientation was significantly augmented when Oliver Tambo led a delegation to Vietnam to study the experiences of the NLF under the astute leadership of General Võ Nguyên Giáp. The delegation was impressed with the lessons they learnt from Vietnam, and once again underscored the old adage that the armed struggle in South Africa was not like other armed struggles and could not succeed without creating strong underground political structures that would mobilise and organise all sections of our people.

The Vietnam delegation reported to a joint meeting of the RC and NEC held in Luanda, Angola, in 1979. Dr Dadoo, who was a member of the RC, was unable to attend and asked me to represent him. Naturally, I was thrilled because I was now entering the engine room of decision-making that dealt with internal reconstruction and critical strategic and political matters. When I arrived, I was politely but firmly informed that there was no formal provision for members of the RC to be represented by 'proxies' and I could therefore not attend. Still, I drew some consolation from the fact that I was in the company of so many of the comrades involved in the work of the RC, many of whom I met during lunch and supper breaks. In fact, some comrades stayed in the same residence, which proved helpful since they were able to keep me posted on what had transpired in the discussions.

The Luanda meeting decided that we had to make some far-reaching structural adjustments. It thus decided to institute the Politico-Military Strategy Commission (PMSC), which produced a report otherwise known as the 'Green Book', aimed at addressing our own strategic deficits and tactical shortcomings. The PMSC made significant recommendations that greatly influenced the course and direction of our struggle by incorporating critical lessons of the Vietnamese revolutionary experiences. These included elaborating on an overall strategy for more effective mass mobilisation; creating the broadest national front for liberation; strengthening the ANC's underground machinery; and developing military operations from political activity. It was especially the relationship between political and military struggle where the PMSC's recommendations proved very instructive. The armed struggle had to be based on mass struggle and popular resistance, and had to emerge from mass political support involving all sections of the population. As such, military activity had to, at every stage, be guided and determined by the need to generate and promote political action, organisation and resistance. As the Vietnamese victory had demonstrated, it was only through the combined synergy of sustained political and military action that the enemy's grip on power could be weakened.

In fact, the Green Book became such an important charter document that it was later adopted by a meeting of the NEC. There was further agreement that there should be a joint planning command and control mechanism to guide all aspects of the struggle in both a political and military sense. It was becoming increasingly clear that if we wanted to build effective MK military structures in South Africa, we had to work on a long-term strategy driven by the perspectives of a people's war. We therefore had to prioritise the development of political structures that would serve as the support bases for the military cadres being infiltrated into the country.

The impact of the Green Book

We were now moving away from infiltrating some of our best cadres into South Africa in order to carry out targeted 'armed propaganda' actions. We had achieved some major successes, but had come to the realisation that necessary political structures, such as safe bases, were not in place. These were necessary because cadres who carried out the armed propaganda activities would need to be able to retreat to safe bases among our people.

We also had to take into consideration the nature of the terrain and the absence of safe bases for MK cadres, and work on the principle that the 'people are our jungles and mountains'.

On the basis of the PMSC findings, the NEC decided that the PMC would replace the RC, and the PMC thus became the executive arm of the NEC relating to all matters involving the conduct of the political and military struggle. The PMC was charged with coordinating the activities of the political headquarters, the military headquarters and the intelligence department.

The PMC in Lusaka met regularly at least once a month and was mandated to deal with broad strategic planning and to continuously assess developments in the country. The Executive Committee of the PMC, in turn, met on a daily basis. Various higher organs in the Frontline States were replaced by regional political and military committees and their new mandate gave them the authority and responsibility to make 'operational decisions', including the selection of targets. Previously, such decisions could only be made from the ANC headquarters in Lusaka.

The regional PMCs were mandated to coordinate political and military activities in all the 'forward areas' for which they were responsible, but also had to establish area PMCs in South Africa. These area PMCs had to be responsible for providing local leadership on both political and military matters, as well as collecting intelligence and training political and MK cadres in South Africa.

London was designated a forward area and I became secretary of the RPMC. All forward areas were instructed to intensify efforts to meet leaders and key activists from all internal formations representing political, trade union, student, cultural, academic, religious, sports, business and civic organisations. The objective was to generate momentum for consolidating the four pillars of struggle: mass mobilisation, strengthening the political underground, escalating the armed struggle and strengthening international solidarity. A Political Code of Conduct, a Military Code of Conduct, and Rules and Regulations Governing the Handling of Weapons and Explosives were also adopted.

We used these documents, which became invaluable in our work, to prepare lectures for cadres being recruited for political and/or military work. They were also timely because, unlike the 1960s, many of the new generation of members who had swelled the ranks of MK had not come from within the ranks of the ANC. They had very little experience of political struggle and therefore did not have sufficient understanding of the ANC's political outlook and its theoretical and practical perspectives. Large numbers of young people had not gone through the discipline of revolutionary struggle, and the Codes of Conduct, for example, emphasised the shaping of a new citizenry in a non-racial democratic dispensation. The codes also dealt with the issues of security, discipline and the dangers of drunkenness in response to growing indiscipline among some of the newly recruited youth.

Dissension in the ANC camps

In the 1970s there was great anxiety among the ANC leadership about the rising levels of infiltration into the organisation's ranks. The movement was conscious that after 1976 the apartheid system had been quite scrupulous – and alarmingly successful – in infiltrating our ranks, as well as those of other components of the liberation struggle.

In 1978 I visited Lusaka and spent a considerable amount of time with Comrade Mzwai Piliso who was the head of the ANC's intelligence department and a close friend. He informed me about developments in Lusaka and, importantly, about what was taking place in various MK camps in Angola. He told me about deliberate plans by the regime to eliminate the ANC through a well-organised programme of infiltrating our ranks, driven independently by Defence Intelligence, the National Intelligence Agency (NIA) and Special Branch. The ANC had received information that the main purpose of this infiltration was the systematic elimination of our senior leadership based in Lusaka, Luanda and other areas. Already, well over 60 enemy agents had confessed and many more were under suspicion. I learnt a lot from Comrade Mzwai, especially since from my London base I never fully appreciated the security threats faced by our movement.

One of the most egregious consequences of enemy infiltration was the total destruction of the MK camp at Novo Catengue in Angola by a South African Air Force attack in March 1979. The five Canberra jets targeted specific facilities housing our armories, senior commanders and Cuban instructors. This could not have taken place without information provided by infiltrators, and I was told that heavy casualties were only avoided because we had intercepted South African Defence Force (SADF) messages in time and so defensive measures were taken. In 1977, in an incident referred to as 'Black September', the food at Novo Catengue was poisoned and affected almost 500 people. If Cuban doctors had not reacted with alacrity and urgency, many of our cadres would have died. And then, in 1983, serious problems and mutiny erupted in the MK camps in Angola.

The Stuart Commission

It is important to offer a full account of the Stuart Commission – established by the Working Committee of the ANC in February 1984 – whose mandate was to investigate the unrest in the Angolan camps and to make appropriate recommendations. The commission was convened by James Stuart (a *nom de guerre* for Hermanus Loots), with Anthony Mongalo, Sizakele Sigxashe, Mtu Jwili and me as members.

The commission's terms of reference were to investigate and report on:

- the root cause of the disturbances;
- the nature and genuineness of the grievances;
- outside or enemy involvement, their aims and methods of work;
- connections in other areas; and
- the ring leaders and their motives.

In February 1984 the commission travelled from Lusaka to Luanda and, over a period of three weeks, we visited and interviewed almost all the occupants of the military camps except those at Funda. We also interviewed the 33 ring leaders who had been detained in the Luanda Maximum Security Prison, as well as members of the Military High Command, the Regional Command and the ANC Chief Representative in Angola.

On a lighter note, I remember the drive from Luanda to the camps in other provinces, where our drivers were moving at such breakneck speeds on roads that had many pot holes that we were convinced we would be killed before we reached our destination. Of course, we were entirely ignored when we complained, but were later informed that the reason for driving so fast was because we were in UNITA rebel territory where our convoys were constantly ambushed. And when we returned to Lusaka from Angola, the members of the commission – with the exception of me – had contracted serious bouts of malaria and had to be confined to bed. I, with more than a hint of sarcasm, reminded them that when we reached the Caxito camp, they had all rushed to occupy the 'suite' – only to find that the room was infested with mosquitos. With the others struck down, however, it was then left to me to compile the final draft report.

To correctly understand the disturbances, we had to analyse specific events in the context of the growing problems that had arisen in our camps in Angola over the previous few years. When we first established our camps in Angola, we experienced a number of obstacles. However, since the leadership was based in the camps with the MK cadres and was supported by cadres who came into exile in the early 1960s as part of Luthuli Detachment – the majority of whom were experienced and tried-

and-tested comrades – it was possible to solve the problems politically and timeously. The disciplined and politically correct relationship between the various levels of leadership and the cadres also allowed redress without any serious consequences. The Novo Catengue camp symbolised the vision and mission of a people's army: logistics were well organised and care was taken to ensure adequate and varied food supplies. If and when there were shortages, which is always a distinct possibility in war conditions, then both the leadership and the cadres suffered. There was no preferential treatment. Indeed, conditions in our camps during this period were 'good', not only in relation to food supplies, but also because there were well-organised medical, recreational and cultural activities. The military training conducted by MK veterans assisted by Cubans was both thorough and professional. The priority orientation to political education and development was impressive, and discipline was maintained through 'constructive punishment', with cadres themselves being involved in disciplinary processes. In fact, the Novo Catengue camp was fondly referred to as the University of the South.

The relationship between the administration and the rank-and-file therefore rested on a firm but comradely footing characterised by a revolutionary atmosphere which was based on discipline, high morale and combat readiness. Such an environment made it easier to deal with problems as they arose and before they reached crisis proportions. Crucially, there were limited opportunities for the many infiltrators to exploit. However, after the South African Air Force destroyed the Novo Catengue camp in 1979, our remaining camps had to be moved to unfavourable and often more hostile terrain surrounded by UNITA forces in southern Angola. This had a profound effect on camp dynamics: there was a considerable increase in complaints relating to the 'availability of food and cigarettes', 'womanising by the camp leaders', maladministration, nepotism, improper deployment and a rising number of casualties following skirmishes with UNITA. These complaints could have been dealt with politically if living conditions were better and if the quality of political leadership and education remained at the level at which we started in Angola.

Our report concluded that despite Angola being a 'rear base', it had been used as a 'dumping ground' for enemy agents, suspects, malcontents and generally undisciplined cadres. The key question that arose in the commission's findings related to why enemy agents who had been rounded up throughout southern Africa – and even those who had been sent from within the country – were all congregated in Angola. This endangered our movement and had to be stopped immediately or our camps in Angola would continue to become convenient points of enemy penetration and centres of subversion. This did not, however, solve the sticky problem of what to do with enemy agents, whether confirmed or suspect, and I do not think the commission satisfactorily answered this question.

We also found that confessed agents were in many instances deployed to sensitive positions in the camps. They were typically cooks, medical officers and even commissars in some cases. Some suspects had been in our camps for as long as eight years, and became key instigators of the disturbances that broke out. Clearly we had not yet been able to adopt a more strategic and methodical approach. There are many examples of other struggles in Africa, Asia and Latin America where confessed or suspected enemy agents were summarily executed, but because of its revolutionary morality the ANC chose not to follow this path and I am not sure that there is even a textbook solution to this problem.

A Committee of Ten had been formed in February 1984 to represent the grievances of cadres at the Viana camp, where some of its leading members, as well as some of those closely connected with them, had a long record of anti-movement activities and dissension. They had for years exploited every opportunity to foment factionalism and to undermine the organisation's leadership and policies. Some even harboured illusions of power and had chased leadership ambitions in their quest to achieve reactionary and counter-revolutionary goals. But we did not have sufficient evidence to conclude that the Committee of Ten was part of an organised conspiracy on behalf of the South African regime.

While understanding that there were some genuine grievances, we were strongly critical of the tactics some cadres had used to resolve their grievances. Under no circumstances could the movement condone the indiscriminate shooting and terrorising of Angolan citizens, the total rejection and contempt of authority, the breakdown of military discipline and the drinking and marijuana smoking as a means dissent and protest. Indeed, some of those involved in the disturbances were very conscious of the consequences of their activities.

Another important contributing factor behind the disturbances was the quality of our cadres. Generally, because of the influx of many 'walk-ins' into our ranks, the level of political consciousness had deteriorated and this made it easy for cadres to be influenced and manipulated. Under these circumstances, they were also vulnerable to South African propaganda that was beamed mainly through Radio South Africa. This type of propaganda effectively convinced some of our cadres that the majority of youth in the country wanted the armed struggle to escalate, but that our leadership instead chose to emphasise the political struggle because they were leading 'a very comfortable life abroad' and 'had no serious intention of confronting the enemy'.

Also, magazines like *Africa Confidential* (which I suspected had some links to British Intelligence) and South African and foreign radio stations found their way into our camps and became important sources of disinformation. This material, and its mostly negative content, were used as a basis for distorted and misconstrued political discussions. And, of course, the camps did not have access to sufficient alternative material and there were no regular briefings by the administration about political developments in South Africa and elsewhere.

The vast majority of the MK cadres came from urban areas and many were students. The commission reiterated the ANC NEC's conclusion of the need to strengthen our internal organisational machinery so as to enable us to recruit more workers and peasants and therefore create a more balanced people's army. We had to face the reality that without improving the quality of our cadres and ensuring that there was greater class and social representation in the army, we would be almost certainly subjected to further disturbances initiated and exploited by enemy agents.

Our main recommendation urged the leadership to initiate a well-organised political education campaign in all our Angolan camps. This would help to restore necessary confidence and trust in the leadership and in the leadership's ability to lead the struggle to ultimate victory. It would enable us to raise the levels of political consciousness and thereby provide our cadres with a better understanding of the progress we were making and the challenges we were confronting in trying to advance our armed struggle, but also explain the concerted military and political offensive the apartheid regime and its international patrons had launched against the ANC and other liberation movements in the region.

We also made other important recommendations. One was the strengthening the modalities of political leadership among the camp administrations and the Commissariat, as well as the security, information and logistics departments. This was based on our conclusion that investigations in Angola had highlighted problems that could exist in many other areas where ANC cadres were located. In another set of recommendations we advised that a Revolutionary Tribunal be established which would be provided with formal guidelines for trying all security cases; and that disciplinary problems be handled by camp commanders and commissars and not by the intelligence department. It had become clear that after 1981 the influx of recently arrived young cadres into the Intelligence had led to some abuses. Our final recommendation was that the NEC appoint a National Preparatory Committee with a clear mandate to organise a national conference to deal with rapidly evolving developments in South Africa, the region and the world in order to plot the way forward.

I believe the Stuart Commission's work helped give the leadership a more comprehensive understanding of the objective conditions in our camps, the dangers of enemy agents exploiting problems in the camps and therefore the urgency to deal decisively with the problems in Angolan camps. It also helped us think more strategically about our existential dilemmas as a movement in the context of fast-changing circumstances at home and abroad.

The bottom line was that unrest and protest action that erupted across our various Angolan camps in December 1983 resulted from the very difficult and challenging circumstances under which a liberation movement such as the ANC had to function. It was a sobering reminder that we were not a government, but were operating in exile and as such were prone to making mistakes in our conduct and judgement. We did not have the capacity, the equipment or adequate detention centres to deal with the rising and toxic levels of infiltration. It is unfortunate that these incidents, which included the loss of life, and the levels of dissension they provoked, were used as a propaganda offensive to discredit the ANC and to depict our leadership as authoritarian 'Stalinists' who showed scant respect for the rules of war, combatants' welfare, human rights and so forth. In fact, the ANC is the only liberation movement that is a signatory to the Geneva Convention of 1949, which comprises four internationally binding treaties and three additional protocols for defining humanitarian conduct during war.

Developments in the SACP

While in London in 1967, I was recruited into the structures of the SACP. This was a totally new experience for me but allowed me to grow in personal confidence and political maturity. Party membership gave me a new political vantage point, because in its small units I acquired a much better understanding of the dialectical relationship between the class and the national struggle and the concomitant importance of progressive nationalism. Party membership taught us about the importance of discipline, commitment and responsibility. One always felt that being a member of the party placed greater demands on you as a revolutionary; and one was always aware that the party did not tolerate indiscipline and bad working habits. Most importantly, being a member of the party made us better members of those ANC structures to which we belonged. We understood the dangers of reactionary nationalism and the need to confront them by ensuring that ANC policies remained driven by progressive ideas and vision.

The unit I was in was a well-organised and tight-knit group and included

Rusty Bernstein, Berry Feinberg, Mannie Brown, Stephanie Sachs, Hillary Rabkin (the sister of David Rabkin who was killed in a training camp in Angola when a sabotaged weapon exploded while he was training) and Brigitte and Garth Strachan (Ronnie and Eleanor Kasrils' daughter and son-in-law).

Given the realities of the exile community in London, there were some concerns that Party membership was predominantly white; that contact with CC members in Africa was sporadic and not good; that the CC was not functioning effectively; that contact between the CC and its membership was limited; and that formal relationships with the ANC were not effective. The main tasks of the London party units were to intensify solidarity work, advance Marxist-Leninist thinking to all sections of the Alliance and to distribute Party literature. The London leadership also maintained contact with the communist parties of the Soviet Union, Europe, Africa and the US. In 1966 the SACP organised two meetings with several African parties to discuss a socialist agenda for Africa. Against this background, there were constant debates about whether the party should play a 'low-profile role' or take a more 'public posture'. Some of our leadership in Africa argued for a low-profile role.

A CC meeting of the party in 1968 decided that it would be re-established in South Africa. In addition, it was agreed that there was a need for closer cooperation between the SACP and the ANC, and that strengthening the socialist outlook in the movement could be a source of strength and could shape the future of the country in combating racial, tribal and other divisive and reactionary influences. Subsequently, the Morogoro consultative conference in April 1969 took a decision to formalise the relationship between the ANC and the SACP, thereby resolving in part an increasingly divisive debate in the Alliance structures about who leads the struggle, the role of minorities, the leading role of the ANC and so on. Contrary to the widely held view of extreme theoretical and doctrinal tensions between the ANC and SACP, I must stress that any differences that did exist were mainly to do with what Marxists would call 'praxis' – in other words, how we translated our common understanding of struggle into ensuring that our structures, policies and operations produced practical outcomes on the ground.

Then, in 1970, the party organised an extended and enlarged CC meeting in Moscow and I was invited to attend. This was a remarkable experience, for here I was with old stalwarts such as Ruth First, Dr Dadoo, Brian and Sonia Bunting, Michael Harmel, Joe Slovo, Moses Mabhida, Josiah Jele, Ray Alexander Simons, Chris Hani, Rusty Bernstein, Eric Mtshali and Dan Tloome, as well as comrades I had not seen for many years and had known from my time in South Africa. At the conference, a number of issues were discussed and resolutions adopted, among them relations with the ANC, the armed struggle and organisational work. It was also decided to improve the work of the CC and to establish new party units. On the armed struggle, the resolution continued to argue that guerrilla warfare had to be launched from the rural areas. Clearly we were still influenced by the classical concept of guerrilla warfare. Chris Hani, Josiah Jele and Moses Mabhida were elected to the CC. During the Moscow meetings, I had the unique distinction of staying in Joseph Stalin's *dacha,* the huge lounge and bedrooms of which I shared with Thabo Mbeki. Besides our usual political discussions, Mbeki kept reprimanding me about my limited understanding of classical music and spent quite a bit of time trying to educate me, introducing me to Berlioz, Verdi and other famous composers and musicians. To this day, I love to listen to classical music.

However, despite the 1970 meeting, working and operational relations between the party and the ANC remained strained. In September 1972 the CC met to discuss the offensive against the party by 'dissidents' and the exclusion of party representatives from an important ANC meeting in Lusaka in 1971, which examined 'strategic questions related to new developments inside the country'. In his report, Slovo expressed concern that the party was seen to be a formation for coloured, Indian and white members and that 'all Africans are the almost exclusive property of the ANC – an impression has become even more entrenched that we are a minority organisation ... [And as such] we have only a qualified right to mobilise people at home under the Party's banner.' He went on to say, 'We hear attacks against us every time it leaks out that we take a collective stand on an important issue even in support of the ANC Executive.' He concluded on an apocalyptic note that if this trend continued 'we might as well decide here and now to liquidate the Party'. I believe that Slovo, based in London, was strongly influenced by the exposure of the Okhele initiative, which was alleged to be a plot by Johnny Makhathini involving the writer and poet Breyten Breytenbach and other South Africans to organise the 'new left' in Europe as a counter to the SACP, and was exaggerating the problem of marginalisation. I never believed that Okhele could be a serious threat to the SACP. Leading CC members held important positions in the ANC and there was no serious danger that anti-SACP thinking would dominate the ANC. Also, ANC-SACP relations at that stage had not been properly worked out, and if the matter was not handled sensitively it could play into the hands of reactionary anti-party elements.

Admittedly, critical issues discussed in the ANC-SACP meeting in 1969 remained unresolved. This included party recruitment in the exile community, and in the ANC leadership there was still opposition to the SACP's role in establishing structures, especially within MK, and fears that the party was imposing its ideological and political lines. These were certainly trying times and the SACP's strategic response was to strengthen its support for CC members based in Africa, increase the number of units in East Africa and support the organised formation of SACTU in exile. The leadership capacity of the party was also significantly enhanced with the election in 1973 of Dr Dadoo as Chairperson to replace the recently deceased JB Marks; Moses Mabhida as the new General-Secretary; Chris Hani as Assistant General-Secretary; and the appointment of Eric Mtshali as a full-time party functionary. The party's educational and propaganda work was also to receive greater attention, with a focus on improving the 'Inner-Party Bulletin' (established in 1970) and the party magazine *Inkululeko-Freedom* (established in 1971).

In 1979, the second extended meeting of the CC was held in the GDR, where Moses Mabhida was re-elected General-Secretary. Mabhida was adamant that the party's internal reconstruction work had to be driven from Africa, because by this time more of the CC leadership was based in Africa. Given these developments, it was agreed that the headquarters would be moved to Africa, and in 1982 the party headquarters relocated to Maputo and then, after the signing of the Nkomati Accord between South Africa and Mozambique, to Lusaka. A number of regional structures were also established across the continent, including in Angola, Swaziland, Botswana, Lesotho, Mozambique, Tanzania and South Africa. Senior CC members were assigned various party regions in Africa. Mabhida was assigned Angola and Tanzania; Slovo, Zimbabwe and Luanda; Hani, Lesotho; John Nkadimeng, Mozambique and Swaziland; and Dan Tloome, Botswana.

The move of the SACP headquarters to Africa and the strategic deployment of senior party leaders to regional structures had a positive effect on the party in that they ensured that the working relations between the party and the ANC took place on a more consistent and coherent basis. As a result, relationships between the Alliance structures became less antagonistic. In 1982, agreements were reached that the ANC and the SACP would meet formally at least twice a year and that the party could establish units within MK structures in Angola. However, although formal working relations between the ANC and the SACP had improved, there were still some tensions, especially relating to the roles of SACP units in MK and in the ANC and SACTU structures.

In September 1981, a CC meeting crafted a resolution entitled 'Party Work in Fraternal Organisations'. It affirmed 'the right and duty of communists working in the national movement to discuss and decide on their common approach to all matters which affect the basic direction and content of the revolutionary struggle, and to ensure that they advance and support such decision in any organ that in which the matter arises'. And further that 'every Party cadre who is active in any level of a fraternal organisation is accountable to the Party collective to which he or she is a member for his or her work and conduct in that organisation'. Comrades were cautioned that disciplinary measures would be taken against anyone who breached this resolution.

But the resolution, which required party members to account for their work in ANC and SACTU structures, was complex and fraught with political problems. Some party members within the Alliance structures incorrectly interpreted this to mean that party units were elite structures acting as a 'caucus' and 'managing' the Alliance structures. This concern was compounded by some party cadres who were not involved in ANC work demanding constant briefings of work being done in ANC structures – which was problematic particularly when dealing with the sensitivities of underground work. In response, the party leadership cautioned all members that newly formed party structures within MK and the ANC should not be misused by demanding reports from cadres working in other Alliance structures, taking sectarian positions or by challenging the leading role of the ANC within the Alliance. Our SACP comrades had a special responsibility to articulate the correct understanding of the relationship between the national and class struggles.

The Cuban experience

I was part of the SACP delegation – which included Joe Slovo, Ronny Kasrils and Sizakele Sigxashe – that visited Cuba in the early 1980s and met with senior leaders of the Cuban Communist Party, including Fidel Castro. This visit was particularly enlightening because the strategic perspectives conveyed to us by the Cubans were fundamentally different from the constant propaganda portraying them as 'militarists' who believed strongly in power through 'the barrel of the gun', and who were totally committed to nationalisation and expropriation. The Cubans explained how after the Bay of Pigs invasion, a US-orchestrated attempt to overthrow the Cuban government, they had had to resort to more drastic economic measures, although they appreciated that the conditions were not right.

In relation to South Africa, they discussed the clauses of the Freedom Charter and indicated that some of these – the nationalisation clause, for instance – were far beyond what could be realistically achieved in South Africa, given the world political and economic situation. They shared with us their experiences when they were forced to nationalise, which resulted in the assets of Cuban big business leaving the country. These capitalists patented major Cuban products in the US and elsewhere, and used the labels without permission from the Cuban authorities. They also withdrew enormous financial and other resources. As a result, Cuba lost skilled expertise and had to face economic, military and political subversion. The Cubans indicated that in a world that was becoming increasingly globalised, the issue of nationalisation was not realistic and that, especially in the South African situation, we should revisit the clauses dealing with nationalisation, for example.

Of course, our delegation defended the Alliance policies on the economic clauses of the Freedom Charter and explained that the Charter was adopted at the Congress of the People. We explained the specific nature of the South African economy, which was dominated by a small white minority, and that it was therefore appropriate to nationalise in the context of the vast discrepancy of wealth between the 'haves' and 'have-nots' and the ownership of the means of production by a very small minority, which excluded the vast majority of our people. The Cubans, however, continued to offer examples of the consequences of nationalisation in Cuba and in many other Latin American countries. It was important to get a different perspective from Cuban comrades, and the discussion had a profound impact on my thinking. I concluded that the Freedom Charter was not 'cast in stone' and that perhaps we may need to reconsider some clauses within the context of the changing international and national situation. However, I understood that any changes to the Freedom Charter could only be made by an ANC conference.

At this point, the Cubans were providing specialist military training to some of our best cadres. In discussing the armed struggle in South Africa, their analysis was that the country was heavily urbanised and developed, and that the regime had one of Africa's strongest military and security machineries and enjoyed the support of all the major Western powers. In these conditions, the armed struggle would thus have to be based on political mobilisation and, according to them, a conventional type of people's war was not realistic. They highlighted not only their own experiences, but also the experiences of the liberation movements of Latin America and elsewhere. We explained the specific characteristics of the South African struggle that forced us to adopt the 'armed propaganda' approach. The Cubans did not waver from their broad strategic approach to armed struggle in South Africa, and arranged for us to meet with representatives of the Farabundo Martí NLF, operating in El Salvador. This was an attempt to reinforce their counter-arguments about our approach to armed struggle.

Naturally, one of the highlights of the visit was our meetings with Fidel Castro, who proved to be an immensely charismatic and intelligent leader. I had read a lot about him and the Cuban Revolution, and was impressed by his book, *Conversation with Christians*. This was an excellent treatise on how Marxists and Christians should cooperate to fight poverty, nuclear warfare and dictators, and have a common understanding of democracy, human rights and the rule of law. We also had extensive discussions on the Cuban internationalist support for Angola's MPLA government. Practically every Cuban family had a family member who had fought in the war against the SADF troops and UNITA in Angola, and many had died. We discussed the Cuban missile crisis, Cuban relations with the Soviet Union and the Sino-Soviet dispute. The result was that many of my earlier concerns were dispelled during these dialogues.

We also got a better understanding of the US counter-revolutionary activities against Cuba. Until my visit to Cuba, I had condemned the US attacks on Cuba without fully grasping the nature of the Cuban Revolution and the extent of US aggression against this nation-state. I left Cuba convinced that I had deepened my own understanding of the challenges and dangers of creating a socialist system in a developing country, facing counter-revolution orchestrated by the most powerful imperialist power in the world. In fact, our visit allowed me to gain a better understanding of the political and economic developments in the whole of Latin America. I also better understood the nature of subversion of progressive forces in Latin America, Asia, the Middle East and Africa. And so it was that when I returned to London I took every opportunity, in the party units and in ANC structures, to put forward the perspectives of the Cubans, the depth of analysis and the genuine commitment to fundamental transformation, opposition to dogmatism and sectarianism. All my subsequent trips to Cuba could only be a further elaboration of the foundations I had developed during the visit of the SACP delegation.

The Moscow Congress

In 1984, the SACP held its sixth congress in Moscow. Moses Mabhida was re-elected General-Secretary and Joe Slovo, who had been acting chairman since the death of Dr Dadoo in 1983, was elected Chairperson. It is difficult to describe my emotions when I was elected to the CC, the leading organ of the party.

This sixth congress – which debated and adopted the Party Constitution – heralded another critical turning point in the life of the SACP, as it took place against a background of major developments unfolding in South Africa. These included the growing crisis of the regime and the emergence of the Mass Democratic Movement (MDM). At the meeting there were intense, constructively critical discussions on improving the quality of work of all party structures, especially the CC and the PB; but it was the discussions about a People's War that dominated proceedings. Following the ANC delegation's visit to Vietnam and the adoption of the Green Book, it was now accepted that the idea of a guerrilla war launched from the rural areas was not sustainable and we had to plan non-traditional methods of guerrilla warfare in urban areas. Our 'forests and mountains' had to be the masses. The Party Constitution stated unequivocally that the SACP is the leading force of the South African working class and 'is in the vanguard in the struggle for national liberation, socialism and peace in our time'. To ensure that there was no confusion about the notion of the 'vanguard role', it was agreed that the party 'was to participate in and strengthen the liberation alliance of all classes and strata whose interests are served by the immediate aims of the national democratic revolution'. This alliance was expressed through the liberation front, headed by the ANC.

This conclusion was a significant response to the sharp ideological discussions taking place during the 1970s and '80s. Some 'left' liberals on one hand, and young militant activists, on the other, had joined the ANC, while others had been recruited into the SACP. 'Vulgar Marxism', which tended to distort the essential logic of the struggle for political power, was a polemical current of this period and debates were further complicated by the self-serving and factional activities of 'African Nationalists' like the Gang of Eight. It was necessary, based on a better understanding of Marxism-Leninism, to have greater clarity about the relationship between the national and the class struggles, and to counteract and weather the worrying tendencies developing within the Alliance structures.

In London, a small group of 'leftists' had infiltrated the SACTU office and used this as a base in their attempt to confuse, disorganise and divide the ANC and SACTU structures, as well as the broader anti-apartheid movement. They tended to talk left, but in reality nothing that they proposed would have taken us in a direction that could be considered progressive. My experiences with the Sussex Trotskyites and ultra-leftists put me in a good position to understand this phenomenon within our ranks. If these elements had succeeded, our movement's progress would have been severely retarded. Some communist parties in Latin America, Asia, the Middle East and Africa adopted policies that ignored the concrete stage of the NDR and ventured to 'go it alone'. But they paid a heavy price and the worldwide progressive movement also suffered as a result. In terms of this formulation, it was vital for all of us to pay special attention to fighting and defeating the 'leftist' tendencies that were emerging predominantly within the London office of SACTU. However, even in the SACP there was a 'leftist', but totally myopic perspective of advancing 'socialism now', and some comrades were even beginning to raise the issue of the party spearheading this hegemonic tenet on its own. This reinforced my conviction that it was critical that we improve the ideological literacy of our work in the Alliance. For the future of our non-racial and democratic revolution, it was important to defeat the dogmatism and erroneous tendencies of exponents of the 'socialism now' orthodoxy.

As a party, we thought it important to encourage debate within a framework of democratic centralism. As a basic postulate of all communist parties, this meant combining free political expression in the party and the open election of leaders with strict hierarchical discipline in executing decisions reached by democratic means. This helped to ensure that the party always prided itself on being a 'Party of the best and tested Comrades'. The slogan that drove our recruitment policy was 'fewer but better'.

In his speech to celebrate the 60th anniversary of the SACP in July 1981, Oliver Tambo brilliantly and succinctly reflected the perspectives that I and many other comrades had learnt from the ANC:

> To be true to history, we must concede that there has been difficulties as well as triumphs along our part, as, traversing many decades, our two organisations have converged towards a shared strategy of our struggle. Ours is not merely a paper alliance, created at conference tables and formalised through the signing of documents and representing only an agreement of leaders. Our alliance is a living organism that has grown out of struggle. We have built it out of our separate and common experiences.

The Havana Congress

The seventh Congress took place in Havana, Cuba, in April 1989 and was attended by 49 delegates, which included those from South Africa and the party's underground structures. The 'Path to Power' dominated proceedings, but in my view the document ignored critical realities: the Berlin Wall had collapsed; the Union of Soviet Socialists Republics (USSR) and other socialist countries were experiencing serious contradictions and crises; China was adopting 'Socialism with Chinese Characteristics'; and communist parties in the West were in retreat. Yet the SACP's analysis was that the world was going through an era of transition from capitalism to socialism, which would be the catalyst for a People's War that would result in the seizure of power – all of which was totally erroneous. The 'Path to Power' stirred some controversy, especially since it was an extensive ideological and analytical elaboration of revolutionary processes, the thesis of 'colonialism of a special type' and the transition from capitalism to socialism.

Soon after the seventh Congress, on 2 February 1990, FW de Klerk announced the unbanning of the ANC, the SACP and other organisations. At that time, some comrades were not aware of the many secret talks that had taken place between Nelson Mandela and representatives of PW Botha's regime, as well as the secret talks in the UK and Switzerland, all of which provided tremendous impetus for De Klerk's announcement and the subsequent negotiations between the ANC and the government (I discuss the nature of these secret talks more fully in subsequent chapters).

Later in February 1990, an extended Politburo meeting took place in Lusaka to discuss the consequences of legalising the party. One view – represented by Slovo, Hani and Kasrils, among others – argued that the party should become a mass party, while another view – whose proponents were Mbeki, Zuma, me and others – argued that the current stage of the NDR demanded that the ANC remain the leading force behind the struggle, but that the party should continue to play its historical role of deepening the content of the NDR. Becoming a mass party posed too many dangers. Firstly, it did not take into account the virulent strain of anti-communism that prevailed not only in South Africa, but also elsewhere in Africa and the world. Then there was the potential for unhealthy competition within the Alliance, the threat of 'vulgar Marxism', a lack of appreciating the historical juncture of the NDR, as well as the negative impact a mass character would have on the ideological integrity of the party. After lengthy debate the meeting resolved that 'the outcome, speed, and social content of the democratic revolution necessitate the existence of the party as a legal, public, and independent political vanguard of the working people. The reconstitution will need speed and bold steps.' The majority decision (with the exception of some senior SACP leaders) was that the SACP would become a mass party and that an 'internal leadership core' would make their membership public. They would be selected from a list of names that included Govan Mbeki, Ahmed Kathrada, Andrew Mlangeni, Elias Motsoaledi, Billy Nair, Chris Dlamini and Sydney Mufamadi. A final list of 12 out of 20 CC members was agreed to for this purpose.

I remain convinced that the historical experiences and strategic congress decisions, which underpinned the party's development, were ignored after it was legalised. Indeed, mass recruitment into party structures has fundamentally affected the class character and quality of its membership and leadership. It has also resulted in 'entryism' and the failure to correctly understand the relationship between the national and class struggles and the role of the party at this stage of the NDR. The party's increasingly hybrid character and movement away from its founding heterodoxy helps to explain why after 1994 it experienced a serious crisis of political legitimacy and ideological relevance.

I, in the meantime, continued – sometimes subconsciously, it has to be said – to integrate these developments with experiences from my own life, to weave what transpired on regional and international platforms with my own quest for personal growth and my participation in the struggle. By this point, it was clear to me that I could not divorce the two, and straddled worlds that may have appeared to be diverse, but were in fact tightly interwoven.

Chapter 4

Intensifying the struggle and the crisis of apartheid

The 1980s will be remembered for mass-militant struggle that reached unprecedented heights in South Africa. This resulted in a nationwide state of emergency between July 1985 and June 1986, which gave the police sweeping powers of arbitrary arrest, detention, torture and interrogation, as well as the banning of meetings and preventing any media coverage of unrest. The level of state tyranny was particularly severe on anti-apartheid political organisations, in what was really a desperate attempt by the Botha regime to impose martial control on the country. More than 30 organisations were banned during the state of emergency and unofficial estimates were that as many as 30 000 people had been detained. In addition, between 5 000 and 8 000 soldiers were deployed across the seething townships in order to supplement the overstretched police in enforcing the draconian emergency regulations. The regime, it seemed, hoped that this level of control would provide the political leverage to impose its 'reform' agenda without much hindrance from opposition forces.

In the southern African region, the apartheid regime was also engaged in a violent destabilisation campaign that had far-reaching implications. Between 1980 and 1989, according to a British Commonwealth committee, this campaign resulted in the deaths of one million people, had left more than three million destitute and homeless, and had caused billions of dollars worth of damage and destruction to the economies of neighbouring countries. The consequence was greater international pressure to tighten sanctions against South Africa.

There were – and still are – commentators, such as academics, journalists and analysts who concluded that the ANC in exile was 'totally out of touch' with events in South Africa, and that the organisation had no or very little influence on internal developments. While we must not exaggerate the role of the ANC, the SACP and SACTU, it would be a gross distortion of history to deny that the Alliance – through its propaganda activities, armed actions and growing organisational network in the country – did not exercise a significant impact on the increasing militancy, strength and consolidation of the internal struggle. We should also remember that political prisoners had been released, who had been sentenced in the 1960s and who had been forged in the crucible of the 'University of Robben Island' while serving long jail terms. They and many of the ANC cadres who had not gone into exile started to participate in political activities. Moreover, military action by MK operatives and the effects of political trials during this period also became important platforms for the mobilisation of our people and the popularisation of the ANC's armed activity. Every trial in the repressive climate, punctuated by two states of emergency declared by PW Botha, was used as a platform to advance ANC policies and to project the image of the ANC, which was complemented by the distribution of Alliance literature and leaflet bombs.

However, PW Botha's 'Total Onslaught' strategy necessitated a change in approach where, for instance, some comrades argued that the Indian Congress should be reactivated so that it could participate in the tragicomedy of the Tricameral Parliament with coloureds, while Africans were relegated to the atomised Bantustans or farcical urban apartheid municipal councils. Dr Dadoo was asked to organise meetings with Indian comrades in London to discuss future ANC responses to the imposition of institutions such as the Tricameral system and the general mobilisation of this community in the work of the ANC. In 1979 a delegation of NIC leaders, which included stalwarts such as Pravin Gordhan, Ismail Meer and Thumba Pillay, travelled from South Africa to meet with the ANC leadership. They were joined by another NIC member, Roy Padayachee, who happened to be in London at the time. The RC delegation was led by Dr Dadoo and included Mac Maharaj, Essop Pahad and myself. Among the group of NIC leaders were 'participationists' who based their argument on Lenin's thesis of 'Two Tactics' in order to tackle and weaken the apartheid edifice from within the system. After two days of intense and heated debates, we strongly advised against participation in the Tricameral Parliament because it would set a wrong and dangerous precedent in legitimising what was, after all, a spurious and disingenuous attempt by the apartheid regime to engineer political reform by co-opting the coloured and Indian communities.

Growing popular resistance

During the 1980s we were thus facing a fundamentally changed situation. A popular groundswell throughout the country challenged, in a highly organised manner, the repressive excesses of the apartheid regime at every level, including in schools, workplaces, cultural societies, and religious and sporting bodies. It was also a period when the armed struggle was intensified. This was clearly reflected in the May 1983 bombing outside the Nedbank building in central Pretoria that killed the two ANC comrades who had planted the bomb, as well as 19 civilians, and injuring close to 200 people. There were other attacks, too, which indicated that armed actions were escalating. These included, in 1980, an attack against the SASOL refineries in Secunda and Sasolburg; and in 1981, attacks against the Arnot and Camden power stations and the Voortrekkerhoogte military base (this was the first time that artillery was used and also signalled a shift from economic to military targets). In December 1982, there was the spectacular attack on the Koeberg nuclear power plant; and in May 1983 an attack on the South African Air Force building on Church Street in Pretoria. For the first time white South Africa was suffering civilian casualties and MK cadres were using more sophisticated weapons. The apartheid regime could not ignore this reality.

In 1983 the United Democratic Front (UDF) was launched. Prior to the formation of the UDF, OR Tambo, in the annual January 8th Statement of the same year, had called for the formation of a united democratic front organisation in South Africa. Many discussions had also taken place between the ANC in exile and political, trade union, religious, academic, sporting and cultural leaders from South Africa. At the UDF launch, Allan Boesak, president of the World Alliance of Reformed Churches, mesmerised the crowd with his rhetorical eloquence when he used what he called 'three little words' that expressed our seriousness in the struggle: '*All Here Now* – we want all our rights, we want them here and we want them now.' He went on to state that the time had come for white people in this country to realise that their destinies were inextricably interwoven with ours and that they shall never be free until we are free. Until its banning, the UDF proved to be an inspirational and imaginative political formation of many different groupings in the country, all united in their struggle against apartheid. Within a year of its launch, it had 600 affiliates and represented some three million people.

I was fortunate that, in preparing for the launch of the UDF, I was part of the ANC group in exile which had many discussions with the UDF's internal leadership, who we met in several European countries before and after the party's formation. In fact, prior to the launch of the UDF, Thabo Mbeki and I had met Allan Boesak in London and discussed what his opening address at the launch should contain. There were also some tactical issues where we sought to iron out our differences because some UDF comrades did not fully understand the potential divisiveness of certain matters. For example, they were being advised by their 'friends' in the country, as well as abroad, to establish international UDF offices. We had extensive discussions in order to convince them that this was part of an orchestrated scheme to promote alternatives to the ANC and to weaken the democratic forces. As a result, this plan did not go ahead. Also, the UDF leadership was receiving invitations from foreign governments and non-governmental organisations alike. Some were genuinely interested in supporting its efforts, while others had ulterior motives in seeking alternatives to the ANC.

We had also been involved in intense discussions taking place in the country about the formation of the Congress of South African Trade Unions (COSATU). In 1984 senior delegations of the progressive trade union formations came to London to meet the senior Alliance leadership. I was a member of this delegation. We met at the home of a British sympathiser in South London where over 30 of us crowded into one room. The meeting started around 10 a.m. and continued till about 8 a.m. the following morning. The meeting concluded that it would be in the interests of the NDR for COSATU to be formed. As irony would have it, an enemy agent was part of the trade union delegation and was later exposed. He had, however, given a full report to his handlers and in his report I was condescendingly referred to as an 'Indian-looking man'!

Soon after the visit to London, in 1985, the formation of COSATU was announced publicly and it became a powerful force of struggle, with strike action reaching the highest levels in decades. The federation worked closely with the UDF, and both organisations managed to build strong links with the ANC in exile. The growing influence of COSATU was demonstrated when it called a strike on May Day in 1985 and 2.5 million workers responded to the call to stay at home. At a time when industrial relations were decidedly in favour of employers, it was no surprise that employers retaliated brutally. Many workers were arbitrarily dismissed and one strike by the major COSATU affiliate, the National Union of Mineworkers, resulted in 50 000 miners being dismissed. The exponential increase of strikes, coupled with other forms of mass action, were having a severe and deleterious effect on the economy. In 1986 there were nearly 800 strikes, which was a record for South Africa, and some 2 700 trade unionists were arrested. The government thus introduced the Labour Relations Amendment Act, which enabled bosses to sue for losses of profits resulting from industrial action and which imposed restrictions on strikes. In September 1988 the government banned unions from engaging in any activities that had an ostensible political orientation.

As part of the repressive apartheid vortex, in September 1984 there was another massacre in Sharpeville in which six people were killed in clashes with the police, and as an expression of popular anger, three people identified as collaborators were murdered by the demonstrators. In typical fashion, the state then deployed thousands of troops to carry out reprisal attacks in Sebokeng, Sharpeville and Boipatong townships. It was not long, however, before the cycle of state-sponsored violence spread to other parts of the country, and in March 1985, during a huge demonstration of about 4 000 people in Port Elizabeth, the police opened fire yet again, killing 20 people. This prompted Archbishop Desmond Tutu, the Anglican Archbishop in Cape Town, to call on all churches to participate in the struggle, and he made a public appeal to the international community to impose sanctions on the regime. Not unsurprisingly, the massacre in Port Elizabeth sparked retaliatory action by anti-apartheid activists and those identified as collaborators became prime targets. This was the period when 'necklacing' was adopted by some sections of the youth: a tyre was placed around the neck of a suspected collaborator, doused with petrol and then ignited.

These increasingly unacceptable and inhumane retaliations were condemned by the movement because they were not only contrary to our values, but could also be exploited effectively by the apartheid government. We were concerned that the regime would use its very effective overt and covert propaganda machinery to portray senior leaders and members of the MDM as collaborators, thus making them vulnerable to attacks and necklacing as well. Internationally, necklacing was used to project the ANC and MDM as 'ruthless thugs' intent on creating chaos and disaster. The horrific pictures of victims were sensationally splashed across international media and even some of our staunchest international supporters expressed deep concern. We were conscious that in the face of the regime's total onslaught and aggression, collaborators had become the most hated elements in our society and that the anger of some youth in the townships would be vented against them. We were opposed to necklacing, but also realised that we had to confront this issue in a manner that did not alienate township youths. We therefore communicated the message to the democratic movement and underground ANC structures that necklacing had to cease forthwith. Later, at the Harare Children and Repression Conference in 1987, attended by over 200 delegates from South Africa, including the late Beyers Naudé, Oliver Tambo spoke out strongly and unequivocally against this practice.

In its January 8th Statement of 1985, the ANC called on the people to make 'South Africa ungovernable', and the objective conditions were such that people responded to this call with much enthusiasm. The army was deployed to support the police, and by July 1985 the situation had reached such crisis proportions that PW Botha imposed a state of emergency across South Africa – the first of its kind since the Sharpeville massacre 25 years earlier. The police were given sweeping powers, but what was different now from the 1960s was that state violence and repression could not contain the militant mass action that was taking place throughout the country. Within three months, an estimated 14 000 people had been arrested, 5 000 were held in custody, and nearly 700 killed and 20 000 injured. It was clear that a mini-insurrection was taking place.

The Kabwe Conference

In June 1985 the ANC held a national consultative conference in Kabwe, Zambia, which brought together four generations of ANC leadership going back to the 1940s. The conference dealt with many issues that confronted Alliance structures since the banning of the ANC. Correctly understanding the documents and debates at Kabwe would be an important step in helping us to better manage the challenges our movement faces today. As was usually the case prior to a conference such as this, all ANC regional political committees – including London – had to prepare and thoroughly canvass draft discussion documents. I was the secretary of the London Regional Committee and had to ensure that the discussions contributed to enriching our draft documents.

The most critical consideration of the conference was the political developments in South Africa and mapping out perspectives for dealing with the upsurge of mass-militant struggle and the growing crisis of the regime. For obvious reasons, we could not expect much of a contribution from our comrades on Robben Island or those who were still surviving in the very difficult, harsh and oppressive conditions in South Africa. However, the Kabwe Conference was nevertheless a landmark event for the ANC. The NEC report delivered by the then president of the ANC, Oliver Tambo, and in which Thabo Mbeki played an important role in its drafting, was excellent. It showed a deep strategic and analytically sophisticated understanding of developments inside the country, the relationship between our struggle and developments in the region, and the role of international imperialism. Tambo prophetically captured the historic moment when he proclaimed:

> The days we will spend here will live forever in the records of that struggle as marking a turning point in the history of all the people of South Africa. The beginning of the end of the apartheid system has commenced and everywhere there is an open recognition of the fact

that this pioneer of the African Revolutionary Movement, the ANC, is and will be at the centre and the head of the process which will result in the overthrow of the white minority regime and the suppression of the crime against apartheid.

The report further analysed the global offensive of imperialism, focusing on the war in Vietnam and Indo-China, the imperialist subversion of the Palestinian cause and the support for Israel during the 1967 war. It also examined other important matters, such as 'freedom fighters' from Czechoslovakia being recruited in their hundreds to South Africa in order to strengthen and further consolidate the apartheid system, the implications of the continuing fascist dictatorships in Portugal and Spain and the US-sponsored *coup* in Chile, which resulted in the killing of President Salvador Allende.

In relation to South Africa, the imperialist strategy was integrally linked to the USA's 1969 National Security Study Memorandum 39 on Southern Africa under the tutelage of Henry Kissinger. This memorandum, as seen in the quoted text that follows, was very instructive regarding the strategy:

> For the foreseeable future South Africa will be able to maintain internal stability and effectively counter insurgent activity. The whites are here to stay and the only way that constructive change can come about is through them. There is no hope for the blacks to gain the political rights they seek through violence which will only lead to chaos and increase opportunities for the Communists. We can through selective relaxation of our stance toward the white regime encourage some modifications of their current racial and colonial policies. At the same time, we would take diplomatic steps to convince the black states of their area and that their current liberation majority rule aspirations in the South are not attainable by violence and that their only hope for a peaceful and prosperous future lies in closer relations with the white dominated states.

The memorandum went on to dismiss the liberation movements of southern Africa as 'ineffectual and not realistic or supportable alternatives to continued colonial rule', precluded any further possibility of victory by these movements and questioned the depth and permanence of black resolve.

The document was a stark reminder of the perspectives not only of the US, but of the governments of the UK, Germany, France, Spain, Portugal and others. These governments not only called for the isolation of the liberation movements, but also brought pressure to bear on neighbouring countries in Africa to cooperate with the white regime in order to perpetuate and prolong apartheid. Imperialist countries were thus seeking to protect their interests in Africa by using the apartheid regime as its *de facto* policeman in the region – and the Kabwe Conference showed a cogent understanding of these dynamics.

The NEC report urged delegates to strive for maximum political and organisational unity and to mobilise all our members in order to advance our struggle. It will be recalled that the Morogoro Conference that took place in Tanzania in 1969 had decided that all ANC structures except the NEC should be open to *all* South Africans, irrespective of race, ethnicity, colour, religion or class. At Kabwe, some of our senior leaders from the UK, in particular Brian Bunting and Kader Asmal, continued to argue that the NEC should not be opened to minority groups, because they believed that at this stage of the NDR the main objective was the liberation of the African majority. Their views provoked intense debate, and in the final analysis were opposed by the majority of delegates. I was also surprised that Brian and Kader had articulated a position that did not represent the perspectives of the ANC or SACP structures in the UK. In terms of the letter and spirit of this decision, delegates were giving real content to the clause in the Freedom Charter that proclaimed that South Africa belongs to all – black and white. It was also a recognition that opening the NEC to all races reflected developments and changing realities in South Africa where all sections of the South African population were increasingly drawn into participating in the struggle.

In line with our objectives and philosophy of 'unity in action', the NEC report called on the conference to define its attitude towards the BCM.

In 1973, the NEC had concluded that 'in the last few years there has come into being a number of black organisations whose programmes by exposing the black anti-racists dispositions that the ANC fights for, identifies them as the genuine forces of the revolution'. The Kabwe statement in 1985 further elaborated on some important positions: 'The assertion of the black identity of the oppressed people is not an end in itself. It can be a vital force of the revolutionary action, involving the masses of people, for it is in struggle, the actual physical confrontation that people gain a lasting confidence in their own strength and in the inevitability of final victory. It is through action that the people acquire a true psychological emancipation.' Proceeding from these positions, the ANC sought to establish relations with the BCM and, in particular, sought to encourage the movement to grow – but as an instrument for the mass mobilisation of our people into struggle.

By 1976 the ANC had decided that it was time to meet with the leaders of the BCM, especially Steve Biko. It was clear to the ANC that Biko and his colleagues had adopted and acknowledged certain positions: firstly, that the ANC was the organisational leader of our revolution; secondly, that the BCM should concentrate its efforts on mass mobilisation; thirdly, that the BCM should function within the broad strategic parameters of our movement; and finally, that a meeting between the leadership of the BCM and the ANC was necessary.

The ANC made several attempts to meet the BCM, but due to prevailing circumstances these meetings did not take place. In 1977 Barney Pityana, a BCM leader who was to lead a delegation to meet the ANC, was arrested. Most tragic of all, Steve Biko was murdered by the apartheid regime on 12 September 1977, at a time when he was planning to meet the ANC leadership. The notorious government spy Craig Williamson had infiltrated the International University Exchange Fund (IUEF) in Geneva, which had been funding various elements of the BCM. He was responsible for their travelling and scholarship arrangements and it is alleged that it was his information that led to the arrest and murder of Steve Biko.

Some circles, particularly outside South Africa, were also working to ensure that the BCM consolidated itself as a political formation to replace the ANC or that it would emerge as a parallel movement that enjoyed the same levels of legitimacy as the ANC. There were also attempts to create an anti-ANC coalition made up of some elements of the BCM, the PAC, the Unity Movement and the ANC Group of Eight, which had been expelled in 1975. However, despite the severe setbacks we had suffered during the 1960s, all efforts to weaken and defeat the ANC had failed. Oliver Tambo reported that notwithstanding attempts to set up 'Third Forces', the ANC had encouraged the establishment of a number of mass democratic organisations of youth inside South Africa. The arrest and detention of many of the activists in 1977 gave them an opportunity while in prison to get a better understanding of the ANC, and of our strategy and tactics. And it was significant that many of the leaders of the then-banned South African Students' Congress (SASCO) came to the conclusion that the ANC was the authentic representative of our people.

Many of the delegates at Kabwe had played a leading role in the formation of the BCM and discussions were very lively and of a high calibre. The Conference agreed that the ANC should maintain direct and dynamic contact with the BCM in order to ensure that we defeated any manoeuvres to turn the latter into an anti-ANC 'Third Force'. It is a great irony, therefore, that some commentators still argue that the ANC did not understand and was hostile to the BCM.

With regard to the Soweto uprising, the NEC report noted that the uprising provided ample evidence that our country was sitting on a veritable powder keg and that such uprisings could become a permanent feature of our struggle. Importantly, it understood that our movement had the responsibility to take advantage of such moments when 'the activity of the masses is increased a thousand-fold, when the masses are prepared to fight to the finish for the destruction of the adversary'. However, it acknowledged candidly that between 1976 and 1977 in organisational, political and military terms, we were too weak to take advantage of the situation created by the uprising. We had very few active ANC units in the country, we had no military presence to speak of and the communications link between ourselves in exile, and the masses of our people was still too disjointed and weak to deal with tectonic changes taking place, such as was posed by the Soweto uprising. It acknowledged the outstanding role played by ANC cadres inside the country, many of whom were former Robben Island prisoners. Through their activities they were able to stamp the ANC imprint, however limited, onto the bloody battles of this period.

The report noted with concern that many forces inside and outside the country were seeking to use the youth and students' uprising to vilify the ANC and to ascribe a vanguard role to students in our struggle. Desperate attempts were made by elements in the US, independent Africa and Western Europe to form political groupings of youth as specific alternatives to the ANC. One such organisation was the South African Youth Revolutionary Council (SAYRC), which sections of the Nigerian military government tried to finance, train and develop as an alternative to the ANC. As the NEC report at Kabwe noted: 'Through struggle in which we put to the fore our policy, strategy and tactics while continuing to engage in actions against the apartheid regime at home and abroad, we defeated this attempt to create a Third Force. The majority of the youth who had left the country had come into the ranks of the ANC, as had the majority of the activists of the BCM.' The report noted that after the Soweto uprising, attempts to set up sinister and duplicitous 'Third Forces' were intensified.

The conference was also meeting at a time when the ANC was confronted with intense pressure from within the OAU to unite with the PAC, but the ANC resisted because of its past experiences with the PAC. It was our firm conviction that unity could not be imposed from above and that it needed to be an organic process. The ANC was also not prepared to lend credibility to the PAC, which had discredited itself as a divisive factor within our broad movement. We believed that the demise of the PAC would help limit the possibilities of counter-revolutionary forces planting agents among the masses.

The report also dealt with factions within the ANC who questioned the ANC and SACP's understanding of the relationship between the national and class struggles, and tried to artificially divide the movement into nationalist and socialist blocs, both politically and organisationally. Some factions in the country were arguing that the ANC should turn itself into 'a new socialist party'. This group was linked to a 'Marxist tendency' within SACTU in London.

The NEC reported that in the context of our strategic approach to the Bantustans, we maintained regular contact with Chief Gatsha Buthelezi. The NEC believed that 'this former member of the ANC Youth League who took up his position in the KwaZulu Bantustan after consultations with our leadership should use the legal opportunities provided by the Bantustans programmes to mobilise the masses and orientate them to focus on the struggle for a united and non-racial South Africa'. We had agreed that this would also necessitate the formation of a mass democratic organisation in the Bantustan that Chief Buthelezi should head – hence the Inkatha Freedom Party (IFP) originated from this agreement.

Oliver Tambo gave the conference a lucid explanation of our tactical approach to the Bantustans, and candidly observed that in some ways what later became negative activities of Inkatha were our fault: 'We have not done enough and are not doing sufficient political work among the millions of our people who had been condemned to the Bantustans. The artificial boundaries purporting to fence them off from the rest of our country do not make them any less a vital and integral part of the popular masses fighting for national liberation and social emancipation of our country.'

The report went on to argue that although we made some progress with regard to the creation of a MDM in the Bantustans, especially in the last 12 years, the reality was that we had not succeeded in building this movement to the level of strength that was both possible and indeed necessary. And we had failed to exploit more fully the presence of ANC stalwarts in the Bantustans.

The report concluded with great foresight and sagacity what was needed to set the stage for a negotiated settlement in the country. It very clearly stated that 'the NEC is of the view that we cannot be seen as rejecting a negotiated settlement, in principle. In any case, no revolutionary movement can be against negotiations in principle'. Apartheid was indeed confronting an existential crisis where there was a growing realisation among sections of the white community about an urgent need to defuse an increasingly volatile climate and retreat from an impending Armageddon. The report noted the increasing readiness of such sections representing businessmen, intellectuals, members of the media and even members of the regime in seeking contact and dialogue with the ANC. This was a new development that demanded careful thought and a unity of purpose in the democratic movement so as to ensure that the development of the struggle was not sidetracked.

The NEC's final clarion call was for maximum unity within the ANC, the broad democratic movement and the masses of our people on the basis of our programme, strategy and tactics. We were confident that despite the challenges we faced, we had defeated all efforts to divide the ANC or to create an effective 'Third Force'.

The Kabwe NEC report and its sound analysis and arguments thus challenged the fatuous view of several experts and academics that the ANC played no role in the major developments of the 1970s and 1980s. It put into proper perspective the role that the ANC played in the development of the struggle inside the country, notwithstanding the weaknesses of our underground structures. The report helped us to get a much better handle on the strategic leadership that the ANC brought to every level of the struggle at very decisive moments. Through various propaganda activities and political trials, the ANC had already begun to emerge as a leading force in the liberation narrative of South Africa. The conference gave us a distinct sense that major changes were possible and that a mood of expectancy and confidence prevailed. Its timely nature galvanised both the ANC of old and the new into one strong, united force. It proved to be not only a lesson in the history and philosophy of the ANC, but also of the broader historical wave sweeping through the country, as well as its relationship to progressive nationalism. The conference helped to identify the positive and negative attributes that came with the swelling of our ranks from the 1970s.

There was now a palpable expectation that we could defeat apartheid. Those who had become despondent found a renewed sense that the movement had, through its strategic and tactical leadership, managed to create the conditions for a decisive advance in our struggle. The resolutions taken at the conference enabled us to decisively change the balance of forces in our favour and to make both strategic and substantive advances in our fight against the regime.

As part of my own evolution in the movement, the high-water mark of the conference was my absolute shock but unbridled exhilaration at becoming a member of the NEC. This must go down as the proudest moment of my life as I had never expected to serve in this nerve centre of the ANC. After so many years in struggle, I had now joined the leadership at the highest level and would be privy to many of its discussions, as well as participate in its decision-making processes. From this vantage point,

I would get a better sense of the perspectives of the movement in the unfolding but highly contiguous revolutionary processes in South Africa.

This was indeed the beginning of a new phase in my life. I had already been head of the London PMC, and now being on the NEC gave my work an added dimension and greater responsibility. I left the conference not only with a sense of purpose and direction, but with the feeling that wherever we functioned, we had made some contribution to the intensification of the struggle in South Africa. Having become a member of the NEC, I felt that I had achieved an honour I had never dreamt of.

PW Botha's Rubicon speech

The mid-1980s was also significant because, in light of the worst crisis of President PW Botha's chequered political career, he had given notice to South Africa and the world that he was going to make major changes to apartheid policies. The then Foreign Minister Pik Botha referred to this as Botha's 'Rubicon speech', which was supposed to herald the beginning of an era of reform in the country. Pik Botha had assured the US National Security Council adviser, Robert McFarlane, that the Rubicon speech would fundamentally change the nature of the South African political system. South African embassies were briefed about the contents of the speech and instructed to win the endorsement and support of Western governments and the private sector on the eve of the speech. The government seemed convinced that the speech would lead to the easing of sanctions, win greater support for the apartheid regime and thereby help to isolate the ANC.

At the time, I was in Lusaka and Thabo Mbeki, Anthony Mongalo and I went to the Zambian Broadcasting Corporation's headquarters to listen to Botha's speech, which was delivered at the Durban City Hall on 15 August 1985. It was estimated that a global audience of over 300 million people would be listening in and we were alerted to prepare for some important announcements. The speech, however, turned out to be anti-climactic and was an intemperate and irascible defence of apartheid. Botha indicated that he 'would not lead white South Africans and minority groups to abdication and suicide' and warned the world that they should not 'push us too far'. This speech was a clear demonstration that both PW Botha and sections of the Afrikaner establishment were not ready to cross the metaphorical 'Rubicon', which by definition is a journey from which one cannot turn back. There was a lot of conjecture about what caused Botha to renege on what was widely thought to be a historic watershed and some averred that the speech was changed at the last minute. Until his death, PW Botha insisted that his cabinet had fully agreed with the speech as delivered.

As it turns out, the Rubicon speech led to precisely the antithesis of what we assume Botha initially intended: the renewed pressure for international sanctions and the total isolation of the apartheid regime. The confidence of foreign investors was likewise dampened. In late 1985, following the lead of Chase Manhattan Bank, the Paris Club – which handled international debts, including those of South Africa – decided not to roll over the country's debt, thus increasingly cutting off the regime's access to international capital. Combined with the massive outflow of capital (legally and illegally) by South Africans, this meant that the country was on the verge of financial collapse. Some of South Africa's allies nevertheless tried to save the apartheid regime. Dr Liet Wille – a major Swiss financier and a close friend of the British prime minister Margaret Thatcher – visited South Africa for urgent talks with PW Botha. It is interesting that this financier, who had come to South Africa to help, refused to see Mandela, accusing him of having communist connections. Wille's initiative was a blatant attempt to try to stave off increasing economic sanctions, especially in the financial sector. He also conveyed Thatcher's message that some political changes were necessary to sustain international support for the regime. Botha assured him that he would make some far-reaching reforms, which ultimately turned out to be a damp squib. Many South African captains of industry, including Anton Rupert, a leading Afrikaner business tycoon and member of the Afrikaner Broederbond (Brotherhood), secretly travelled to Switzerland to meet with bankers in a futile effort to stem the effects of financial sanctions.

Instead, the pace of disinvestment was considerably stepped up. Major companies, like General Electric, General Motors, IBM, Coca-Cola and Werner Communications, all withdrew from South Africa, and banks and pension funds stopped supporting companies that had South African connections. By 1986, the economy had contracted by 2 per cent and unemployment began to spiral. It was conservatively estimated that three million blacks were unemployed, while in the first half of 1988, nearly $3 billion flowed out of the country. By a Chamber of Mines estimate, between 1985 and 1990 the total cost of disinvestment had reached R40 billion. Most significantly, US Congress banned new investments and loans to South Africa and barred imports of agricultural products, as well as uranium, coal, textiles, iron and steel. South African Airways was also denied landing rights in the USA. This was a particularly significant development because the US Congress had in fact acted in defiance of President Reagan's policy of 'constructive engagement' with South Africa. The Congressional Black Caucus and the anti-apartheid movement in the US played an important role in influencing this decision.

Botha's Rubicon speech also provoked our people to greater anger and gave rise to intensified resistance. By the middle of 1986, people had captured control of many of the townships. The unrepresentative black urban councils and administration boards in many of the major townships collapsed and 'semi-liberated zones' were set up under street committees under the leadership and direction of UDF cadres. However, it soon became apparent that gangsters and racketeers were exploiting the situation and were consolidating their positions in the townships. This opened the space for other forces and criminal elements, secretly supported by the state's security services to initiate a murderous phase of 'black-on-black' violence. We categorically rejected this notion of black-on-black violence with the contempt it deserved since it was our belief that elements of the police and defence establishment were the architects behind it. Later, during the Truth and Reconciliation Commission (TRC) hearings, it became clear that our suspicions were not unfounded.

Meanwhile, both the UDF and COSATU accepted the Freedom Charter as their programmatic guide. The wave of popular support for the ANC grew apace: its songs were sung, slogans shouted and flag openly displayed at many demonstrations and meetings. Even internationally, apartheid South Africa's mainly Western patrons could no longer ignore or continue demonising the ANC after it became abundantly clear that the edifice of apartheid and the 'white united front' that held it together was disintegrating.

Although the Thatcher government had continued to label the ANC a 'terrorist' organisation, in October 1985 the ANC was for the first time asked to present its case to the Foreign Affairs Committee of the House of Commons. The majority of this committee was CP members. I was a member of the delegation that accompanied Oliver Tambo and Thabo Mbeki to this meeting. To a hostile audience, which saw the ANC as terrorists and/or communists and 'lackeys of the Soviet Union', Oliver Tambo was frank and forthright in putting forward the ANC's positions.

In response to the question of whether the ANC would renounce the use of violence if we were allowed to contest an election as a political party, Tambo eloquently responded:

This is what we are insisting on. We call for a government that must be a government of the people of South Africa. It should be an elected government, elected by the people of South Africa, not by a small white minority. This is at the very heart of our story. Now the ANC is not a political party; it is a national movement and has within it people of all political persuasions. It is a national movement but it seeks to establish in South Africa a democracy, precisely so that the country should be run according to the will of the majority of the people, who would seize upon an opportunity for elections to take place so that we elect a government of the people of South Africa.

This is a message that the ANC has conveyed for many years. However, it was the first time I believe that the House of Commons Foreign Affairs Committee listened to a leader of the ANC putting it so succinctly.

On the issue of rejecting the conditions set by Botha for Mandela's release, Mbeki responded:

It is a very simple thing for Botha to instruct his jailors to open the gates and let the prisoners out, but clearly, Botha is not interested. The conditions he has placed, like the political prisoners having to undertake not to engage in political activity which is likely to lead to their arrest are ridiculous when you have an apartheid system continuing because if Mandela decides I am not going to carry this reference book any more, he is liable to arrest.

He then went on to explain the political environment and the banning of the ANC, which led the ANC to resort to violence. Mbeki argued strongly that the release of political prisoners was not sufficient a basis for a peaceful solution, but had to be accompanied by other measures, including dismantling apartheid, lifting the state of emergency and unbanning the ANC and other political organisations. This would then obviate the need for violence on the part of the ANC.

The input of the ANC delegation appeared to have considerable impact on the committee members, and we began to see some changes in how sections of the British establishment responded to the South African situation generally, and to the ANC specifically. This meeting was also significant because it would have signalled to the regime that some of the British establishment attitudes towards the ANC was changing positively in our favour.

The debate on the balance of forces

In January 1986 the UDF met with the ANC in Stockholm. UDF delegates included Arnold Stofile, Mohammed Valli Moosa, Cheryl Carolus and Raymond Suttner. The ANC delegation was led by OR Tambo and included Alfred Nzo, Thomas Nkobi, Thabo Mbeki, Mac Maharaj and myself. The ANC representatives analysed the internal political developments and concluded that the increasing mass-militant action and the international sanctions campaign had created a crisis in the apartheid state. In our view, it was important for the UDF to have better regional and national cooperation. It should employ more full-time organisers, especially in the rural areas, and formulate a Programme of Action based on the rejection of the Tricameral Parliament and the increasing demands for non-racial local government. The ANC recommended that the UDF launch a national rent strike, demand the release of political prisoners and launch a campaign to reject the government's proposal to 'reform' influx control; and recommended that the UDF increase its cooperation with COSATU and intensify efforts to involve democratic white structures.

When the UDF delegation returned to South Africa, it received increased funding from the Swedish government, and it employed rural organisers and started implementing aspects of the Programme of Action discussed in Sweden, driven by the primary objective of creating organs of people's power.

In the late 1980s and in the wake of increasing repression and crackdown by the apartheid regime, a delegation of UDF leaders travelled to the UK to discuss the domestic balance of forces and the need for a 'tactical retreat'. This group included Yunus Mohamed, Valli Moosa and Sydney Mufamadi. I was part of the ANC's PMC delegation that met with the UDF delegation at a luxurious hotel outside London and delivered a paper on 'The Crisis of Imperialism and the Balance of Forces Internationally'. For their part, the UDF presented a paper that argued a position similar to that of the NIC delegation several years earlier: that there was a political stalemate in the country. Hence democratic forces had to seriously consider participating in the new apartheid dispensation, in what was after all the balkanisation of the country, in order to extend the apartheid regime. In her book *Anatomy of a Miracle*, Patti Waldmeir writes that by 1987 Valli Moosa 'was fed up with what he saw as the ANC's romantic approach to revolution ... The Lusaka leadership carried on cheerfully plotting insurrection but the UDF was increasingly reluctant to do the legwork'. Waldmeir notes that Valli Moosa remembers a meeting between the UDF and the ANC 'in a nice old castle about an hour's drive from London', where the UDF proudly presented its analysis of the crisis in the country and argued that 'we have done everything and we can do a bit more of everything but there is a stalemate ... Something else now needs to happen. The Boers are cleaning us and it is not conceivable that we are going to be able to overrun Pretoria.' She goes on to quote Valli Moosa as saying: 'We were attacked by the [ANC] leadership for even suggesting that there could be a stalemate. We were given a lecture on insurrection and sent back to prepare for it. And of course that's what we did.' Waldmeir, however, is either quoting inaccurately and out of context, or she did not correctly appreciate the many discussions about the 'stalemate' that were taking place both internally and externally and which were often very acrimonious.

Josiah Jele, a member of the ANC NEC and the SACP, led our PMC delegation and chaired the two-day meeting. He introduced our response to the UDF paper. (When Jele was presenting our response, I was not aware that the comrades in Lusaka had obtained a copy of the UDF paper and had prepared an extensive response.) Jele critically analysed the UDF paper and concluded that it was not time for 'tactical retreats' but an opportune moment to intensify the struggle. We explained that we were in contact with many sectors of South African society and were aware of the unprecedented reign of terror launched by the regime. We argued that, unlike in the 1960s, our people were not being cowed into submission, and indeed South Africa was becoming ungovernable. Also, as the regime intensified repression, the sanctions campaign was growing in strength. Any acceptance of a stalemate and participation in government-created institutions at this time would have played into PW Botha's co-option strategy. We were also aware that this debate was dividing the UDF. We concluded that there was no stalemate and that the balance of forces did not favour the regime. At this time the UDF leadership was also not fully aware of 'talks about talks' with Afrikaner representatives that had already commenced with Mandela in prison and the ANC in exile.

In retrospect, if we had accepted the fatalist argument about a 'stalemate' and the need for a 'tactical retreat', I doubt we would have seen a democratic transformation in 1994.

While the ANC, the SACP and the MDM continued to wrestle with key strategic, organisational and, indeed, existential questions, an important initiative by the Commonwealth was unfolding that would thrust the South African question squarely and urgently into the international spotlight. This initiative would ultimately have an important bearing in shaping both the parameters and promise of a negotiated settlement – as it would, of course, not surprisingly, inform my own life, the course it would take and the role I would play in the broader context of South Africa and the road it was destined to take.

Chapter 5

The Commonwealth and strategic engagement

It was against a background of mass-militant activities in South Africa, the Kabwe Conference and the growing intransigence of the apartheid regime that the Commonwealth Heads of State Summit took place in Nassau in the Bahamas in October 1985. The ANC expected the summit to make far-reaching decisions regarding sanctions against South Africa. In the end, despite the view of the vast majority of the participants at the summit, and because of the obstinate opposition of the British prime minister, Margaret Thatcher, it was agreed, as a compromise, to appoint an 'Eminent Persons Group' (EPG). The EPG would visit South Africa between March and May 1986 to assist with facilitating a negotiated political solution from what was fast becoming an impending catastrophe in the country.

The non-aligned countries were well represented in the EPG: from Africa, there were Olusegun Obasanjo of Nigeria and Johan Malecela of Tanzania; Nita Barrow came from Barbados and Sardar Singh from India. In addition, there was Lord Anthony Barber from the UK, Archbishop Ted Scott from Canada and Malcolm Fraser, the Australian prime minister. Obasanjo was co-chair of the EPG with Malcolm Fraser.

The discussions the group held with the National Party government, Mandela in prison, the ANC in exile and different formations of the MDM are all crucially important. They provide remarkable insight into the positions of major role players; but most importantly, demonstrate the consistency of the positions of the ANC leadership in exile, Mandela's position in prison, as well as of those of the MDM. These were the strategic and tactical approaches that guided us in all our interactions, overt and covert, with South Africans from all sectors of society. The discussions also provided a useful prelude to the approach and thinking of the many white delegations we were to meet, as well as the regime's strategic and conceptual framework for negotiations during the critical transition periods of the CODESA I and CODESA II, between 1991 and 1993.

Crucially, the important contribution of the EPG to the country's democratic processes has not been fully appreciated. When the setting up of the EPG was announced, I and other comrades in the ANC were worried that the initiative could have a negative impact on the growing militant struggle in the country on one hand, and the international sanctions campaign on the other. Since the 1960s, the ANC had been subjected to systematic and well-orchestrated pressure to renounce the armed struggle. We were therefore justifiably concerned about any international initiatives that would deprive us of an important instrument in any future negotiations with the apartheid regime. It was thus with a certain measure of trepidation that we monitored the setting up of the EPG and how it pursued the objectives of its mandate as defined in the Nassau Accord.

The ANC and government positions

There were expectations in sections of our ranks that the apartheid regime would reject the EPG initiative. I, however, was convinced that this underestimated the reality that the regime was aware that, because of Thatcher's strong opposition to sanctions, the EPG was a compromise and, in the letter and spirit of this compromise, the regime could not blatantly and overtly reject the EPG. They could, however, try to subvert its stated objectives and interaction with it could also be used by the regime to project a new image of 'reasonableness and willingness' to cooperate in seeking a negotiated solution. If they skilfully and adroitly dealt with the EPG, they could also succeed in their strategy to 'expose the ANC as the obstacle to a peaceful solution'.

Consequently, and because of these strategic and tactical considerations, the South African government did not reject the initiative. In fact, they even gave the EPG a position paper that explained their understanding of the group's mandate – a document that provided valuable insights into the regime's approach to both their overt and covert discussions with the ANC in the years that followed. The position paper stated:

It is a conviction of the government that any future constitutional dispensation providing for participation by all South African citizens should be the result of negotiations with the leaders of all communities. The government will not prescribe who may represent black communities in negotiations on a new Constitution for South Africa. The only condition is that those who participate in discussions and negotiations should forswear violence as a means to achieve political objectives. The agenda for political reform is open. In the process of negotiations the government will not prescribe and will not demand; give-and-take will be the guiding principle.

The government's broad approach to negotiations seemed 'reasonable', but it was qualified by many unacceptable provisos and qualifications, a subterfuge in approach that the regime had used for many years and had refined into an art form. Examples of the regime's duplicity, unrealistic tactics and naivety included:

- while apartheid was declared 'outmoded, finished and indeed dead', the exercise of political rights and freedoms would have to be within the ascriptive framework of 'groups' or 'communities';

- the document asserted that South Africa could not be compared to other countries, and Western democratic norms and practices had no relevance. It was 'a nation of minorities' and any future constitutional arrangements would have to accept individual aspirations within the confines of ethnic groups. This meant that group rights would take precedence over individual rights and the government would have written assurances preventing the domination of one group by other groups. They argued that they wanted to prevent the replacing of 'white apartheid with black apartheid';

- while the government expressed commitment to a united South Africa, this did not include the four 'independent homelands' or the other remaining self-governing 'states', which were also going to become 'independent';

- a 'common citizenship' for all South Africans excluded all black South Africans resident in the 'homelands';

- the issue of 'universal franchise' had to be exercised within the group context, which ruled out developing a common electoral role; and

- 'full political participation' through power-sharing and political cooperation on matters of 'national concern' would be subject to 'self-determination for each group in respect of its own affairs'.

It was absolutely staggering that the government believed that these positions would be acceptable to either the international community or to the ANC. The regime's isolation and patent lack of understanding of domestic and international realities clearly influenced what can only be seen as a tactical approach. The government's positions were, incidentally, similar to those held by many of the white delegations we subsequently met with in our overt and covert meetings and the positions taken by the government in the CODESA talks, which I address in subsequent chapters.

After meeting the government delegation, Obasanjo's group met with Mandela in prison. Thereafter, the group visited Lusaka to meet with an ANC delegation led by Oliver Tambo. The ANC representatives informed them that we had expected the Commonwealth to take firmer decisions on the further isolation of the apartheid regime. There was an inherent danger that the group and its work could be a pretext for weakening the international sanctions campaign, as well as defusing the mass-militant actions taking place in South Africa.

However, if the EPG proceeded on the basis of its mandate as outlined in the steps of the Nassau Accord, and if this was accepted by the South African government, then favourable conditions could be created for negotiations. The Nassau Accord called on authorities in Pretoria to take certain steps as a matter of urgency, including:

- declaring the system of apartheid as one that had to be dismantled and that the government take specific and meaningful action to achieve this;

- terminating the state of emergency;

- immediately and unconditionally releasing Mandela and all others imprisoned and detained for their opposition to apartheid;

- establishing political freedom and, importantly, lifting the ban on the ANC and other political parties; and

- in the context of the suspension of violence on all sides, initiating a process of dialogue across lines of colour, politics and religion with a view to establishing a non-racial and representative government.

The ANC informed the group that these were precisely the demands that the ANC and its Alliance partners in South Africa had been making for years, but the regime had consistently rejected these demands. If Botha's government accepted the processes outlined by the Nassau Accord, and his ruling regime was genuinely committed to resolving fundamental issues through concrete policies and actions within a relatively short period, there would be no need to continue with the armed struggle. However, the position on violence was not a precondition for any progress in the negotiations process. There were many examples and precedents of negotiations that took place while hostilities and warfare still continued, as was the case in Angola, Mozambique, Vietnam and Zimbabwe.

The group's members were reminded that the ANC was not in principle opposed to dialogue, but categorically refuted the regime's claim that it was embarking on a serious reform programme. Although the National Statutory Council (NSC) had been established by the regime to 'develop modalities for a new constitution', this council was merely a consultative and advisory body without powers.

The EPG was advised to address the fundamental issue of dismantling the apartheid system in its entirety. The ANC delegation strongly argued that the release of Mandela and other political prisoners was an important prerequisite and *sine qua non* for the ANC to seriously consider starting negotiations with the regime. The ANC was aware that a campaign had been initiated to draw parallels and to equate the regime's violent responses with the ANC's armed struggle, as if they were morally equivalent. The ANC also explained that since 1948, when the National Party swept into power, we had been subjected to a system that the UN had declared a Crime Against Humanity. We had then responded to apartheid terror and deeply entrenched institutionalised violence with non-violent mass action, which included the historical markers of resistance such as the Defiance Campaign in 1952, militant trade union activities, strikes and various boycott campaigns. In 1956, and after militant but peaceful resistance, many of our leadership was arrested and charged with treason.

Still we continued on the path of militant but non-violent activities, even though it was clear that the National Party regime was intent on destroying all political opposition with ruthless violence and repression, and through recourse to draconian legislation. Given these cold and harsh realities, we had been left with two choices: submit or fight. And it was only then that the ANC made the very difficult decision to embark on an armed struggle. MK, the people's army, was created and sabotage activities were conducted by MK units throughout the country.

The world therefore had to appreciate that our armed struggle was an extension of the political struggle. This logic dictated that, without the necessary space to carry out any political activity, we were left with no alternative but to embark on the armed struggle. Moreover, in terms of the moral imperative and just war precepts, apartheid violence could not be equated with the ANC's armed struggle.

The EPG process

During the EPG visit, it became evident that some members of the group had never previously had such a thorough discussion with an ANC leadership collective. The group thus left Lusaka much better informed about ANC political and economic policies and, equally importantly, perspectives on the history of our struggle. Being better informed also had a positive impact on EPG members who had advertently or inadvertently accepted the carefully orchestrated anti-ANC propaganda.

Our delegation further advised the group that there were many examples of the regime coming to agreements and then failing to implement them. The Nassau Accord called for a six-month timetable and it was thus important to adhere to this timeframe to defeat any subterfuges and sleight of hand by the apartheid regime.

I, however, remained convinced that the regime would not accept the provisions of the Nassau Accord and would rather try to use the EPG process to gain acceptance for its version of a 'reform' programme.

On returning to South Africa from Lusaka, the EPG met with representatives of the UDF, COSATU and the Azanian People's Organisation (AZAPO). The UDF and COSATU broadly represented and endorsed the same positions as the ANC, our common approach clearly indicating that functional mechanisms had been established for consultations and communication between the different strands of the democratic forces in South Africa and the ANC in exile. A normative unity of purpose and a common strategic approach to negotiations had thus emerged, which enabled us to speak with one voice.

After these consultations, the EPG produced a negotiating concept paper that called on the government to:

- remove the military from the townships, provide for freedom of assembly and discussion and suspend detention without trial;

- release Mandela and other political detainees; and

- unban the ANC and PAC and permit normal political activity.

The concept paper was given to the government for its consideration, but it was soon evident that Botha and his senior officials had Machiavellian motives and were participating in this EPG political exercise in a manner that lacked commitment and integrity.

On 24 April 1986, in a letter to the EPG, Foreign Minister Pik Botha indicated that the South African government had given serious consideration to salient features of the possible negotiating concept. On the issue of releasing Mandela, the government's basic concerns were that this action should not be accompanied by or result in further violence. The cessation of violence by the ANC held the key to the government accepting the negotiating concept.

Pik Botha reiterated the government's position that the apartheid system was fundamentally changing. The state president PW Botha had made a commitment in Parliament in early 1986 that fundamental reforms would be introduced by 1 July 1986. Moreover, the government intended to repeal or amend more than 34 Acts and proclamations that would ensure that the movement of people would not be subject to discrimination on the grounds of colour or race.

Finally, he proposed that the EPG meet with other representatives of the South African government to exchange views on how to proceed further, particularly on the modalities for achieving a 'suspension of violence' and facilitating discussions. Botha's letter, however, failed to address any of the fundamental issues raised by the EPG.

The concept paper, for instance, called for the withdrawal of security forces from all townships, while the reply only referred to some black townships. The response was silent on the issues of political freedom and the suspension of detention without trial and suggested that the government was not considering the release of all political prisoners and/ or detainees. It was also not clear whether the negotiations would lead to new constitutional arrangements within the context of genuine power-sharing arrangements or in the context of the existing structures.

Pik Botha's suggestion was disingenuous to say the least. He explained that in the 'event of difficulties in the negotiations process and continued violence, the government would have to take preventative action, and that such action should not lead to the imposition of more sanctions as this would understandably not be acceptable'. Notwithstanding the EPG's critical assessment of Botha's letter, they continued with their engagements.

A daily log of events as they unfolded reveals not only their significance to the negotiating process later, but also offers some insight into the unbridled cynicism and contempt with which the South African government approached the EPG initiative.

On 13 May 1986, the EPG met with Pik Botha, and the following day with the Minister of Justice and Prisons, Kobie Coetsee. The next day PW Botha made a speech to Parliament in which he listed many 'non-negotiables' and also issued a strong warning about outside interference, obviously directed at the EPG. The speech was not so much a hardening of the government's positions, but rather a true reflection of its intransigence. The government was steadfastly adhering to its old position of managing and choreographing change based on 'power-sharing' and 'group and racially defined' realities.

On 16 May, the EPG presented the concept paper to Nelson Mandela. He accepted the concept paper as a basis from which to start discussions and explained that this was his own position. He was in isolation and it was important for the EPG to get the reaction of the ANC leadership in exile. He also suggested that it would be important for him to consult with his comrades in Pollsmoor Prison and on Robben Island, as well as with other key figures in South Africa. Mandela again confirmed the ANC view that to put an end to violence, the necessary conditions had to be created for meaningful discussions between legitimate leaders of the oppressed and the government. The fears of escalating violence if he was released were, he said, unfounded, and that such an eventuality could be controlled.

He stressed that his release would not be sufficient in itself and that, as the concept paper had correctly indicated, it would be necessary to withdraw all security forces from the townships. In addition, he and his comrades should be able to move freely throughout the country so that they could use their powers of persuasion and influence to help create the conditions for stability that would allow the negotiating process to begin.

The EPG must have been impressed by the fact that Mandela, who had been incarcerated for so many years, was able to broadly reflect the positions of the ANC leaders in exile as well as those of the MDM.

The EPG again met with Pik Botha and briefed him fully on the Mandela meeting. His response was that his government was not dealing only with the ANC; there were many other political groupings in South Africa and all these would have to be involved in any future negotiations. According to Botha, the government had serious misgivings about repealing the laws that provided for detention without trial because this would necessitate introducing new legislation and, in the present circumstances, this would not be easy to achieve. On the issue of the suspension of violence, Pik Botha repeated that they understood this to mean a permanent cessation.

These were spurious points. There was no evidence to show that Mandela, the ANC in exile or the MDM had argued that other political parties would be excluded from negotiations. The ANC and the MDM had also never suggested that every time there were differences in negotiations that we would resort to violence. To the contrary, we had consistently argued that the issue of suspending or ceasing violence would be determined by the progress made in the negotiation process. The government's insistence on wanting serious signs of the 'deescalation of the violence' that engulfed many parts of the country before any negotiations could start was literally asking us to end all forms of struggle. The continuing emphasis on the potential for violence if prisoners were released ignored all the undertakings of the ANC and the MDM.

However, notwithstanding the obstructionist tactics of the regime, the EPG was still determined to keep the Commonwealth initiative on course.

It therefore agreed to meet with the cabinet's Constitutional Committee to determine whether any progress could be made and what the extent thereof might be.

On 17 May, the group returned to Lusaka and the concept paper handed to the regime seven to eight weeks previously was now given to the ANC. The EPG informed the ANC that the government was 'seriously' considering the concept paper and 'had not accepted or rejected it'. They also gave the ANC a comprehensive briefing of their meeting with Nelson Mandela.

Oliver Tambo's answer was that the ANC could not provide an immediate response, but reiterated that if the concept paper was in line with the principles and demands of the Nassau Accord, he could not see any difficulties with the ANC accepting the concept paper as a basis for starting discussions. He emphasised that the ANC in principle had no objections to negotiations, but that the regime had to show genuine commitment to the implementation of the principles enunciated in the Nassau Accord. If the regime continued to harbour illusions that it could get away with simply tinkering with the apartheid system, then negotiations would be a non-starter. He informed the group that the ANC would provide a formal response to the concept paper within the following 10 days.

When the EPG subsequently returned to South Africa they met with the different formations of the internal MDM to inform them about the concept paper and the negotiating dispositions of the government and the ANC. The internal formations generally agreed that the document could be a starting point for discussions, but indicated that they would have to consult their various constituencies. The EPG must have understood that their main consultations would occur with the ANC Alliance in exile.

On 19 May, in a dramatic development and just hours before their planned meeting with the Constitutional Committee, the EPG was shocked to hear on the national broadcaster, the South African Broadcasting Corporation (SABC), that the SADF had attacked ANC bases in Zimbabwe, Botswana and Zambia. This naked aggression against three Commonwealth countries by the apartheid regime was a blatant violation of its commitment to 'help bring about stability and peace in the region' and highlighted the level of insincerity and hypocrisy about its stated commitment to a negotiated solution. We believed – as did the UDF, COSATU and other internal organisations – that the government's stated responses to the concept paper and military attacks against three neighbours exposed their dishonest intentions, especially their deep commitment to 'group affairs' on the one hand and the near-zealous pursuit of destabilising the region on the other. Indeed, because of the increasing internal repression and regional destabilisation, their rhetoric about finding peaceful solutions rang hollow.

It remains a subject of ongoing conjecture about why the defence force under its hawkish minister, Magnus Malan, was instructed to carry out the attacks; although it was later revealed that PW Botha himself had authorised them without even informing his foreign minister, Pik Botha. The EPG, believing that their task remained important, decided that they should still meet the Constitutional Committee. It comprised of the Minister of Constitutional Development, Chris Heunis, who acted as the chair; the Minister of Foreign Affairs, Pik Botha; the Minister of Education, FW de Klerk; the Minister of Law and Order, Louis le Grange; the Minister of Cooperation and Development, Gerrit Viljoen; the Minister of Finance, Barend du Plessis; the Minister of Home Affairs, Stoffel Botha; and the Minister of Justice and Prisons, Kobie Coetsee. The meeting, however, yielded little of consequence since the committee members naively and arrogantly continued to restate their same positions.

I had always understood and vigorously argued that the regime's notion of 'change' was very distant from that of the ANC's, the vast majority of the Commonwealth members and more specifically the EPG's. The concept paper basically represented the antithesis of PW Botha's government's understanding of what would constitute a democratic South Africa and how this could be achieved. The government had entered into discussions solely for the purpose of creating tactical space to manipulate the EPG process in the interests of shaping the discussions on its own terms. Given the internal and external dynamics, it would have been suicidal not to do so. In the end, their responses and military actions exposed their true intentions and resulted in an upsurge of resistance. It also led to increased international condemnation and the intensification of the sanctions campaign.

On 29 May, Pik Botha again wrote to the EPG, essentially repeating the government's earlier stated positions and conditions for entering negotiations. Once again, the onus of violence was placed on the oppressed people of South Africa. Botha and his government still maintained that it was the oppressed who had to 'end the violence' and not themselves. They rejected the written and verbal presentations made by the ANC in various forums about the nature of our armed struggle and our commitment to a peaceful solution. So, while they talked about a constitutional dispensation, it was clear that they had little grasp that this could not be imposed by them and had to be a consequence of a process in which all South Africans participated. Pik Botha's letter ignored the Nassau Accord's call for normal political activity and freedom of assembly and discussion.

Indeed, inherent in Pik Botha's letter was a rigid adherence to constitutional dispensations and power-sharing arrangements in the context of

My family, 1963: my parents Goolam and Amina, my eldest brother Ismail and his wife, Rockeya, and their children Yasmin and Shehnaaz. Standing behind (L–R) is Nassim, Juned, Essop and me.

Farid Adams (on the left), Shanti Naidoo, Ann Nicholson and me at the Transvaal Indian Congress Office preparing supplies for detainees.

Treason Trial halts, 1958: Me with Nelson Mandela and Winnie Madikizela-Mandela outside the court (Courtesy of Abe Bailey Archives).

Wolfie Kodesh (far left), Hilda Bernstein, Abdul Minty and me at an anti-apartheid demonstration outside South Africa House in London, 1989.

With Dr Dadoo on his 70th birthday (1979). Dr Dadoo died four years later from cancer.

The Cuba-SACP delegation in Hemingway Restaurant in Havana, Cuba, in the 1980s with Joe Slovo, Ronnie Kasrils and Sizakele Sigxashe.

The SACP Central Committee Meeting in the 1980s: Front row (L–R): Thabo Mbeki, John Nkadimeng, Joe Slovo, Dan Tloome, Ray Simons, Francis Meli. Middle row (L–R): Sizakele Sigxashe, January Masilela, Henry Makgothi, Aziz Pahad, Reg September. Back row (L–R): Ronnie Kasrils, Mac Maharaj, Brian Bunting, Chris Hani, Josiah Jele.

Our ANC meeting with IDASA and South African and Soviet Academics in Leverkusen, Germany, 1988. Joe Slovo, Jonny Makhathini, Irina Filatova, Thabo Mbeki (holding a proof copy of *Vrye Weekblad*), Prof Solodovnikov, Alex Boraine, Van Zyl Slabbert, Simon Makana, Tony Seedat, Vyacheslav Tetekin, Jackie Selebi and Aziz Pahad.

Our last Mells Park Meeting in the UK, June 1990: Seated (L–R): Willem Pretorius, Aziz Pahad, Thabo Mbeki and Dawie de Villiers. Standing (L–R): Joe Nhlanhla, Wimpie de Klerk, Mof Terreblanche, Tony Trew, Willie Esterhuyse, Michael Young and Attie du Plessis.

After his release from prison, Nelson Mandela's first meeting with Oliver Tambo and ANC NEC members in exile; Sweden, March 1990. Standing (L–R): Alfred Nzo, Aziz Pahad, Ruth Mompati, Ahmed Kathrada, Chris Hani, Anthony Mongalo, Thabo Mbeki, Joe Nhlanhla; Seated: Nelson Mandela and Oliver Tambo.

Meeting of the ANC leadership and leaders of the Mass Democratic Movement with Oliver Tambo in Sweden, March 1990: Billy Modise, Thabo Mbeki, Nelson Mandela, Archbishop Trevor Huddleston, Oliver Tambo, Chris Hani, John Gomono, Winnie Mandela, Joe Nhlanhla, Mohammed Valli Moosa, Ahmed Kathrada, Adelaide Tambo, Alfred Nzo, Zanele Mbeki, Cyril Ramaphosa, Abdul Minty, Trevor Manuel, Anthony Mongalo and Aziz Pahad.

With Thabo Mbeki and Joe Nhlanhla at the ANC's preparatory meeting before its first talks with the government, 29 April 1990. This photograph is on display at Vergelegen Estate, Somerset West. (Courtesy of Anglo-American/Vergelegen)

Ministers and Deputy Ministers in the Government of National Unity, 1994. On the day of the photoshoot I was on a diplomatic mission abroad, hence the insert.

Swearing-in ceremony: being congratulated by President Thabo Mbeki and Deputy President Jacob Zuma on my re-appointment as Deputy Minister of Foreign Affairs, April 2004.

Ronnie Kasrils, Minister of Intelligence, conferring the Friend of Intelligence Services medal on me (and Joe Nhlanhla) at a function held in our honour by the Department of Intelligence Services, Pretoria, November 2007.

With my wife, Angina, and Nelson Mandela at his home in Houghton, 2007.

group rights. Clearly, his regime was not ready to 'cross the Rubicon' to move towards genuine and sincere negotiations. It still believed that the EPG would fundamentally change its concept paper to suit the premises and rationale of the regime's negotiating posture and political interests.

The EPG and the unbending regime

And yet, despite all of this, I was surprised that the regime continued to believe that its tactics would weaken or even confuse the anti-apartheid movement both at home and abroad and furthermore, that this would create more favourable conditions for major Western powers to exert increasing pressure on the ANC. For the regime's approach to be accepted in ending what was becoming a growing crisis of apartheid rule, it continued to pursue a path that was manifestly unsustainable under the prevailing circumstances. Only die-hard racists and reactionaries would accept such fallacious arguments, and even their staunchest supporters at home and abroad found themselves in a very difficult predicament.

In the regime's scheme of things, the EPG concept paper represented everything that it opposed and, as an existential dilemma for maintaining the entire apartheid system, it would not be in its interests to accept the principled elements of the paper. Pik Botha's letter was a clear exposition that the National Party government would not be willing to accommodate the fundamental principles of either the Nassau Accord or the concept paper.

On 29 May the EPG replied to Pik Botha, indicating that his letter was a re-statement of what the Constitutional Committee ministers had raised at the meeting on 19 May. The group repeated its conviction that it was possible to bring about a democratic South Africa through negotiations, but only if the government was genuinely committed to such a process and was willing to create the conditions that would allow for the participation of leaders who had the mandate to fully participate in such negotiations. They expressed their frustration in understanding the government's conceptualisation of the suspension of violence because they had informed the government on several occasions about the views and perspectives of Mandela, the ANC in exile, the UDF and COSATU.

The EPG also argued that violence would decrease if the government took certain important measures, and that a key element of this was the government's own actions to suspend the violence fomented by its state machinery. They further stressed that, in the wake of the attacks against three Commonwealth countries, the government would have to give a firm commitment to refrain from carrying out further aggression against its neighbours. They indicated that the responsibility to end intimidation rested firmly with the government because only it could address the circumstances in which normal political activity and freedom of assembly and discussion could take place, and that this constituted an important element of the concept paper.

The group pointed out that they saw no point in continuing with the discussions if the government remained 'doggedly intransigent and continuously prevaricated'. The Nassau Accord had proposed, in the context of the suspension of violence on all sides, the initiation of a process of dialogue across lines of colour, politics and religion, with a view to establishing a non-racial representative government. The alternative to a negotiated solution would be 'appalling chaos, bloodshed, and destruction'. Their considered view was that despite appearances and statements to the contrary, the South African government was 'not yet ready to negotiate such a future except on its own terms' – and those terms, both with regard to objectives and modalities, fell far short of reasonable expectations of the majority of South Africans and widely accepted democratic norms and principles.

They asserted that apartheid went beyond the institutionalisation of discrimination and economic exploitation; indeed, the system was primarily a means of ensuring and maintaining ultimate political and economic power in the hands of the white minority. Any reservations by the government about the dismantling of apartheid would inevitably – and understandably – be viewed by the vast majority as a ploy for perpetuating white power in a new guise, and hence this explained its willingness to change its form but not to abandon its substance. The group drew the following conclusion:

> While the government claims to be ready to negotiate, it is in truth not ready to negotiate fundamental change, nor to countenance genuine democratic structures, or to face the prospect of the end of white domination and white power in the foreseeable future. Its programme of reform does not end apartheid but seeks to give it a less inhuman face. They wanted power sharing but without surrendering overall white control.

On the modalities of negotiations, the government was willing and ready to negotiate with 'responsible leaders' who would come to the negotiation table to strike a deal, but only if violence and intimidation abated. In the South African government's view, these 'responsible leaders' were those from the homelands and Bantustans. In the EPG's view, 'with the exception of Buthelezi, the homeland leaders had no real standing or following, and would not in our view be credible parties in negotiations to resolve South Africa's deepening crisis'. But, above all, the EPG argued in their final report that:

> [t]here can be no negotiated settlement in South Africa without the ANC. The breadth of its support is incontestable and this support is growing. Among the many striking figures whom we met in the course of our work, Nelson Mandela and Oliver Tambo stand out. Their reasonableness, absence of rancour, readiness to find negotiated solutions which while creating genuine democratic structures would still give the whites a feeling of security and participation, impressed us deeply. If the government finds itself unable to talk with men like Mandela and Tambo, then the future of South Africa is bleak.

They confirmed the people's identification with the ANC through the symbolism of banners, dances, and songs at funerals and churches, which in their view supported the assumption that if elections were held then on the basis of universal franchise the ANC would win. This would fundamentally depend on the government's willingness to create an environment conducive for free political activity. However, in their disillusionment with the government, the EPG was aware of the extent to which legitimate leadership would be prevented from emerging due to apartheid's repressive regime and the belief that the precarious status quo could be maintained indefinitely by force. In a country with a black majority, they held that this was 'an act of self-delusion'.

The international reaction

The interventions of the EPG had an influence not anticipated by the regime and its international supporters. Margaret Thatcher and other supporters of the apartheid regime in the Commonwealth had either been misinformed about the realities of the South African situation or had contemptuously believed that the EPG could be manipulated into producing a report favourable to the regime – this would not only have impacted negatively on the international anti-apartheid movement, but also on the struggle in South Africa, and thus further demonise and isolate the ANC.

However, the experience of the EPG and its final report played an important role in destroying the myth that the regime was committed to a negotiated solution and that the obstacle was the ANC, which was bent on a violent seizure of power. The EPG process had, in fact, enabled the ANC to comprehensively explain its strategic approach to the struggle for freedom and justice in South Africa, including the armed struggle, as well as to articulate its position on negotiations to the entire world. We had successfully defeated the demonisation of the ANC within the ranks of many Western governments and establishments. The regime's total isolation, misreading of the African and international mood, and lack of interaction with the ANC and others genuinely committed to finding peaceful solutions, helped to carve a mindset far removed from reality and greatly influenced by its own propaganda.

The final EPG report thus gave added impetus to the international sanctions campaign and firmly established the leading role of the ANC. In fact, the significant role played by the EPG under very trying circumstances has not been fully appreciated in that it not only opened the space for South Africans to openly meet with the ANC in exile, but also influenced major Western powers to appreciate that the ANC had tremendous support in South Africa and could no longer be ignored. Most significantly, it helped to create an international political and normative consensus that a genuine negotiated solution, with the crucial participation of the ANC, was the only viable option.

In early 1987 the Americans proposed that Oliver Tambo meet with Chester Crocker, the Assistant Secretary of State for African Affairs, but – given the level of US representation – some of our leadership in Lusaka was strongly opposed to this meeting. It was only after the intervention of President Kenneth Kaunda of Zambia that the ANC agreed to the meeting in London, which we insisted take place at the Zambian High Commission. I was part of the delegation and when the meeting started, Crocker angrily informed us that he was aware that we had not wanted to meet with him. He reminded us that he represented a superpower and had been involved in strategic discussions on Angola and Namibia. The only reason, he said, 'the US was talking to the ANC was because they [the USA] had major interests in South Africa and Africa and they did not want instability in the country to affect these interests'.

Needless to say, my comrades and I were outraged at Crocker's imperious attitude; we even went so far as to suggest that we walk out of the meeting. But once again, Oliver Tambo's leadership was outstanding and he instructed us to continue with the meeting and, in the end, we all concluded that it had been a constructive engagement. Significantly, it paved the way and helped prepare for the meeting with the US Secretary of State, George Shultz.

In 1986 Oliver Tambo, as president of the ANC, also met with the head of state of the Soviet Union, Mikhail Gorbachev. This was the first meeting between an ANC president and a Soviet head of state, and it took place soon after the meeting between Gorbachev and US president Ronald Reagan in Reykjavik, Iceland; after which they indicated in a press conference that they had agreed to cooperate in dealing with regional conflicts.

Tambo's meeting with Gorbachev was an important one because we were able to gain significant insights into the discussions that had taken place between Gorbachev and Reagan. The ANC strongly believed that the future of South Africa depended on negotiations between South Africans themselves and that we should as far as possible avoid outside involvement. We were thus anxious that Thatcher and Reagan should not be the driving forces behind the processes for a negotiated solution for South Africa. Tambo, therefore, proposed to Gorbachev that the Soviet Union investigate the possibility of a joint USA-USSR programme to find a negotiated solution for South Africa. We believed that this would give us extra political protection and tactical cover against the US policy of 'constructive engagement'. If there was to be any outside involvement in our negotiating processes, we wanted to avoid a situation in which Reagan and Thatcher became the only interlocutors in any future talks.

It was thus two months after the meeting with Gorbachev that Tambo – accompanied by Thabo Mbeki – met for the first time with the US Secretary of State, George Shultz. I was informed by Thabo Mbeki that it was a good meeting and for the first time the ANC was able to explain its perspectives and views directly to an American Secretary of State. Given the realities in southern Africa, the crisis of ungovernability in South Africa and growing international solidarity for our cause, this meeting brought about a significant change in successive US administrations' approach and attitude to resolving the complex conundrums of our country.

The EPG visit and report, as well as the international engagements with two major powers, also provided the impetus for significant changes in the mood of the Afrikaner and business establishment in South Africa. The curtain of fear was finally broken and inspired the many encounters and discussions between a wide spectrum of the white establishment and the MDM, which met across Africa and other parts of the world.

In the aftermath of the EPG visit and its final report, the chairman of the Broederbond, Pieter de Lange, produced a discussion document titled 'Basic Conditions for the Survival of the Afrikaner'. Historically, the Broederbond had been instrumental as a secret policy think-tank and leadership repository for the ruling National Party. De Lange therefore had the requisite stature and authority to play an integral role in initiating discussions within the Afrikaner establishment, including the intelligence services, about the need to reform the apartheid system.

In June 1986, De Lange attended a meeting in New York organised by the Ford Foundation to discuss the South African situation. Representing the ANC were Thabo Mbeki, Mac Maharaj and Seretse Choabi. By this time there was some awareness in our ranks of this new ferment among the more enlightened factions of the National Party establishment. However, Choabi – failing to grasp the significance of this shift in thinking among some of the more enlightened Afrikaners – viciously attacked De Lange for being a representative of the oppressors, and Mac Maharaj had to intervene in order to calm the situation. Later that evening, De Lange and his wife dined with Mbeki, which provided an opportunity for further engagement and discussion. A good understanding developed between Mbeki and De Lange, and when De Lange returned to South Africa he used every opportunity to convey the views of the ANC to his fellow Broederbonders.

If anything, the EPG had played an important role in demystifying the ANC in the minds of the South African public, but especially among the white ruling elite. In addition, it had been an important harbinger in demonstrating the efficacy of open dialogue among adversaries. This had interesting consequences for a series of open yet dramatic encounters between the ANC and various white South African constituencies. Of course, it also opened up all sorts of possibilities for me personally, allowing me to follow a course for which I seemed to have been preparing myself all of my life – both in my youth and my early days as an activist, in both South Africa and abroad.

Chapter 6

The ANC's dialogue with white constituencies

The developments in the 1980s in South Africa and the region persuaded major supporters of the apartheid regime, including Thatcher, Reagan, and the French and German governments, that a veritable 'revolution' was unfolding in the country that would have a serious impact on their economic and geo-strategic interests on the African continent. This much was already evident from the EPG's final report.

A public indication of the growing reality that the ANC could not be ignored was an article by Ton Vosloo in *Beeld*, one of the prominent Afrikaans newspapers in the Transvaal. He wrote that the ANC was the major opposition group in South Africa, that millions of black South Africans supported the ANC and that the government had to consider talking to the ANC. But Vosloo then cited certain preconditions, namely that the ANC had to accept a confederation or federation model (without indicating what this would be); that it would have to recognise the Bantustans; and that it had to renounce communism. It was interesting that Vosloo did not mention the issue of the ANC 'renouncing violence', as was the mantra of the Botha regime. The National Party government was trying to create an impression – aimed primarily at its international supporters in the West – that it was committed to a peaceful negotiated solution. This was tantamount to flying a trial balloon to see how the white population would respond, but at the same time establishing preconditions for any talks.

In August 1983, Robert Cabelly, assistant to Chester Crocker – US Assistant Secretary of State for African Affairs during the Reagan administration – met with Thabo Mbeki in Lusaka in what was one of the first informal discussions between the American administration and the ANC. Cabelly informed Mbeki that the ANC's call for sanctions was 'wearing thin' and that, according to him, even Mozambique and Zimbabwe had told the US in private discussions that they were opposed to sanctions. After Cabelly's trip to the region, he reported to his government that the ANC was not a military threat and that the Frontline States were 'jiffy' about the ANC – in other words, not very excited or impressed with our organisation.

In May 1984, the South African ambassador in Paris, Robert du Plooy, intimated that given the rapidly changing developments in southern Africa, talks with the ANC were possible if the party ended the armed struggle, recognised the 'sovereignty' of the South African government and ended its links with the Soviet Union. I am certain that an ambassador would never make such a public statement without clearance from his Foreign Minister, in this case Pik Botha.

A year later, in February 1985, Crocker's deputy, Frank Wisner, visited Lusaka and informed the ANC and Thabo Mbeki that some elements within the South African government were willing to talk to the ANC. At a meeting in June of the same year, the US government indicated that it would be ready to officially meet the ANC and asked us to propose the time and venue. Wisner gave no indication that any conditions would be attached to such a meeting.

However, in October, Cabelly returned to Lusaka and informed Mbeki that an 'official' meeting with the administration was not possible unless the ANC changed its policy positions on the armed struggle and joined 'the process of reforms' initiated by the PW Botha regime. He warned that if the ANC did not respond favourably, it would be forced out of the region to countries as far as Egypt. But he indicated that the US government would continue to have 'unofficial' contact with the ANC as distinct from official relations.

In the meantime, the UK government – because of its aversion to the armed struggle and because it considered us a 'communist front' – publicly maintained that there would be no official contact with the ANC. However, it allowed British Intelligence operatives based in Lusaka to maintain contact with us. Sandy Harding, their intelligence representative in Lusaka, had several discussions with Thabo Mbeki, and I in fact participated in some of these, using the opportunity to explain ANC positions in the knowledge that these would be conveyed to the British government. It is interesting to note that many of the issues Harding raised were the same ones later put forward by the South African big business delegation to Lusaka, and again in other meetings with South Africans in Lusaka, Zimbabwe, Dakar, Paris and Leverkusen (West Germany). These issues were also brought up in the secret meetings with Professor Willie Esterhuyse's Afrikaner group in the UK.

It is thus against this backdrop that events started gathering momentum. In August 1984, Professor HW van der Merwe, a senior academic at the

University of Cape Town, contacted the ANC. Van der Merwe had good connections with leading people in the ruling apartheid establishment and internationally, as well as with members of the AAM and the British establishment. He had two meetings with the ANC, first in Tanzania, and then a follow-up in Zambia in December 1984, when he was accompanied by Piet Muller, a senior journalist from *Beeld.* The ANC delegation consisted of Thabo Mbeki, Johnny Makhathini and Penuell Maduna. Van der Merwe and Muller proposed that the ANC meet some members of the South African Parliament, either in Lusaka or in the north of France. But for this to happen, the ANC had to sever all its contacts with the socialist countries and the SACP, and we had to abandon the armed struggle and give serious consideration to safeguarding minority-group rights.

When I later met Van der Merwe in London, he again raised the same issues. I patiently explained that the ANC was a revolutionary nationalist organisation and had a historical alliance with the SACP that had been hammered on the anvil of struggle. I informed him that SACP leaders and its members were also leaders of the ANC, a strategic and political connection that we greatly valued. Like other genuine liberation movements, it was no secret that we received military training, arms and humanitarian support from the Soviet Union, the GDR, Cuba and other socialist countries. Moreover, many of our cadres received professional training in the socialist countries and I was not aware of any conditions attached to such support. We had also obtained solidarity support from many countries and organisations outside socialist countries, especially from Scandinavian governments and the broader international anti-apartheid movement. I further indicated that we were not a communist party but a broad-based movement that encompassed many political ideas and diverse perspectives and, as such, we would never become party to divisive Cold War tactics of anti-communism. I reminded him that the ANC had only embarked on an armed struggle when all other forms of resistance became illegal and were brutally suppressed. Above all, we had never rejected negotiations in principle.

Van der Merwe returned to London for a follow-up meeting and we continued our discussions. Soon after our meetings in Lusaka and London, he publicly started calling for dialogue with the ANC. At this time, *The Argus* newspaper based in Cape Town reported that, according to an opinion poll, there was increasing evidence that the ANC had widespread support among the oppressed majority of South Africa and that 43 per cent of white South Africans favoured negotiations with the ANC. Curiously, while PW Botha continued fostering the illusion that he favoured negotiations, he prevented a National Party youth delegation from visiting Lusaka.

The ANC could not, however, ignore the reality that the apartheid regime had launched an offensive to project an image of itself as a government that understood the realities of South Africa and was committed to reform. By trading on the notion that it was willing to find a negotiated solution, the regime hoped to defuse the growing struggles in South Africa and thereby divide our people and isolate us from the burgeoning support emanating from broad sections of society and many governments internationally. This was also a ploy to confuse and weaken the increasing international solidarity movement that had been gaining in strength since the 1960s.

We were, of course, aware that intensive pressures were being exerted on us by major powers to enter into talks, but knew too that these talks would take place on their conditions which, in subtle or more overt ways, would effectively support the apartheid regime. We were also conscious of the very strong warnings directed at us by the US that if we did not accept talks, we would be pushed out of Africa and exiled as far away as Egypt, as Cabelly had reported. They had consistently reminded us of the Nkomati Accord, which compelled us to cease all our activities on Mozambican territory and to withdraw our cadres from there. This was cited as an example of the harsh 'realities' confronting us. We were continuously informed that negotiations between the South Africans and the Angolans were going well and that this would lead to favourable developments in Namibia and Angola; and that as soon as the Angolan talks were concluded, we 'would be forced out of Angola' as well.

They reminded us that ZAPU and Zimbabwe African National Union (ZANU) had entered the Lancaster House talks with a warning from the Frontline States that, if they did not come back with a solution they would be prevented from operating from neighbouring territories and would be expelled from those countries. The subtext here was that the ANC would have to enter into talks on conditions determined by others.

In all of these developments, we could not ignore the broader systemic context and the changed international setting. Important developments in this regard were the end of the Cold War, the collapse of the Berlin Wall, and the new global capitalist order spawned by the forces of globalisation and mercantilism. A major consequence of this change, epitomised by Francis Fukuyama's triumphalist 'End of History' thesis, was serious structural crises in socialist countries and the emergence of a unipolar world with the US at its epicentre. However, many 'experts' have again exaggerated the pressures that the Soviet Union put on the ANC to engage in talks. In fact, prior to 1984 our relations with the Soviet Union were with its Communist Party and Solidarity Committee, relationships that were initially developed through the SACP, but later directly with the ANC. It must be stressed that we never received or were given formal government recognition by the Soviet Union. It was only towards the end of 1984, and under the leadership of Mikhail Gorbachev, that the Soviet Union for the first time decided to have formal state relations with the ANC, with an ANC delegation being received by its Foreign Ministry.

In this fast-changing environment, we knew that we could not simply reject the principle of talks – we had to defeat the regime's strategy with greater political and strategic finesse and through a more nuanced approach to the issue of negotiations. In response to this challenge, the ANC's extended National Working Committee (NWC) meeting in 1983 explored scenarios for negotiations. A committee, chaired by Pallo Jordan, was established and included Thabo Mbeki, Joe Slovo, James Stuart and Simon Makana. Their brief was to craft and develop negotiation scenarios.

The committee concluded that there were three sets of circumstances under which negotiations could commence: firstly, an outright defeat of the apartheid regime; secondly, a stalemate; and thirdly, a 'Patriotic Front dilemma', which referred to the situation in 1979 when the Frontline States gave the Zimbabwean liberation movement an ultimatum to go to Lancaster House and return with an agreement or be forced to leave their countries. The moral of this scenario exercise was that we had to prepare our cadres for the possibility of negotiations.

Preparing for talks

In July 1984, when speaking in Gaborone, Botswana, Oliver Tambo said, 'We had not been approached for talks, but we know that the question of talks between the ANC and Pretoria is being discussed.'

Tambo indicated that the ANC would indeed be prepared to meet PW Botha, but only if we were sure that there would be serious dialogue aimed at bringing an end to apartheid. He suggested that the release of Nelson Mandela, the unbanning of organisations, the release of all other political prisoners and the end of the state of emergency would signal that the regime was serious about dialogue. This had been discussed in the NEC, as well as various other structures of the movement.

Following the Kabwe Conference in Zambia in June 1985, a draft ANC discussion document analysed the debates taking place within NP think-tanks about the future constitution of South Africa. The paper argued that the Freedom Charter needed 'greater elaboration and popular appeal so that it could be better understood by a wider audience'. It also argued that the world needed to be reassured of our position on political pluralism. It went on to suggest that the ANC needed to develop a Bill of Rights and a set of constitutional guidelines that set out the kind of democratic political regime that South Africans could expect under an ANC government. Oliver Tambo thus appointed a constitutional committee that was mandated to answer the question: 'We know what we are against, but what are we for and what kind of country do we want?'

The committee was very impressive. It was led by Zola Skweyiya and included Kader Asmal, Penuell Maduna, Brigitte Mabandla, Simon Makana, Albie Sachs and Jack Simons. The team was confident that they could complete their task quickly, but soon realised that it would be more problematic than they had anticipated. Their dilemma was that they had to write a draft constitution in advance without knowing the circumstances in which liberation would be achieved. Secondly, they believed that politically it would be incorrect to produce a draft constitution by a committee of the ANC. A constitution by its very nature had to come from the people of South Africa through a properly constructed and elected constitution-making body.

However, since there was enormous pressure to obtain the ANC's perspectives, the committee had to find an alternative to a draft constitution and proposed four constitutional principles – political pluralism, a mixed economy, participatory democracy and a Bill of Rights – that had to be taken into consideration by any future constitution-making body. At this stage, these principles had not been fully spelled out and there was an understanding that a process of popular consultations would be initiated. Tambo participated actively in the discussions and contributed to the debates. From this point onwards, and in all the annually issued January 8th Statements, Tambo expressed our commitment to multi-party democracy and a Bill of Rights.

Tambo's commitment, together with the ANC's principled stance on participating in negotiations, was not an easy one to accept because sections of the leadership and cadres, especially in MK, did not trust the regime and firmly believed in the 'armed seizure of power'. However, it was obvious to some of us that the government was planning to participate in negotiations on its terms, based on group rights and a national convention of homeland leaders and 'moderate' blacks. The group-rights concept was being marketed internally and internationally, but was simply the equivalent of a Trojan horse for maintaining white minority privileges. It was important, therefore, for the ANC to produce a Bill of Rights as an alternative that would counter the group-rights thesis and serve as the best guarantee and protection against the abuse of individuals and minority rights. We had already seen that the Botha strategy of co-opting coloureds and Indians into a Tricameral parliamentary system had been rejected by these communities and ended up as a monumental failure in constitutional engineering. The Indian Congress and the coloured Labour Party had rejected participation – although the latter did later join the Tricameral system in order to promote change from 'within the system'. From the ANC's perspective, this was a gross tactical error, but we refrained from public condemnation of the Labour Party and its leadership under Allan Hendrickse.

Some activists and academics in South Africa were also concerned about a Bill of Rights because they saw it as an instrument to protect the property of minority whites. We had to consistently argue against such views. We believed that a Bill of Rights would deal with 'white fears' in the context of 'black aspirations' and, as such, enlarge the scope of freedom for everyone. This would thus be an effective safeguard against the abuse of power by any future government. As we prepared for the eventuality of negotiations, we stayed rooted in the four pillars of struggle: mass mobilisation, building the underground, intensifying the armed struggle, and intensifying the international sanctions and isolation campaign.

This was the broad political and policy backdrop against which high-profile visits and discussions between the ANC in exile and different groups of the white establishment in South Africa began to take place; the types of engagements that stirred great controversy and contestation in the country.

Meeting with the captains of industry

When mining giants Anglo American and Anglo Vaal fired 14 000 and 3 000 workers respectively in May 1985, MK responded by bombing their corporate offices. This bombing campaign, linked to the strike action, began to unite the elements of our struggle, namely, the worker and the political and armed dimensions. At the same time, the ANC was intensifying the campaign for the isolation of South Africa and for mandatory UN sanctions.

The South African Foundation, which represented almost all top South African companies, started talking about reforms. Anglo American had extensive business interests in Zambia, with substantial investments in its copper mines. And Gavin Relly, the then director, had been based in Zambia in the early years of independence and had forged good relations with President Kaunda. Kaunda suggested to Relly that South African big business leaders should meet with the ANC in Zambia.

Big business was responsive to President Kaunda's overtures, because by the mid-1980s growing internal resistance and financial sanctions were beginning to take a heavy toll on the South African economy. The steady legal and illegal flow of capital from South Africa had a haemorrhaging effect on the economy, and workers' strikes were becoming more politically inspired and growing in strength and magnitude. Also, the combination of workers' strikes and UDF-organised mass-militant action and the increased sophistication of the armed struggle were creating a serious crisis of governance for the regime.

So it was that Relly started consulting some major South African business leaders, especially those representing big Afrikaner capital, such as Anton Rupert of Rembrandt and Sanlam's Fred du Plessis, but also Barclays Bank director Chris Ball, Tony Bloom of Premier Milling and Barlow Rand's Mike Rosholt. They all agreed that a meeting with the ANC should be arranged.

When PW Botha angrily attacked this initiative by big business, Rupert and Du Plessis withdrew from the delegation. But Harald Pakendorf, editor of *Die Vaderland* – a newspaper that had once been edited by the architect of apartheid, Hendrik Verwoerd – Tertius Myburgh, editor of the *Sunday Times* and Hugh Murray of *Leadership* magazine, ignored Botha's intemperate warnings and agreed to take part. Zach de Beer, previously leader of the Progressive Federal Party (PFP) and a member of the Anglo American board, also agreed to join the delegation.

On 13 September 1985, these business leaders ignored PW Botha's hostility to the initiative and travelled to Zambia to meet the ANC at a game lodge in the Luangwa Valley owned by the Zambian government. Sensing that change was inevitable, these individuals had the foresight to understand that their interaction with the ANC leadership was about trying to influence the direction of a future democratic South Africa.

The ANC delegation was led by Oliver Tambo and included Thabo Mbeki, Chris Hani, Mac Maharaj, Alfred Nzo and Pallo Jordan. The meeting started rather tentatively – and understandably so, because this was the first such meeting between the ANC and the major captains of industry. And so to lessen the tension, it was decided that the delegations should not sit on opposite sides, but in a mixed formation so that they could get to know one another. The meeting was an important harbinger and opportunity for frank discussion between South Africans from different perspectives, backgrounds, classes and racial groups.

Tambo set the stage by explaining some basic ANC policies – even these top businessmen were quite ignorant of the ANC's history, philosophy, and its strategy and tactics – and went to great lengths to elaborate on the Freedom Charter. The participants then openly and frankly discussed the merits of capitalism versus economic justice, the idea of group rights and majority rule based on 'one person one vote', the armed struggle and the ANC's attitude to 'soft targets'. Also up for discussion was the relationship between big business and trade unions, and the importance of big business joining the campaign for the release of political prisoners.

Relly raised the possibility of official negotiations because he believed that Botha was 'honest and sincere' in wanting genuine negotiations. The reality, however, was that the ANC, in the present circumstances and in the absence of signs indicating that the government was seeking a negotiated solution, had no option but to escalate the struggle. Tambo warned that this would lead to many deaths and South Africa's destruction, unless the regime and the international community decided to take more meaningful measures to bring about necessary fundamental changes in South Africa. Tambo argued that business was a powerful force in South Africa and that the government could not ignore its views.

The perennial questions of the influence of the SACP and the use of violence were raised and, predictably, turned into a major area of debate. Tambo explained that in the early days he and Mandela were among those who had opposed any cooperation with the SACP and, indeed, they spearheaded the move to expel its members from the ANC. However, such views were defeated by the majority of the ANC leadership who better understood the relationship between the class and national struggles, and understood the important contribution of members of the Communist Party. He informed the delegation that highly respected SACP members were also leading members of the ANC and that he was convinced of their loyalty to the ANC. He explained that the ANC was a broad national movement that had within its ranks people of all religious and ideological persuasions, including Muslims, Christians, atheists and communists. As such, the ANC was willing to have anybody in its ranks who accepted its constitution, and its strategy and tactics.

The business leaders had come to the meeting convinced that the ANC was a 'tool' of the SACP, which was in turn 'driven and controlled by Moscow'. They must have been surprised then that the president of the ANC was able to so openly and frankly discuss the relationship between the Communist Party and the ANC and the futility of playing the 'red bogey' card.

On the issue of future economic policy and specifically whether a new South Africa under the ANC would be communist or capitalist, the ANC delegation explained that we could not ignore the reality that the country would never be stable or secure if the huge discrepancy between the rich and the poor was not squarely and honestly addressed. The issue of nationalisation was policy and, if any changes in policy were necessary, these would have to be discussed at a conference in the country when the ANC was unbanned. However, the ANC indicated that we preferred the option of a mixed economy.

So it was that, for the first time, the captains of industry were being exposed to the full spectrum of ANC policy positions, which led to demystifying and de-demonising the ANC in the eyes of the delegation. This was a critical element of our tactical approach to breaking the regime's hegemonic control of information and its tendentious impact on our white compatriots.

After the delegation returned to South Africa, Relly told a press conference that he had a feeling that 'the ANC leaders wanted to come home and that South Africa had to find ways for them to come home'. A week later, an advertisement appeared in several newspapers. It was signed by 91 business leaders under the title 'There is a better way'. The signatories advocated abolishing all racially discriminatory laws, negotiating power-sharing with acknowledged black leaders, granting citizenship rights to all people of South Africa and restoring the rule of law. Abstracts from this advertisement were also published in the UK and the USA, where 10 major CEOs of multinational companies endorsed the message. The message contained aspects that in any normal society would not be startling, but in apartheid South Africa – and coming from such a powerful lobby – they certainly created a sensation and began to shake up the 'white laager' mentality.

Our strategic and tactical approach to lifting the regime's curtain of ignorance, disinformation and fear around the ANC was to arrange an organised programme of activity with all sections of the South African population. The business delegation's visit to Zambia significantly opened up space for South Africans to ignore the government's threats and, consequently, hundreds of South Africans from all sections of society and walks of life began to travel to different parts of Africa, Europe and North America to meet with the ANC. The psychosis of regime propaganda directed at the ANC was coming to an abrupt end and people were losing the 'fear factor'. This was certainly evidenced in our next major meeting with a very heterogeneous group of Afrikaners in Dakar, Senegal. They essentially inaugurated the much-needed spirit of honest and open dialogue with the ANC, something the ruling regime was still struggling to come to terms with politically and ideologically.

The Dakar talks

After the meeting with the captains of industry, and following the growing interactions between the ANC and internal groups, it was decided that the ANC should meet publicly with a high-level group of 60 mostly Afrikaans-speaking South Africans, whom Tambo referred to as the 'New Voortrekkers'.

It started in 1986 when Frederik van Zyl Slabbert, leader of the PFP, and Alex Boraine, a Member of Parliament, resigned from Parliament. In an interview, Oliver Tambo commented that to get out of the party and join the extraparliamentary forces of change was a 'very correct move', and he called on the rest of the members of the PFP to leave Parliament to work for real change.

After having exited Parliament, Slabbert and Boraine established the Institute for a Democratic Alternative for South Africa (IDASA), in order to create a platform for extraparliamentary dialogue across political and racial divisions. At the time, this was a revolutionary development that had a significant impact on the thinking of groups of white South Africans. IDASA argued strongly that no peaceful solution was possible without talking to the ANC leadership in exile. After consultations, it was agreed that we should organise such a meeting in Dakar, Senegal, and this duly took place between 9 and 12 July 1987. This initiative was funded by the American philanthropist George Soros, a few Scandinavian countries and the German Friedrich Naumann Foundation.

The wife of President François Mitterrand, Danielle Mitterrand – who headed the France Libertés foundation – was also a staunch supporter of the initiative. The writer and poet Breyten Breytenbach, who was a close friend of both Van Zyl Slabbert and Ms Mitterrand, was living in Paris and he too played an important role in garnering support for it. Thabo Mbeki and I had a few meetings in London with Van Zyl Slabbert, Breytenbach and businessman Dick Enthoven to prepare for the Dakar meeting.

Most of the IDASA group had not visited any African country before. And, similar to the business delegation, the government reacted with great displeasure when news of the Dakar initiative leaked and, not surprisingly, many of the IDASA group was apprehensive.

At our first get-together on the night of their arrival, the IDASA group and our delegation shared introductions and got to know one another better over drinks. The next morning all participants were addressed by the Senegalese President Abdou Diouf – the first time that a white group from apartheid South Africa had been so lavishly hosted by an African head of state. The IDASA group was surprised that they were so warmly welcomed by the Senegalese people, and it seemed that many found themselves in emotional turmoil after discovering that they were 'Africans and welcomed in Africa'.

Our joint visit to Gorée Island was an unforgettable experience. This was the island used to 'export' hundreds of thousands of African slaves to Europe and the USA, which brought into sharp focus the sheer inhumanity shown towards Africans and their dehumanisation. As we gathered around the 'Gate of No Return', the departure hole for slaves, we all stood in silent prayer and meditation as we united in our conviction that we had to intensify our efforts to end the apartheid system.

The Dakar conference addressed four specific issues: strategies for bringing about fundamental change; the building of national unity; the structure of government in a free South Africa; and the economy of a liberated South Africa. And once again I was surprised that such a high-level grouping, which included many senior academics and journalists, was as unfamiliar with ANC policies as were the businessmen who came to Zambia.

Thabo Mbeki's speech to the group took an hour and Max du Preez, a journalist, stated thereafter that it was:

> ... probably the most honest, direct and comprehensive explanation of the ANC's positions ever given to people outside the organisation. He spoke freely about the ANC's concern with uncontrolled violence; the difficulties of controlling guerrillas inside the country; the role of the Communist Party; a negotiated settlement versus a transfer of power; the suspension of violence; the unhappiness of radical youth in the townships; attitudes to other groups such as Inkatha ...

The atmosphere was electric and the IDASA group was visibly impressed by the speech. Du Preez further commented that 'Thabo Mbeki bowled everyone over with his sincerity, sense of humour, intellect, clear thinking and straight talk, his charm and charisma ... this was a spectacular performance.'

However, while we were in Dakar, MK carried out a daring attack against the Witwatersrand Command Centre in Johannesburg. There was a great amount of consternation and nervousness in the ranks of the IDASA group, especially since before they had departed for Dakar the group had been harshly criticised in the media and even in its English-speaking sections, for being 'naïve individuals foolishly talking to the ANC "terrorists". After the bombing, the government and the media launched vicious attacks against the group. Within days, Cassius Make, a member of the MK High Command based in Swaziland, was assassinated. This came as a great shock to me since I had become very friendly with Cassius while we were both based in Angola.

These military actions added further urgency to our heated and intense discussions about the armed struggle and presented a poignant moment for doing so. The ANC delegation gave a detailed exposition of the circumstances that led us to adopt the armed struggle and we strongly defended the concept of a 'just war'. In any such war, civilian casualties were unavoidable. However, we expressed our concern about hitting 'soft targets', and explained that this was not ANC policy and that such actions were counter-productive. Rather than winning over our white compatriots towards a non-racial democratic South Africa, such attacks would simply push them deeper into the laager. However, the member of IDASA also had to understand the frustration and anger of our people and the unrelenting repression. We explained that we faced many challenges in managing MK units operating in South Africa. We informed them that there could be a cessation of the armed struggle if the government was genuinely committed to a negotiated solution, but that the ANC could not declare a unilateral cessation.

Some in the IDASA group very directly and candidly wanted to know how the ANC expected 'support' from them when they and their families could well be victims of our bomb attacks. Our response was that our people, both inside the country and in exile, lived under the constant threat of death. Of course, necklacing was another issue that was also strongly condemned by the IDASA group, and we explained that we were politically and morally against such methods. We also opposed it because it could so easily be exploited by agent provocateurs, and pointed out that Oliver Tambo had publicly condemned this heinous practice at the Children and Repression Conference in Harare.

The discussions revealed the wide gap existing between the two delegations. In a press briefing, the Stellenbosch University philosopher André du Toit stated on behalf of IDASA: 'I don't think they have answered this [suspension of the armed struggle] to our satisfaction. This concerns not only the proliferation of uncontrolled violence. It concerns the actions of all those people who claim to act on behalf of the ANC, whether or not they are part of an organised and disciplined hierarchy of political control.' He expressed concern about the moral ambiguity of accepting responsibility for the bombing that took place while we were in Dakar, especially where there were civilian casualties. He argued that this required that we take an even more unequivocal stance in repudiating and renouncing such acts of violence. Many of our white compatriots seemed entirely unaware of the repression and killing that had taken place in black townships over many decades – apartheid had insulated them from the many extreme realities of life that the black population had to endure on a daily basis.

Another very intense discussion was about 'bi-communalism'. Hermann Giliomee, another Stellenbosch University academic and historian who had a reputation as a *verligte* (enlightened) dissident, passionately argued for a group-based solution. I believed, however, that he had incorrectly interpreted the conflicts between the Israelis and Palestinians, on one hand, and the Catholics and Protestants in Northern Ireland on the other, as motivation for the 'co-existence of competing nationalisms' in a future South Africa. His reasoning was that the vast majority of whites would never accept a non-racial democratic South Africa based on majority rule because this would result in a winner-takes-all dispensation. And white resistance would only lead to greater repression and violence, which would have destructive consequences for the country. By this logic, bi-communalism provided the only political formula for accommodating the conflicting interests of 'Black nationalism and Afrikaner nationalism'.

This was nothing more than a thinly veiled academic justification for the National Party's spurious 'reform' processes. Many of the internal delegation supported Giliomee's position, however, and this led to intense discussion on minority rights, and the protection of religion, cultures and languages. This again revealed the extent to which these powerful and influential representatives of the Afrikaner community, including the academics, were not familiar with basic ANC policy documents.

Overall, the three days in Dakar proved to be a remarkable encounter and had a major impact on all of us who attended. Quite crucially, and similar to reshaping the world views of the business delegation, the Dakar talks made an important contribution to the ANC's fight against the unwarranted demonisation and vilification of our organisation. The IDASA group got the message in crystal-clear terms: white South Africa was a pariah state, not because of racial considerations, but because of apartheid policies. As we got to know one another, trust developed and inhibitions and fears were allayed. The participants of IDASA felt more confident about raising their fundamental concerns in an uninhibited manner; nothing was sacrosanct. We were able to discuss white fears and black aspirations in a comradely manner, and while the discussions were intense and heated, there was never any aggression or acrimony.

We then started receiving media reports from South Africa about the 'Dakar Safari', with the SABC, *Die Burger*, *Volksblad* and *Beeld* conducting an orchestrated vilification campaign against the 'useful idiots' that constituted the group. Criticisms in the English press were less hostile, but also palpably negative. The IDASA group had remained in touch with their families and friends and received reports of intimidation experienced by the latter. When the atmosphere became more jovial, we teasingly inquired how it felt to be demonised, which had been our lot for so many years. However, I do not think we fully appreciated the fears, tensions and concerns that permeated through the group; it was they who had to return to the 'belly of the beast' to face the wrath of their communities and the regime.

In the informal discussions, Beyers Naudé asked how they were going to respond to the fact that the Afrikaans media had become an uncritical mouthpiece of the National Party. It was becoming increasingly evident that consideration should be given to launching an alternative Afrikaans-language newspaper that would be able to counter the propaganda and distortions of mainstream media. But because this initiative would inevitably unleash further venom from the political and security establishments, it was not enthusiastically supported. Van Zyl Slabbert was not confident that the necessary funds would be forthcoming and told Max du Preez – who was interested in taking the idea forward – that he was 'straddling a tiger'. Van Zyl Slabbert did, however, along with Braam Viljoen, support the project, and Braam suggested that the paper be named *Vrye Weekblad* ('The Free Weekly'). The ANC delegation also believed that this was a good initiative and committed to help raise funds for the project, which Thabo Mbeki subsequently did.

From Dakar to Burkina Faso and Ghana

From Senegal, a smaller group travelled to Ouagadougou, the capital of Burkina Faso, for further discussions. On arrival, the group was once again overwhelmed by the welcome. Thousands of Burkinabe filled the streets to greet them. Prior to the visit, the local media had written extensively about the IDASA group and, as a result, the Burkinabe had a sense that they were contributing to the demise of apartheid. Host President Thomas Sankara freely interacted with the members of the group and he and his cabinet even sang some of their folk songs. In response, the South African group provided a rendering of 'Sarie Marais' – but since many of them were suffering from diarrhoea, the singing was neither melodious nor overly enthusiastic.

Sankara gave a lengthy speech on his philosophy and ideals, while many of our joint group struggled to stay awake. Then he stopped suddenly and asked everybody to stand and clap their hands. After a few minutes he smilingly said, 'The ANC gentleman in the front row is now awake.' He resumed his speech thereafter. But after a while, Mbeki politely interrupted and said, 'Comrade President, this has been a wonderful evening and we deeply appreciate the honour. We are aware of the heavy demands on your time and know that you need a good night's sleep.' After a brief silence, Sankara responded with 'Speak for yourself' – and promptly continued talking for another half-hour!

From Burkina Faso, the group made its way to Accra, Ghana, where the laws actually had to be amended in order to allow South African passport-holders to enter. The group was nevertheless confronted by hostile journalists who demanded to know why the 'ANC trusted these whites'.

131

Mbeki boldly stated, 'I am an Afrikaner' and explained the non-racial aspects of our struggle, and indicated that whites were also members of the ANC.

In a meeting with over 200 Ghanaian luminaries at Freedom House, many speakers questioned the genuine commitment of 'whites' to democracy and non-racialism. The IDASA group was visibly uncomfortable and disconcerted. Van Zyl Slabbbert was especially fazed by the hostility and rather defensively – and arrogantly – responded that he had not been paid to visit Ghana and could have remained in the white establishment, but had decided to fight apartheid. In contrast, the ANC delegation eloquently explained the non-racial character of our struggle and told the Ghanaians that our white compatriots were as African as they were and, furthermore, that whites had formed an integral part of the armed struggle. This was loudly applauded by the Ghanaians.

Senior journalist Allister Sparks wrote that until Accra 'many of the whites had remained sceptical about the ANC's commitment to non-racialism'. However, that scepticism began to dissolve as whites heard how ANC delegates vigorously defended the same position over and over again before critical African audiences. Like the others, Sparks had been surprised by the hostility experienced in Ghana and was greatly relieved to hear the sincerity and candour of the ANC's public response. This was a position that the ANC had consistently taken in its internal debates – for example, during the formation of the PAC, in the OAU and other international forums, in the Treason and Rivonia trials, as well as in many other political trials. The IDASA group could not therefore say 'I did not know' about the ANC's total commitment to non-racialism.

Consequently, the visit to three African countries by the *boers* was widely and favourably reported in African and international media. Graham Leach, a British journalist of note, wrote in his book *The Afrikaners: Their Last Great Trek*:

> It was a landmark. If one day the South African government does decide to negotiate with the ANC, it may only be possible because the Slabbert delegation and others following, have paved the way [for] the beginning of a process which will slowly make it acceptable and respectable for Afrikaners to talk to the ANC.

The domestic impact

PW Botha declared to Parliament that he had been aware of preparations for the Dakar meeting and had been briefed fully about it by his spies. He claimed that 'the group who went to Dakar were totally unprepared to debate with a carefully selected ANC team'. Meanwhile the right-wing Afrikaner nationalist, Eugéne Terre'Blanche, sent Botha a telegram supporting his vehement criticism and called for legislation that would be 'putting an end to discussions with the enemy'.

It came as no surprise, then, that when the delegation returned home, they were met by hostile demonstrators organised by Terre'Blanche's neo-Nazi Afrikaner Weerstandsbeweging (AWB). The group members were variously labelled 'traitors', 'communists' and 'terrorists', and the demonstrators demanded that they be charged with high treason. It was a very volatile situation and members of the Intelligence services had to board the plane in order to secretly escort the IDASA group out of the airport. Niel Barnard, the head of the National Intelligence Service (NIS), later jokingly remarked that it was the 'first time that they had to protect such a group of people'.

Indicative of the kind of wrath, intimidation and censure members of the group had to face and endure was the establishment of a special commission by the government-supporting Dutch Reformed Church in Pretoria to investigate its student chaplain Theuns Eloff, who had also made the trip to Dakar. The commission subsequently decided that he should resign from IDASA, the Reform Study Group of Africa and the Reformations Movement of South Africa, of which he was chairperson. Many of the other group members faced similar recriminations.

And yet, even in the face of such unbridled antipathy, it is worth recounting the views and opinions of some of the IDASA participants since these were reflective of the spirit, impact and outcomes of our discussions. It also highlighted the importance of 'enemies' talking frankly and honestly in order to build mutual trust. Van Zyl Slabbert wrote in his book *The Afrikaners*:

> The fact that the meeting played a significant role to launch the politics of negotiations and to legitimise negotiations with the ANC internally only dawned on them and us much later. It 'secularised' the ANC of most of the stereotypes the government had created. It equally undermined the prejudices the ANC had about Afrikaners, especially the monolithic, brainless, *pap-en-wors*, bully from the Bushveld variety.

Jacques Kriel, Professor of Medical Education at Wits, observed:

> Afrikaners played a role in cementing relations. It was very moving to discover how many of the ANC people could speak Afrikaans (a home language for some) but actually enjoyed learning it again. Afrikaans ...

was what we had between us and what an Englishmen or a Senegalese or an American did not have ... The experience of being able to discuss and debate in spite of radical differences and to maintain respect for one another was the most liberating insight ...

Tom Bedford, an architect and former captain of the Springbok rugby team, stated:

Even for the most pessimistic and negative members of the IDASA delegation, the Dakar initiative ... was without doubt a learning experience of invaluable proportions. It was besides one hell of an adventure ... who could remotely have foreseen that the intensive debates ... would have resulted in the dynamics of argument, agreement and disagreements – not necessarily on a 'we' and 'they' basis, but rather as concerned black, brown and white South Africans discussing and agonising on the future of their country.

Professor André Brink, author and head of the department of Afrikaans/ Nederlands at Rhodes University, wrote that:

... the disappearance of all my Dakar notes at the airport should provide the authorities with much-needed information about the true nature and aims of our organisation destined to play a decisive role in the liberation of South Africans, white and black ... To several of the white South Africans it came as a jolt of discovery when one ANC delegate after another announced: 'I was born in Germiston ... in Bloemfontein ... in Cape Town ... in Schweizer-Reneke ...' One realised anew that the apartheid mentality is demonstrated not only in the lunatic excess of the AWB or the ranting and ravings of Botha but in the more subtle distortions of the mind ... The thorough knowledge of history (both world history and South African history) among members of the ANC stood in alarming contrast with the lack of true historical insight among most of the 'internal' group members.

Advocate Brahm du Plessis noted:

Dakar has meant that the ANC has become less remote ... my being part of the IDASA group has contributed to the demystification of the ANC for those people with whom I have contact ... The days which I spent in Senegal made me realise more than ever before, what we South Africans of all races and cultures have missed out as a result of apartheid. The high standard of debate not generally seen in South Africa and the positive interaction were on their own sufficient evidence of the impoverishment as a result of state-enforced barriers and the censorship of ideas ...

The scope, depth and profound importance of the Dakar meeting are reflected in the IDASA group's concluding statement, where it noted that although there were differences between them and the ANC, the group recognised the rationale behind the ANC's turn to armed struggle after it had exhausted peaceful avenues of change in South Africa. Concern was expressed about uncontrolled violence, white fears and especially maintaining the integrity of the Afrikaans language and culture. The statement recognised the serious obstacles to national unity that arose as a consequence of the deeply entrenched racial, economic and ideological divisions in the country, but expressed hope for a political dispensation based on a Bill of Rights, a multi-party system and economic redistributive justice.

Dakar and other similar experiences had indeed been liberating, and demonstrated the possibilities inherent in frank and open talks with the ANC in addressing the challenges of national reconciliation and nation-building. Nevertheless, it now remains one of those ironies of history that, after 1994, hundreds of our white compatriots who had interacted with the ANC and attended so many other meetings became so disillusioned and destructively critical of the organisation.

Beyond Dakar: The Paris and Leverkusen meetings

After Dakar, another meeting between the ANC, MDM, and representatives of business and other sectors was organised in Paris. This time more English-speaking whites from the business elite made up the delegation, and we discussed many of the same topics examined in Dakar and with the captains of industry in Lusaka.

I recall two unforgettable moments. Our delegation had been invited to visit the Élysée, the heart of French establishment. After speeches and drinks, members of the South African group started singing freedom songs and dancing the protest toyi-toyi until the floors and chandeliers were shaking. The French dignitaries and staff had not experienced anything like that before, and I concluded that the only reason the dancing was not called to a halt was because it was indeed a 'historical moment'.

After the reception, some of the MDM and a few business people decided to continue the celebrations in the city, while the rest of us returned to the army camp where we were staying. Late that night when our comrades returned, they were asked for identification papers and a serious argument erupted. In the heat of the argument, somebody called one of the French guards a 'fascist' and all hell broke loose. The commander of the camp had to be woken to resolve the crisis and, after profound apologies, our comrades were allowed in. I believe that the tensions were not fully resolved until we left.

IDASA then organised another important meeting with white South Africans in Leverkusen in Germany. The objective was to expose these important political and academic actors to their counterparts from the Soviet Union and to deal with strident anti-Soviet propaganda. The discussions dealt with the internal dynamics in the Soviet Union and other socialist countries, the international balance of forces and the impact of these developments on the South African democratisation process. It proved to be yet another unforgettable experience.

Besides these high-profile meetings, there were over 200 others between the ANC and internal South African groups, which were held in Zimbabwe, Zambia and across a range of European capitals.

Niel Barnard, who later became an important interlocutor in the secret talks (see Chapter 9 especially), was very critical of initiatives such as the Dakar meeting and others. He said they represented what PW Botha called *vlentergatte* ('ragged arseholes') and 'do-gooders who wanted to be important'. He constantly expressed concern about do-gooders publicly trekking to Lusaka to meet the ANC. His take on the matter was that they were trying to take the initiative from the government and that this was 'very dangerous'. He also confirmed that the NIS had so many sources in Dakar that 'we knew exactly who breathed ... we knew exactly what they were busy with. It was a sideshow and a nice circus, not without good intentions. But they were not close to the true course of events'. He maintained that 'we had to keep them at bay while the state was busy with real negotiations ... the real McCoy had already started with Mandela and the ANC outside.'

I believe that Niel Barnard may have underestimated the objectives of the ANC. The overt meetings with a range of South African groups were not really about negotiations, but about using every opportunity to counteract the demonisation of the ANC and, importantly, to lift the curtain of ignorance and prejudice that white South Africans had been subjected to for so long because of the hermetically sealed world in which they lived under the apartheid system.

The result was that these meetings had indeed lifted the shroud of ignorance from a critical segment of South Africans and had become something of a *cause célèbre* in the country by provoking heated public debate and ambivalent reactions. However, it was the next round of secret meetings in the UK that did much to lay the political and normative groundwork for the actual negotiations. The atmosphere and substance of these meetings between the ANC and a small group of white South Africans with close connections to the regime have not been chronicled in detail and not much exists in the public domain beyond that captured by Robert Harvey in his book, *The Fall of Apartheid: The Inside Story from Smuts to Mbeki*; and by Willie Esterhuyse in his book *Endgame: Secret Talks and the End of Apartheid.* The next two chapters, therefore, provide a thematic account of my involvement in these secret meetings. Quite crucially, given their overall impact and the spectrum of contested issues we canvassed, Chapters 7 and 8 illustrate how instrumental these secret meetings were in the emerging discourse of how a new dispensation for South Africa could be crafted in order to save the country from a looming catastrophe.

Chapter 7

Secret talks in the UK – Laying the groundwork

Different portents provided unambiguous signals that more consequential talks with the South African government and ruling establishment were in the realm of possibility. To begin with, the ANC's NWC had endorsed setting up a President's Committee, proposed by Oliver Tambo in anticipation of such a prospect and with the authority to manage the interface of any talks and negotiations. The committee consisted of Tambo as its chair, Secretary-General Alfred Nzo, Treasurer-General Thomas Nkobi, Joe Slovo, Dan Tloome and John Nkadimeng. Most importantly, the committee was charged with maintaining confidentiality on any 'talks about talks' on the basis of the 'need-to-know' rule.

However, the precursor to the secret talks begins with Willie Esterhuyse, who published a book in 1981 entitled *Apartheid Must Die,* that caused quite a stir in the Afrikaner establishment. Esterhuyse, the son of an Afrikaner farmer, was a *verligte* professor of Philosophy and Theology at Stellenbosch University with close ties to the Broederbond. He had a good relationship with PW Botha, whose daughter Rozanne was his student.

Next there was Fleur de Villiers, a South African journalist working as a consultant for Consolidated Goldfields in London. In July 1987, she proposed to Esterhuyse that he arrange for Afrikaners close to the government to secretly meet with the ANC and that her company would be willing to fund such an initiative. What Fleur de Villiers had actually proposed to Esterhuyse was based on a very important development that took place the month previously. It was then that I accompanied Oliver Tambo, Thabo Mbeki, Jacob Zuma and Mac Maharaj to a meeting in London organised by journalist, Anthony Sampson, and David Astor, former owner and editor of *The Observer.* The meeting was with chief executives of major banks, multinational companies and influential figures in the world of business. They included Lord Anthony Barber, Chairman of Standard

Chartered Bank; Sir Timothy Bevan and Sir Martin Jacomb, respectively Chairman and Deputy Chairman of Barclays Bank; Sir Alistair Frame of Rio Tinto-Zinc; Lord Dennis Arthur Greenhill of the London-based investment bank SG Warburg & Company and the UK's former Permanent Under-Secretary for Foreign Affairs; Sir Evelyn de Rothschild, the British financier; George Soros of the Soros Fund of New York; Sir James Spooner of Morgan Crucible; and Michael Young, former adviser to British prime ministers Alec Douglas-Home and Edward Heath, who represented Consolidated Goldfields.

The meeting took place because British capital had substantial interests in South Africa and Africa, and had become increasingly concerned about the growing instability in South Africa and the impact of the international sanctions campaign on their interests. This was one of the first ANC meetings with leading UK and international business figures. The ANC delegation gave brilliant input and answered all questions frankly and honestly. I was convinced that our delegation had successfully dealt with the demonisation of the ANC, even joking that some of these business magnates seemed impressed that black South Africans could deal so eloquently with complex political, economic and cultural issues.

Michael Young from Consolidated Goldfields subsequently informed Thabo Mbeki and me that he was so impressed with the meeting that he had approached Oliver Tambo and asked what he could do to help with the growing crisis and sense of despondency in South Africa, and that Tambo had told him to arrange for the ANC to meet with leading Afrikaners close to the regime. The seeds of secret but unofficial and informal talks between the ANC and politically connected Afrikaners were thus sown.

I was not surprised by Tambo's request, as Thabo Mbeki had on a previous occasion informed me that Tambo had once told him about a 'nightmare' he had had that one day the regime would send a signal to the ANC 'that they wanted to talk', but that we would not understand the message and would be unable to respond to the signals. The consequences of not being able to respond prudently would, of course, be 'disastrous'.

As a result, Young discussed Tambo's request with the chairman of Consolidated Goldfields, Rudolph Agnew, who authorised up to a substantial million pounds for the project. However, he warned Young that if there were any leaks, the principle of deniability would be applied, and that both the disbursement and accountability for funds resided with Young.

On receiving the go-ahead, Young approached Fleur de Villiers, who advised him to meet with Esterhuyse and his Stellenbosch University colleague, economist Professor Sampie Terreblanche, to discuss the modalities of facilitating secret talks with the ANC's exiled leadership.

Earlier in 1984, Esterhuyse and Terreblanche had accepted an invitation to meet with the ANC in Lusaka, but they had cancelled it after President PW Botha cautioned them not to attend as their visit could be construed as promoting negotiations and that the timing was not right. In a more confident mood, Michael Young travelled to South Africa and met with Esterhuyse and Terreblanche to discuss a new framework for opening discussions with the ANC, and both readily agreed to participate.

Clearly, circumstances were changing. The crisis in South Africa was deepening and international sanctions were intensifying, thus it seemed that the time was right to engage in dialogue with the ANC. Esterhuyse provided Young with additional names of those who could usefully partici-pate in the initiative. Those who agreed at that time were Professor Willie Breytenbach, a senior academic at Stellenbosch University who had close connections with the military establishment and whose brother was head of the Special Operations section of the SADF; and Marinus Wiechers, a senior professor of Constitutional Law at the University of South Africa (UNISA). Professor Pieter de Lange, head of the Broederbond; Tjaart van der Walt, Rector of Potchefstroom University; and Johan Heyns, Moderator of the Dutch Reformed Church, declined to participate for 'political reasons'.

Interestingly, and with their fingers on the pulse, the NIS was aware of Young's visits and discussions and actually advised Esterhuyse to go ahead with the initiative and to report back on the discussions. Esterhuyse agreed on condition that he could inform Thabo Mbeki. In a rather bizarre twist, the NIS provided Esterhuyse with security training! He recalled that he had told his trainer that such training was not necessary since the ANC would not harm him because they needed him as an honest broker. He was surprised when the trainer told him that they were not protecting him from the ANC but from the 'brown shirts' – that is, elements of the Afrikaner right wing!

Niel Barnard, whom PW Botha had appointed to head the NIS in 1979, informed me in an interview for this book that 'during the 1980s the overall global, continental and southern African picture was clear: the country in response to the ANC's call had become "ungovernable"'. His recollection was that 'we were in a situation where we either had to fight it out and inherit a wasteland, or we sit down as South Africans, among ourselves, and try to find a political settlement for the future of all of us'. He argued that there were two distinct views in the South African government: one, supported by Military Intelligence and the Security Branch, was to fight it out – 'Let's tackle Angola and Mozambique with UNITA and RENAMO' – and thus secure the regime; the second view, represented by the NIS, was that 'the main reason for the problems was that the political system could not hold and they had to seek political change'. Barnard recollected telling PW Botha that 'the longer we waited, the harder it would become, the weaker the government's hand became and the stronger the ANC became. The tide was turning against the government. We could still negotiate with the ANC from a position of power, and then later as equals.'

After Young returned to London, I had several meetings with him to discuss his visit to South Africa and to prepare the logistical arrangements and agenda for our first meeting. The points we negotiated were to be tabled again and again at every consecutive gathering throughout the process until both parties and their members were satisfied with the outcome. Naturally, that was easier said than done, and as we moved from one meeting to the next, it became clear that the discussions would require sound negotiating skills and political deftness on both sides. But, right from the outset, we put forward a number of pivotal points that would set the tone – and the intended outcomes – of these all-important talks:

- One of the principle aims of the secret meetings was to create conditions conducive to negotiations – in other words, formal talks between the ANC and the apartheid government. And in order to achieve that we would have to resolve a number of significant and contentious issues, including the release of Nelson Mandela and all political prisoners, the unbanning of all political organisations, the end of the state of emergency and concern around the issue of the ANC and its continued armed struggle.

- Also high on the agenda were the contested ideas about the con-stitutional character of the South African state and the extent to which it would be underpinned by the principles of majoritarianism and 'one person one vote'. In essence, the central issue of concern here was that the Freedom Charter stated that 'the people shall govern', so the question for the Afrikaner interlocutors was: Did this mean that the ANC would govern and, if so, what were the implications of one-party rule?

- Although more of a red herring in our view, we were aware that we had to address concerns about the relationship between the ANC and the SACP and the potential effect this might have of leading South Africa down a path towards a Soviet-style communist regime.

- On the critical matter of the economy, talks would centre on the Afrikaner interlocutors' fear of nationalisation versus our perspective on the imperative of wealth redistribution in order to effectively deal with the inequalities experienced by the majority.

Quite importantly in this regard, we would have to address whether South Africa would be a state-controlled or free-market economy or a mixture of the two.

- We had no doubt, too, that we would have to table important issues regarding international sanctions, which were increasingly responsible for South Africa's growing isolation and economic malaise.

- Finally, we would have to consider varying regional and international dynamics in so far as these were influencing and impacting on the negotiating postures of the ANC and the South African government.

The first meeting: Compleat Angler

The first secret meeting took place at the Compleat Angler, a luxurious manor house set amid beautiful surroundings in Marlow in the south of England, from 31 October to 2 November 1987. Because of unforeseen circumstances, ANC representatives from Lusaka could not attend and I was asked to organise a delegation of comrades based in London. I approached Harold Wolpe, Wally Serote and Tony Trew to join me. The 'Afrikaner group' consisted of professors Willie Esterhuyse, Sampie Terreblanche and Willie Breytenbach. Marinus Wiechers, their constitutional expert, withdrew at the last minute. Esterhuyse informed me years later that PW Botha had told him that if the talks became public he would denounce him in Parliament, to which he jokingly responded, 'Great, because it would give me international publicity.'

Michael Young's other brief was to provide an overview of the international situation at every session. When we arrived at the venue the atmosphere was uneasy, uncomfortable and tense, and I simply did not know what to expect. I was conscious that the absence of our senior leaders from Lusaka could have created the impression that the ANC was not serious about this engagement and had sent a 'B' team. Furthermore, while we were representing the ANC we had no clarity about who the Afrikaner group was representing. All we knew was that they considered themselves to be 'bridge-builders and go-betweens' and had hinted that they were able to 'convey messages to the highest level'. Fortunately, after the dinner and informal discussions around a log fire, everybody felt more relaxed.

Esterhuyse recalls his horror when he was introduced to 'communist Wolpe' and wondered how he could meet with the 'devil incarnate'. He told me that it was because I had greeted them in Afrikaans that tensions had 'dramatically' eased. They were pleasantly surprised to learn that I had majored in Afrikaans at Wits, that in my second year my lecturer was the Afrikaans literary giant, NP Van Wyk Louw, and that I had enjoyed the course tremendously. I also told them stories about how in exile we spoke Afrikaans when we did not want strangers to hear or understand our discussions. We did this often on the tube in London, until one day our conversation was interrupted by a stranger who greeted us warmly in Afrikaans. As it turned out, the stranger was equally astonished to come across a group of blacks on a London tube speaking 'his' language.

The Afrikaner group was also pleasantly surprised to learn that we were familiar with the Anglo-Boer War, and we revelled in telling them that their arch ideological enemy, Karl Marx, had written about the Anglo-Boer War as one of the greatest examples of an anti-imperialist struggle. In fact, Wolpe, a social scientist, went into great detail about Afrikaner history and we had lengthy discussions on the War. We mischievously asked, given such a history, what had gone wrong.

My colleagues and I had been in exile for many years, so we seized the opportunity to ask questions about South Africa, including mundane matters, such as about the weather and sports. It was a surreal experience. There we were as South Africans, black and white, representing two major contending forces, and we were sitting around a log fire in an English manor house drinking the best whiskey and wine, and sharing anecdotes, jokes and personal stories. Harold's stories about how he, Mosie Moolla, Abdulhay Jassat and Arthur Goldreich escaped from Marshall Square prison had everybody in stitches.

I am convinced that the non-racial composition of our delegation and the fact that all of us were able to speak Afrikaans made a huge impact on the Afrikaner group. The conversation fluctuated between English and Afrikaans; not surprisingly, our Afrikaans was not *suiwer* ('pure') but then neither was their English. This added to the congeniality and friendships quickly blossomed. The absurdity that we could not have such social and intellectual interactions in South Africa escaped no one. Michael Young was utterly 'amazed' by what was happening, given the air of uncertainty about the initiative at the beginning.

The relaxed atmosphere over dinner created a more conducive climate for discussions the next day. We agreed that since there were no senior members of the ANC from Lusaka present, we should keep the conversation general. The discussions focused on three thematic areas: the domestic situation, the economy and the release of political prisoners.

General areas of discussion

The view of the Afrikaner group was that the reform process had been blocked. There was no consensus in their group about whether the National Party could be an agent of reform, although there was some agreement that after 1984 the securocrats were taking the lead on constitutional issues. Parliament and the provinces were effectively becoming marginalised, and since the military establishment had all the political power, there was no need for a coup. They advised that the security establishment should not be analysed in a 'simplistic' or 'mechanistic' manner since 20 per cent of Afrikaner voters and 5 per cent of English voters supported reform.

They confirmed that the rejection of the EPG was a disaster and resulted in South Africa not receiving any support or assurances from the G-7 of industrialised countries, led by the USA, at the Tokyo Summit.

The township revolts in 1984, the mass mobilisation under the ANC and the ungovernability of the townships had deepened the regime's crisis. However, this had given the security establishment the opportunity to act decisively in order to restore a measure of stability. They had *de facto* assumed political power and had put an end to constitutional and other reforms that the 'technocrats' were introducing.

There was a perception that the ANC had lost much of its influence and posed less of a threat, and was, therefore, less important to the political process. In their view, the ANC had the tactical edge when it came to mass mobilisation and international solidarity, but it seemed that it was over-reliant on the armed struggle, which was its weakest weapon compared to the military muscle at the regime's disposal.

I suspected that they were conveying the message that a process of transformation had already started, but because of the ANC's mass mobilisation and 'ungovernability' campaign, the security apparatus had taken control and was thus weakening the ANC's internal base. We differed with them on their interpretation of the internal situation and warned them that there would be an escalation of all four pillars of ANC strategy and tactics – mass mobilisation, strengthening of ANC underground structures, the armed struggle and international solidarity – unless the government took decisive steps to end apartheid and lay the foundations for a negotiated solution.

We also discussed the crisis of the economy and the gross inequalities between blacks and whites in the country. I got the sense that they seemed to think that we were 'economic illiterates'. There was a suggestion that with the help of a type of 'Marshall Plan' we could achieve economic growth, and through economic growth achieve political change. We challenged this thinking and explained the ANC's approach to the economic crisis: namely, that only a non-racial democratic South Africa could effectively deal with the mounting political and economic challenges and deep inequalities that continued to haunt the country.

The State Security Council (SSC) was convinced that it had achieved stability and economic growth and, consequently, that Africans could participate at the 'highest level'. The group wanted to know whether the ANC was willing to consider voluntary group rights in 'own affairs', such as education, for example. We again elaborated on our vision of a non-racial democratic society and our firm opposition to any concept of group rights.

We raised the matter of political prisoners and informed them that their release was crucial to create a climate for negotiations, reminding members of the group that the ANC had consistently raised this issue in the meeting with the EPG and all other meetings. They told us that the government's linking of violence with the release of political prisoners put them in a 'tight corner'. However, Govan Mbeki was to be released soon and the ANC's response to the release – that is, not to turn it into a 'damp squib' or 'shift the goal posts' – could lead to other releases, as well as the unbanning of the ANC.

We all agreed that the meeting had enabled us to better understand one another's policy positions and to share broad perspectives about a range of critical political and economic issues. The meeting gave us further insight into white South Africans' perceptions of the ANC and their fears, which we could not ignore if we were to move forward. This demanded that we give serious consideration to the ANC journal *Sechaba* and Radio Freedom in order to develop our own channels so that the nuances of ANC positions could be better communicated. I was convinced that future meetings with the Afrikaner group would enable us to better explain our policies and vision for a democratic South Africa. Notwithstanding our differences, there was consensus that we were all South Africans seeking appropriate solutions. We agreed that another meeting would be organised, which would include ANC representatives from Lusaka, and that they in turn would arrange the participation of a 'stronger' Afrikaner grouping.

In November 1987 Michael Young returned to South Africa to plan for the second meeting. He was aware that the authorities had some information about the first meeting in the UK since Esterhuyse and possibly other members of his group would have briefed the NIS and other sectors of the Afrikaner establishment.

Young met with Tjaart van der Walt, as well as Naas Steenkamp, president of the South African Chamber of Mines – and both supported the initiative. When Young returned to London, he and I met and he briefed me fully on his visit. We then discussed a draft agenda and the logistical arrangements for the second meeting.

The second meeting: Eastwell Manor

The government had banned 17 anti-apartheid organisations, including the UDF, while COSATU was barred from taking part in any 'non-trade union' activities. We knew then that the situation in South Africa was highly volatile. Govan Mbeki had been released on 5 November 1987 and we expected that the release of Mandela and other political prisoners was imminent.

It was against this backdrop that the second meeting took place at Eastwell Manor in Kent on 21 and 22 February 1988. I later learnt that this meeting had occurred three months before Mandela had his first formal secret talks in prison with a special committee of four that had been established for the purpose, and which consisted of Minister of Justice and Prisons Kobie Coetsee, Commissioner of Prisons Johan Willemse, Director-General of Prisons Fanie van der Merwe, and Niel Barnard, head of the NIS (see Chapter 9).

This second meeting was significant in that the ANC delegation was led by Thabo Mbeki and included Wally Serote, Tony Trew and me. The internal group was made up of Willie Esterhuyse, Sampie Terreblanche and Marinus Wiechers. Willem (Wimpie) de Klerk, the brother of FW de Klerk, was also expected to attend but withdrew because of other commitments.

Esterhuyse privately informed Mbeki about Niel Barnard's proposal that he be briefed fully on all the discussions, and Mbeki's agreement was based on the knowledge that if reports of our talks were given to Barnard, as the head of the NIS, he would in turn brief the state president, PW Botha. Clearly Botha had wanted the NIS to use these meetings to gain a better understanding of the external ANC, its strategy and tactics, its perspectives on negotiations, and whether there were serious differences between the exiles, the ANC leaders in prison and the ANC-allied organisations internally.

The atmosphere was more relaxed and the discussions were more specific and candid.

The theme for the meeting was 'creating the climate for change', and included strategies for negotiation; the obstacles to creating a conducive climate; white aspirations and black fears; and the mechanisms necessary to drive a political transition.

The Afrikaner group was adamant that they were not 'involved in negotiations'. For them, the objective of the meeting would be to contribute to 'creating a conducive climate for negotiated change'.

The question of political prisoners

Of course, we had already dealt with the issue of political prisoners in our discussions with the EPG and in other overt meetings, so the government was well aware of our views. Thus I struggled to understand why a group so close to the Afrikaner political, economic and religious establishments was now discussing the same issues without demonstrating any progress and flexibility in their thinking based on our previous discussions. As had been our principled policy positions with other groups in the overt talks, Mbeki reiterated the basic positions of the ANC and the internal organisations for talks to start: the release of political prisoners, the unbanning of organisations and the removal of troops from the townships.

The response from the Afrikaner group was that the government understood that the release of political prisoners and the unbanning of organisations were important, but it had to seriously consider the consequences of any such major decision. It had to deal with the incontrovertible reality that there was the growing white right-wing CP that was increasing its support base. The government believed that if the political prisoners were released, this would lead to 'widespread violence and disorder' and thus strengthen the right wing.

They wanted to know whether, if the government made such major concessions, the ANC would consider calling off international sporting, economic and academic sanctions. According to them, the ANC had to deliver some quid pro quo. Adriaan Vlok, Botha's Minister of Police, had complained that 'they have not received their pound of flesh' for Govan Mbeki's release and that there was a distinct perception that the ANC kept shifting the goal posts. They believed that Govan Mbeki's first press conference after his release from prison had been 'provocative', and that the ANC had exploited his release for 'propaganda purposes' and used this to intensify its 'mass mobilisation' campaign.

We explained that the Bureau of Information had handled the timing and organisation of the release poorly: Govan Mbeki was only told of the media conference when he landed in Port Elizabeth. And after so many years in prison, and at 77 years of age, he 'would have been disorientated'; nor was he given any opportunity to consult with the ANC in Lusaka or the leadership of the MDM at home. Govan Mbeki had understood all too well that he should do nothing to hinder the process of further release of political prisoners. In fact, his prepared statement for the planned rally, which was banned, was one of reconciliation. Soon after his release, Govan Mbeki had started consulting with the internal leadership to ensure that there was calm when Mandela and other political prisoners were released. There was therefore no justification for banning the rally or restricting Govan Mbeki's movements.

It had been widely expected that after Govan Mbeki's release, other political prisoners would follow. Interestingly, Niel Barnard's view was that Govan Mbeki's release was problematic for a number of reasons. In their secret meetings with Mandela in prison, Mandela's advice was that Walter Sisulu should be the first to be released since this would pave the way for the release of Mandela and fellow political prisoners. The NIS agreed with this view, but the government decided instead to release Govan Mbeki. Of course, the suggestion here is that Govan Mbeki's release – who is said to be more headstrong and even more militant than the calm and level-headed Sisulu – would better suit the apartheid government at the time. Any eruption of volatility engendered by Govan Mbeki would then, one supposes, be just cause to delay further the release of political prisoners. Barnard believed that the release of Govan Mbeki had 'made things very difficult for us'. Regardless of Govan Mbeki's undertaking, he made speeches that led to a 'revolt' within government circles. They had informed Mandela that 'agreement had been reached on the release of Sisulu when Govan made one of his "mad speeches" in Port Elizabeth and the [State] Security Council decided not to release Sisulu'. When Barnard informed Mandela about these developments, he was 'furious'. Mandela believed that the '*boere* always stuck to their word'.

We advised the Afrikaner group that the release of another leading but ageing communist, Harry Gwala, on humanitarian grounds would be another indication of the regime's genuine commitment to release Mandela and all political prisoners. The regime was fully aware of the positive effects that such policy changes would have on the country and without such affirmative acts and 'inducements', it would be difficult for the ANC to convince its constituency that the regime was committed to real and genuine negotiations.

The government was convinced, it seems, that prisoners from Robben Island constituted a 'moderate' faction of the ANC and could, therefore, easily be co-opted since they were far removed from political developments. An interesting new element related to this thinking was that the regime believed that once Govan Mbeki was released, the ANC would support participation in the National Statutory Council (NSC), an extension of the Tricameral Parliament of Indians and coloureds, but including African participation. In their view, our refusal to do so rendered further releases more 'problematic'.

I was surprised that the government continued to believe that leaders of the ANC and 'moderate' blacks would be willing to participate in its dummy institutions, including the envisaged NSC. Was this based on reports from their informants in our ranks or on other discussions of which I was not aware?

I am convinced, however, that after these intense talks the Afrikaner group had a better understanding of the centrality of the release of political prisoners in creating a favourable climate for negotiations. They informed us that they had raised the possibility of meetings with the security establishment to discuss the conditions and logistics of prisoners' release, but the government was concerned that news of such meetings could become public and could easily be exploited by the CP and its rabid right-wingers.

Contending political perspectives

The perception among many white people was that the ANC was demanding the transfer of power to itself and not to the people of South Africa. Also, the opinion was that white South Africans did not accept the concept of a multi-party democracy and that the ANC should thus consider a multi-cultural society. There were suggestions that we give serious consideration to group rights and not black majority rule. The Afrikaner group argued that 'one man one vote' in a unitary state was interpreted by whites to mean black majority rule and this hardened group thinking. Basically, then, they were asking us to soften our positions on a one-person-one-vote system. They cautioned us not to underestimate the military, security and economic power of the regime and its ability to divide the ANC and to exert pressure on neighbouring countries. They believed that change should be incremental and involve 'power elites who were more enlightened than their mass constituencies'. Given this reality and logic, they argued, the 'bridge builders' from the contending political forces or the intelligentsia could play crucial roles.

We explained that since its foundation, the ANC strongly supported multi-party democracy. The ANC never demanded a transfer of power to itself but was committed to an inclusive democracy. The Freedom Charter categorically proclaimed that South Africa belongs to all who live in it, black and white, and our membership was open to all groups.

PW Botha was clearly paranoid about the ANC. He no longer made a distinction between Nationalists and Marxists in the organisation, but was now drawing a distinction between the internal ANC and the external ANC. He was convinced that there were divisions between 'handelaars' (those ready to talk and negotiate) and 'geweldenaars' (those dedicated to violence). In terms of the former, he believed that there were elements within the ANC who could give his reform policy and strategy some legitimacy, including getting involved in the NSC, as a mechanism for bringing black Africans into the existing decision-making process, which already involved some coloureds and Indians. This type of participation went to the heart of validating the dichotomy between 'own affairs' and 'group rights'. The regime's position could thus be characterised by four propositions: there would be no national convention; the Tricameral system would form the basis of Parliament where whites, coloureds and Indians would be represented; the National Party would be in control of the constitutional process; and the self-governing Bantustans would remain in place as platforms for black African representation.

It seemed to me that the regime's strategic approach was based on outdated policies aimed at maintaining the status quo while talking of 'change'. There was no consistency in words and actions; indeed, the regime had learnt nothing from its interaction and experiences with the EPG. The experience of the EPG and other discussions had given us a very clear indication of these National Party bottom lines, which they repeated *ad nauseam* as articles of faith.

Thabo Mbeki responded that the National Statutory Council was not acceptable to the ANC or the MDM since the government still had voting control in this new body and, moreover, would be able to determine the future constitution so that any form of power-sharing would still effectively result in white control and domination of the process. Consequently, any discussion about constitutional mechanisms had to occur within the ambit of a transitional process that enjoyed genuine popular support rather than simply being an instrument of maintaining the status quo. The internal 'movers and shakers' therefore had to accept this inherently correct position and chart the way forward.

It was suggested, too, that the ANC had lost contact with the masses, that it was losing support and was being marginalised in the country; and had thus been reduced to 'ideologising' and 'sloganeering'.

In response, Thabo Mbeki explained that it was a mistake to believe that the ANC was being marginalised; on the contrary, the ANC was in dynamic contact with internal organisations, as well as people from all walks of life, and that there were three elements to the ANC's presence in the country. The first was as a vehicle of ideas and aspirations because the ANC represented a particular tradition within South African politics that included non-racialism. As a broad national movement, any assertion that the ANC was being marginalised could thus be directly challenged. The second had to do with the particular position the ANC occupied in people's perceptions of the history and conduct of the struggle. The organisation was seen as the 'mother body' in the sense that popular organisations and leaders from every section of society opposed to the apartheid system took the ANC as their point of reference and regularly consulted with it. COSATU's recognition of the ANC's role in the struggle provided a good example. And, thirdly, ANC membership in the country was drawn from tried-and-tested activists who had proven themselves in the trenches of struggle and who occupied leading positions in popular organisations.

On security and the protection of languages, as well as religion and culture, the Afrikaner group went to great lengths to outline 'white fears'. They argued that there were many in their communities who could not contemplate fundamental changes to the apartheid system because they would have to give up their privileges. The civil service had, for example, become a job-creation mechanism for many Afrikaners and many of the skilled and unskilled white workforce was aware that 'Africanisation' would mean job losses, especially in the bloated civil service. The white population, generally, had developed negative perceptions about post-colonial Africa and believed that 'standards of living crumbled when Africans took over'; among others, 'educational standards collapsed, roads deteriorated, electricity supplies became irregular, corruption became rampant, crime increased, social conditions deteriorated, the economy collapsed, human rights abuses increased, and democracy was trampled on'.

There were certain privileges that many whites saw as their given right and, therefore, they could not envisage a situation in which Africans took over and all the 'good things' that 'they had created' would no longer be available to them. They believed that they had to maintain political control in order to ensure the protection of their economic interests and social security. There were also concerns about their own physical safety when a black government took over, and deep-seated fears that, when in power, blacks would retaliate violently against whites.

The group went on to explain that white South Africans also believed that a black government would disturb the power equilibrium between political, economic and military interests. Whites would, therefore, be willing to agree to changes in which no group had complete control over political, economic or military structures.

The ANC delegation, in turn, explained that universal suffrage and multi-party democracy were fundamental to our demands. The ANC was a broad movement and as soon as political freedom was established, there was a strong possibility that within the ANC there could be groupings of different persuasions and new political formations could be established. Presently, we were united in our opposition to the apartheid system, but in a democratic South Africa it would be possible that different class, national and social forces would join or form new organisations to serve their interests. This has been the experience of many anti-colonialist movements and liberation movements in Africa and internationally.

We believed strongly that the homeland system had to be dismantled, but we were not opposed to devolution of powers, which meant that however the country's political geography might be altered in a future dispensation, provincial and local government would enjoy certain competences and authority. The challenge, of course, was to 'define the lowest level of governance' in an inter-governmental system that would make such powers meaningful, accountable and authoritative.

On the issue of the economy, we explained that the ANC had no intention of adopting policies that would be either destructive or prejudicial; if anything, a democratic South Africa 'would need a growing and vibrant economy in order to close the glaring inequalities and inequities' in our society and improve the lives of our people. This could only be achieved through the cooperation of all South Africans; a mixed economy would necessarily need the involvement of those who were presently controlling it.

When it came to our differing perceptions of politics and world views, it was a truism that our white compatriots were subjected to constant government propaganda that falsified and demonised the ANC. Since we were in a conflict situation, the regime had created a powerful propaganda machine that distorted what the ANC represented and stood for, and even went as far as releasing false statements in the name of the ANC. This was the catalyst and foundation of white fears. The ANC was prevented from openly communicating with South Africans and there was a compelling need to break through the 'iron wall' that controlled ideas and information.

I am not sure whether, at this stage, the Afrikaner group was fully convinced by our arguments, and these points continued to be recurring issues in all future meetings. I was surprised that they were ignorant of the work of the ANC's Constitutional Committee and our perspectives on issues such as a Bill of Rights, and found it strange that they were not informed about the many meetings the ANC was having with diverse sections of South African society where ANC policies on all these issues had been thoroughly canvassed and explained. In fact, one was left to wonder whether the NIS, Military Intelligence and the Security Police – as structures that had infiltrated agents into our ranks – had correctly and adequately briefed the government and group members attending these secret talks. Our interlocutors were senior members of academia and the Afrikaner establishment, and yet were they not privy to ANC and SACP policy documents?

Regional dynamics

In our wide-ranging discussions about dynamics in southern Africa, the group informed us that there were sections in the military hierarchy who believed that politicians were not doing enough to find a political solution to regional conflicts and tensions. This was influenced by the reality that, because the army was in the frontline, it was left to it to carry the responsibility and burden of implementing the government's 'hardline' policies. At the regional level, they were suffering increasing casualties, especially in Angola, and were thus looking for a political solution. Within the military leadership, there were those who supported the unbanning of the ANC, the release of political prisoners and ending the state of emergency. Some of the SADF military leadership heading up the South West African Territorial Force (SWATF) were adamant that the military's role should be restricted to security and regional stability.

In the Afrikaner group's view, the government's policy on Angola suffered from a serious lack of legitimacy, especially given the economic costs and the growing casualties there and elsewhere, which made its indefinite intervention both unsustainable and untenable. Leading figures in the regime were now calling for negotiations to resolve regional conflicts. For example, already underway were discussions on how the Cahora Bassa Dam in Mozambique could be safeguarded as a 'regional public good'. The problem was that there were sharp differences about whether the Nkomati Accord should be honoured or not; some in the regime believed that the agreement should be implemented while others believed it should not and, in terms of the latter position, support for the Mozambican National Resistance (RENAMO) and the destabilisation of the FRELIMO government should be intensified.

The recent appointment of Major-General Willie Meyer as head of the SWATF was significant since it was expected that he would take some major regional initiatives, including full implementation of the Nkomati Accord, SADF withdrawal from Angola and acceptance of UN Resolution 435, which would facilitate Namibia's independence. This would have serious consequences for ANC military camps in Angola and on our activities in Mozambique and other neighbouring countries.

The meeting concluded that the ANC leadership would consider what concessions it could offer in exchange for the release of political prisoners. And secondly, that mechanisms for the control and orderly release of political prisoners had to be explored on both sides. For its part, the Afrikaner group would provide us with feedback at the third meeting about the many issues we had raised. It was also suggested that a representative from the NIS should attend that meeting.

I was confident that some within the Afrikaner group departed with a better understanding that 'white fears' had to be seen in the context of 'black aspirations', and that this would be dealt with in terms of the

Constitution and a Bill of Rights. Also, the ANC was adamant that the release of political prisoners was a prerequisite, as was the unbanning of the ANC. Both these factors could play a major role in creating an environment of peace and stability that would enable the commencement of direct talks between the ANC and the government. We had once again exposed the fallacy of the argument that releasing prisoners would lead to violence. There could be no ambiguity about the ANC's rejection of any participation in government-created institutions.

In terms of the atmospherics of the meeting, we had many opportunities for informal discussions on a one-on-one basis, as well as in larger groups. This casual informality certainly helped us to better understand the issues we had discussed in the formal sessions. It was in these informal talks that each side posed questions that we understood could only be fully answered after consultations in South Africa and Lusaka.

The staff of the Eastwell Manor, who were discreet and excellent, must have been amused or bemused to see a diverse group of South Africans engaged in such earnest discussions in secretive conditions, often speaking a 'strange' language. The sight of us warmly dressed and walking in groups of two or more in the cold British weather, talking and laughing, would also have been a cause for some interest.

The third meeting: Mells Park

For our third confidential meeting, which took place on 21 to 24 August 1988, we again returned to Mells Park. The ANC delegation was led by Thabo Mbeki and included myself and Tony Trew, while the internal group comprised Esterhuyse, Sampie Terreblanche and Wimpie de Klerk. This meeting took place in the aftermath of a car bombing at the Krugersdorp Magistrate's Court in March 1988 in which three civilians were killed and 22 wounded. There had therefore been some concern that this meeting would be postponed. Fortunately, we all recognised the significance of the 'secret talks' and decided that the meeting should go ahead as scheduled. In fact, Esterhuyse informed us that the NIS 'informant' who had infiltrated the ANC's leadership had stated that the latter wanted talks to continue. We had no idea who the informant was and all efforts to elicit his or her identity proved unsuccessful. I do not think Esterhusye had any direct knowledge of the source of the leak in the ANC's leadership but, wittingly or unwittingly, simply wanted to draw our attention to the fact that the NIS had infiltrated the highest ranks of the ANC's decision-making structures.

Esterhuyse informed us that the NIS was keen for one of its members to attend the next session of talks, which surprised us because we had expected that they would attend this session. I suspected, however, that the reason there was no NIS representative was because PW Botha had recovered sufficiently in a political sense and was asserting his leadership, especially within the National Party. Botha continued talking about drastic changes, but was really simply tinkering with the apartheid system. There was a sense, especially among his inner circle, that they had managed to successfully control mass resistance and that the political climate had become more conducive to implementing a 'reformist solution'. Sending a NIS representative could, therefore, have been interpreted as a sign of weakness or capitulation on Botha's part.

Mandela's release

The third meeting demonstrated that strategic and political shifts in the regime's thinking were indeed taking place. We were informed that the government had decided to release Mandela and that this would most likely take place after the local government elections scheduled for between October and mid-December 1988. Some in the government believed that Mandela's age would prevent him from being politically active, while the majority believed that there were serious divisions within the ANC and Mandela could play an important moderating role in isolating the 'communists and militants'.

We were informed that the government no longer insisted that Mandela renounce violence as a precondition for his release. A Committee of Inquiry would be established, which would recommend that Mandela be released on 'humanitarian grounds'.

However, the government continued to be 'concerned' about how the black population would respond to Mandela's release. Before a decision was taken to release him, the government wanted assurance that the ANC would be able to control its supporters and prevent any violence and disorder. Once again the issue of violence was being raised as an excuse for delaying the release of Mandela and other ANC leaders. This issue had been discussed with the captains of industry and the EPG, and in our previous secret talks. We were also aware from the EPG talks with the ANC senior leadership in exile, and later via Mandela's lawyer, George Bizos, who informed Oliver Tambo that this issue had been discussed with Mandela in prison. In our view, this resolved the debate about whether Mandela's release would lead to violence and whether we could control our supporters in the event that it did. As we would eventually witness, the government's concerns were entirely unfounded.

The Afrikaner group asked whether the ANC in exile was really committed to the freedom of Mandela. Their foundation for this was a perception that if Mandela died in prison, it would result in massive support for the ANC both at home and abroad and that the regime would be further isolated internationally. I was sceptical that PW Botha and some members of his inner circle seriously believed that the ANC in exile would benefit from Mandela's demise, and found it perplexing that the Afrikaner group appeared to be surprised when we challenged this misperception. We repeated our position as a matter of principle and policy: the unbanning of the ANC had to be preceded by the release of political prisoners and that of Mandela. The ANC could not accept even the remotest suggestion that the organisation (and others) would be unbanned, while its leaders continued to languish in jail – because unless we came to an agreement up front, that was not beyond the realm of possibility. We were not interested in exploiting the releases for short-term political gain. The stakes were too high for such a myopic approach and, hence, the ANC would not take any action that would delay Mandela's release. We wanted to be informed about the timing so that we could organise a proper reception; the ANC was even willing to make appropriate interventions that would assist PW Botha with solving any perceived problems that might arise with releasing Mandela.

We were asked whether we wanted to talk to the regime directly in order to finalise arrangements for Mandela's release – although, if it was leaked, the government would deny any knowledge of such a meeting – and Thabo Mbeki indicated that we would agree to such talks if it expedited the process. Since the government wanted deniability, a secret meeting could take place with South African intelligence officials to look at the mechanics of Mandela's release. We reminded them that at our previous meeting we had agreed that a NIS representative would join the group precisely to discuss this issue, but there had been no movement from the government's side. We could not give any commitment to direct talks with the NIS; only the ANC leadership in Lusaka could do so, but we assured them that we could foresee no real difficulty with such a meeting. We clearly understood that the proposal for direct ANC and government talks, without any preconditions, was an important step forward to achieve the release of Mandela and other comrades in prison.

Mbeki explained, too, that Mandela could not be released and then be subject to restrictions; it was only logical that as soon as he left prison he would become active in politics. Moreover, Mandela would not comply with any restrictions imposed by the government. These discussions confirmed my suspicions that PW Botha's government still harboured the illusion that Mandela could be co-opted to challenge the leadership of the ANC in exile, largely because he had been incarcerated for so long and isolated from his own colleagues. They believed that he would take a more conservative position of, among others, calling on Africans to participate in the NSC and to even consider renouncing violence before there was any serious progress in negotiations. The regime would thus deal with a 'conservative ANC', which would enable them to control the direction and pace of the negotiation process and, consequently, impose a reformist solution. Why the regime still believed that it could use Mandela in order to succeed with a divide-and-rule strategy to weaken the ANC was difficult to comprehend. Only officials from the regime who were involved in the secret talks with Mandela could provide some clarity on this.

In both the formal and informal discussions, we explained that, historically, even when there were differing approaches to its strategy and tactics, the ANC could not be divided. No individual could stand above the ANC as an organisation. The political background and experience of our leadership was such that we would emerge with one consistent policy for the way forward.

Changes in white politics

In the all-white general elections of May 1987, the National Party maintained its power in the face of growing cleavages within the Afrikaner electorate. The PFP, a liberal party mostly composed of white English-speaking South Africans, lost its position as the main opposition to the CP. For the first time in decades, there was a major split within the Afrikaner ruling elite and electorate, such that a major challenge to the National Party's hegemony had emerged from the right. The CP's growing support could be attributed to the economic crisis and the deteriorating socio-economic situation of whites. As international investment started to decline and inflationary pressures caused public spending to decrease, poverty worsened for both black and white. It became clear that further economic deterioration would be calamitous and lead to the increased militarisation of government in a siege economy. The National Party government thus confronted a serious and potentially debilitating legitimacy crisis since its electoral support base could no longer be guaranteed.

The election had also shown that there were growing divisions within the National Party. The real battle over political influence and control was being fought inside the National Party caucus and among the Broederbond, whose enlightened members were beginning to assert their leadership positions. If white 'leftist' groups were united, they could form an important pressure group in alliance with extraparliamentary groups, capable of forming a multiracial government in the next five to 10 years, which could play a part in the negotiating process leading to a non-racial constitution. In terms of the discussions we were having, I suspected that this would be based on some form of a 'non-majoritarian democracy'.

It was increasingly apparent that some organisations within the Afrikaner community were at last moving out of the confines of their laager. This was reflected by the fact that Afrikaner unions wanted to join COSATU and the South African Rugby Union (SARU) wanted to talk with the ANC in order to fast-track sports integration. In this context, the Afrikaner group raised with us the need to seriously consider ending the sporting and cultural isolation, which 'had a pernicious and harmful effect' on white morale in South Africa.

Democratic transformation

There was a growing realisation within the Afrikaner ruling establishment that a 'total strategy' solution was not the answer and that the only way out of the morass was to find a negotiated solution. A salutary development in this regard was that the majority of the Afrikaner establishment and, as we were informed, at least 45 per cent of the National Party caucus accepted the inevitability of a black government; the challenge was how the interests of the white minority would be accommodated. Here, the government's strategy turned on three possibilities: a semi-dictatorship; socio-economic progress for blacks; and a democratic dispensation that would culminate in power-sharing based on an 'own affairs' government and drawing its inspiration from the consociational model. This model, developed by Dutch political scientist Arend Lijphart, represents a form of 'democratic consensus' in deeply divided societies and was especially attractive to Afrikaner academics and politicians as a vehicle of political accommodation. Characteristics of the model include a grand governing coalition of all major political actors; a mutual veto to ensure majority rule and prevent a minority from blocking the majority; proportionality where representation is based on population strength; and segmental autonomy that protects community, group and identity interests.

In terms of these possibilities, we were told that the government's plans were 'not cosmetic' and that it wanted black participation – but within the framework of an own-affairs arrangement. They believed that complementary socio-economic development of the townships would convince black South Africans to accept the outcomes of the municipal elections and allow for an own-affairs solution. This flawed reasoning was based on the government's conviction that the ANC only enjoyed minority support of about 25 per cent; that anti-ANC forces held 45 per cent; and that there was a middle ground of 30 per cent. This middle ground was contested territory where the government certainly thought it could make inroads. We, however, informed them that they were grossly underestimating support for the ANC, an issue we had discussed many times in the previous sessions.

I continued to believe that, at that stage, the thinking of the establishment was that they could manage and control the reform process such that we could end up with a future South Africa that functioned according to the dictates of group rights. We, however, were involved in an important transformation process and remained confident that, in the end, no reformist apartheid solution would be possible. It was important for us to understand the thinking and perspectives of our Afrikaner compatriots and why it was so difficult for them to accept that a genuine non-racial and fully democratic South Africa was also in their interests. I remained convinced and confident as processes unfolded that no rational or logical thinking person could resist accepting this inescapable reality. The depth and frankness of discussions were critical factors in bringing the Afrikaner group to better understand and appreciate that their long-term interests were intertwined with that of the majority of South Africans.

Armed struggle

The armed struggle was always an issue that was going to raise concerns among the Afrikaner group. This time, there were two incidents. In July 1988, a car bomb exploded at a rugby match at Ellis Park, killing two civilians and injuring 37. This was followed in early August by an explosion at the Hyde Park shopping centre in Johannesburg where three civilians were injured. With these incidents so fresh, the group argued very strongly that such 'indiscriminate violence against civilian targets' made it impossible to arrange any ANC meetings with government and these incidents would have a serious impact on future talks and even lead to their termination.

The bombings certainly helped to lubricate the government's propaganda machinery by stirring up white emotions and creating the perception that the ANC was not in control of MK – and that those who were opposed to talks were in control. The Afrikaner community had been shocked by what it considered to be terrorist actions in the Johannesburg heartland, which provided political traction for the right wing to exploit the situation. They urged the ANC to give serious reconsideration to the cessation of the armed struggle. For them, ending violence was crucial for strengthening the credibility and integrity of those arguing for the acceptance of the ANC.

Thabo Mbeki explained that the ANC understood that attacks on soft targets could intensify and deepen the fears of whites and, after briefing them about our strategic approach to civilian targets, he gave a detailed exposition of the ANC's organisational structures, and especially the command and control hierarchy of MK. He indicated that, in line with policy, the leadership had not sanctioned the Ellis Park and Hyde Park bombings. Our long-standing policy since the formation of MK was to avoid soft targets; hence, only military and economic targets were sanctioned. Mbeki also explained that, given the nature of how we had to function and the difficulties of exercising judicious command and control over our various structures, actions were sometimes taken that were not authorised by the leadership in Lusaka. Only major armed actions were planned from there.

It was inevitable that other decisions had to be taken at lower levels by each unit leader who selected targets, but these had to be within the broad guidelines set by the leadership in Lusaka. Further, he explained that we were not always satisfied with the quality of the training that some of our cadres had been receiving inside South Africa. He gave the example of an armed action intended to destroy three army trucks. Because of inadequate training, the action misfired due to improper calculations and did not achieve the objectives for which the action was sanctioned. In fact, the attack led to the death of some civilians and only one of the army trucks was slightly damaged.

The ANC was confident that generally its command and control structures were very effective and that MK cadres understood that the armed struggle must be based on the political struggle and that civilian casualties must be avoided. However, this policy had not always been implemented correctly.

We gave an assurance that the leadership would in future monitor more strictly all of its operational units and ensure that such monitoring was more effective so that we could prevent attacks on soft targets. However, we stressed that whites too had to appreciate that our units were living in the townships and the people there, largely in response to repression by the regime, demanded retaliatory actions. It was therefore quite understandable that our cadres could not isolate themselves from the mood of our people. While we understood this objective reality, we expressed our concern about the Ellis Park and Hyde Park bombings and asked unit commanders to come to Lusaka for discussions on policies guiding the armed struggle.

The Afrikaner group also wanted an explanation of an interview that the ANC chief of staff, Chris Hani, had given to *The Times* in London and *The New York Times,* in which he had given the impression that 'soft targets' were permissible. It was explained that Oliver Tambo had responded to these interviews both publicly and in private. The armed struggle was a last resort for the ANC and would change into a political struggle *if* the ANC was unbanned and could operate freely within South Africa. Given the supremacy of the political struggle, we would be willing to consider the suspension of the armed struggle if political prisoners were released and the ANC was unbanned and allowed to operate openly and freely.

Mbeki stressed that the cessation of violence could indeed be the subject of negotiation.

We were asked whether such talks could start without any preconditions. Mbeki responded that if we had reached the stage of talks about the cessation of hostilities, this presupposed a common commitment to a process of removing those conditions that had forced the ANC to turn to armed struggle. We were told that the suspension of violence for six months would give the ANC greater legitimacy, but Mbeki was adamant that such a move would be impossible. The government was determined to impose its own schemes by any means and it would be dangerous for the ANC to make moral gestures without the conditions being favourable or, worse, making a mockery of 'talks-for-talks-sake'.

This discussion was long and complex, but it was clear that it captured an important element of the Afrikaner group's concerns – unlike earlier meetings. I suspected that the use of highly sophisticated weapons by MK cadres and increasing civilian casualties would have sent shockwaves throughout white South Africa. However, these actions would have been celebrated in oppressed communities. The session reinforced my view that the white establishment had come to realise that the militancy of our people could not be suppressed. If there were no political solutions, the violence would be uncontrollable and a scorched-earth policy could result in the destruction of everything that whites had acquired under the apartheid system.

It was agreed that each delegation would convey the essence of the discussions to its respective leadership structures, and that responses and reactions would be exchanged at the next meeting so that we could pursue the issues further. I was confident that given the high level of the discussions, much of it would also be reported to important figures in the Afrikaner establishment.

Regional developments

The SADF believed that they could contain SWAPO militarily, but did not believe that a military solution was possible. As a result, the South African government was now considering a political solution to the Namibian issue. However, the future of the 60 000 whites in Namibia who might want to resettle in South Africa would come at a cost and would require the financial and logistical support of both the Americans and the Russians.

By October 1987, South Africans were still not committed to any negotiated solution to the Angolan problem. However, the introduction by the Cubans and Soviets of new military equipment in Angola, especially new mines that could destroy South African armoured carriers, together with increasingly heavy casualties and the growing impact of the financial implications of the war, had compelled the South African government to reconsider its military options. This situation was made worse when a full South African division was trapped by Cuban and Angolan troops and, given Angolan air superiority, it had been difficult to safely extricate the South African troops from their encirclement. All these factors compelled the regime to start looking for a negotiated peaceful solution. South Africans wanted a settlement that would involve Russians, Cubans, Americans and the OAU, largely because a settlement that involved a Cuban and South African withdrawal would enhance South Africa's prestige in the international community and would enable an easing of the growing pressures on the government.

We informed the meeting that while we were conscious that any such settlement would result in ANC bases being closed in Angola, this would not impact our military capacity. Mbeki indicated that if it would help facilitate South Africa's withdrawal we would, as a temporary step, move our bases in Angola further north.

This discussion was important in that it gave us a better sense of events that were to follow, as well as insight into the thinking of the political-military establishment in South Africa. We also better understood the consequences of progress towards a solution in Angola and Namibia, and what they perceived as the 'quieting down' of the political situation in South Africa.

At the end of the meeting, the Afrikaner group identified six points which we would need to report back on to our principals:

- the willingness to engage in informal talks about the 'controlled introduction' of Mandela into political life and the unbanning of the ANC;

- the ANC's willingness to negotiate a moratorium on violence provided the conditions were right;

- the ANC's acceptance that a transitional phase would be necessary for the introduction of a new order, and guarantees that it would participate in the process;

- the ANC's rejection of the use of violence against civilians;

- the ANC's preparedness to have informal discussions with government officials to discuss constitutional guidelines; and

- the ANC's agreement that compromises were an essential part of the process and its preparedness to engage in secret negotiations.

We, however, did not agree with their interpretation of the discussions and proposed the following amendments:

- The ANC would be prepared to meet with government officials to ensure that all obstacles to the release of Mandela were removed and to deal with any problems the government may encounter in this regard. But the release must not be made conditional on the meeting and nor should it be subordinated to the objective of arranging such a meeting. Our demand was for the release of all political prisoners, but since the situation had evolved, we could in the immediate period discuss Mandela's release. The release of all the others would still be a demand. The unbanning of the ANC was not an issue for negotiation. It would be an automatic consequence of the processes set in motion by Mandela's release.

- We could negotiate a cessation of violence only once we arrived at a point where the climate was right and a political solution was possible. But such negotiations would not be about creating a climate as a precondition for negotiations.

- On the transitional phase, we were slowly eliminating an old order and trying to establish a new one. During the transitional phase, we would address whatever fears existed at the time, as well as people's aspirations to ensure that the process is not interrupted.

- A copy of the recent ANC statement on civilian targets would be provided to the Afrikaner group.

- People should discuss the ANC's constitutional guidelines in order to enable as wide a consensus as possible. Here, we were not referring to actual constitutional negotiations with the government, but rather to an important prior phase relating mainly to the release of political prisoners. Discussions among South Africans were welcome, but those were not negotiations and constituted more of an effort to widen the debate and reduce divisions so that South Africans could act together. A broad conference of the people should take place, but the form and mechanisms would have to be worked out.

- 'Negotiations' should be replaced by 'discussions' so that any compromises made could take place against the required background of popular inclusion and consensus. This should be understood to relate to critical matters discussed at the meeting: the release of Mandela; the exchange of prisoners held in ANC detention centres or in prisons in the region for commutation of death sentences imposed on political cadres; and the cessation of hostilities under appropriate conditions.

The Afrikaner group agreed that they would convey the appropriate messages, but suggested that any meetings between the government and the ANC would have to be a completely separate process. The discussions and debates we had at this meeting were important for making progress on the release of prisoners, the unbanning of organisations and what was to follow later in the formal negotiations under the remit of the CODESA.

The fourth meeting: Flittwick Manor Hotel

Our fourth meeting took place at another luxurious venue in the Bedfordshire countryside from 16 to 18 December 1988, with the same nucleus of participants: Thabo Mbeki, Tony Trew and me representing the ANC, and Willie Esterhuyse, Wimpie de Klerk and Sampie Terreblanche representing the internal Afrikaner group.

Review of white politics

What had become clear by this point was that the government was facing crises on several fronts: economically, internationally and as far as its negotiation stance was concerned. It was also saddled with the problem of who would succeed PW Botha. There had been desertion from the 'left' and 'right' as the government struggled to manage a policy environment that had become more discredited and unsustainable.

We began by discussing the extent to which the domestic political situation had changed since our last meeting. The government continued to insist that the ANC should publicly renounce violence before it could be unbanned or before talks with the ANC could take place – although the word 'renunciation' had been substituted with 'suspension'. The ANC would also have to participate in government structures for negotiations, such as the NSC and other government-created institutions.

The October elections did not represent a breakthrough for the right. Its share of the vote was only 30 per cent and could not reach a ceiling of 40 per cent. Although not yet perceived as a serious threat to the government, the right wing nonetheless had the capacity to undermine the government by stirring conflict.

However, tensions had indeed increased within the National Party itself. The 'doves', who were a minority, were arguing for an end to the Group Areas policy of residential segregation, an end to the state of emergency and an indication that reforms were going to be introduced. The 'hardliners' were arguing for the reintroduction of the state of emergency, stricter social and security controls, the preservation of the 'race group' concept as a constitutional building block and reform by co-opting the strategic leadership of other racial groups. The National Party could move to the 'left' of present positions, but would continue to insist on group rights. The Afrikaner group concluded that the 'moderates' had no prospect of success. PW Botha had moved significantly to the right and the ascendency of the securocrats was symptomatic of a hardline approach.

As long as Botha remained president, the National Party would remain committed to old, sterile policies. He controlled the State Security Council while the directors-general of all departments were represented in its working committee, which controlled the entire government bureaucracy. Government policies were still based on ethnic building blocks – so much so that it was strongly committed to a national convention that would unveil a limited power-sharing plan with black Africans. The National Party's massive victory in the October elections proved to be a strong endorsement of Botha's white support base as well as the policies he was pursuing. A Bureau of Information survey had indicated that 40–50 per cent of blacks would support a 'race federation', by which the government believed it could limit the support and influence of the UDF and ANC. The government was obviously aware that there were no resources available to implement a co-option strategy – instead, it continued to believe its own propaganda.

PW Botha was now 'ruling by fear' in a divided government. He certainly enjoyed a new lease of political life and intended to remain in his position for at least another two years before handing over to a new leader. The favourites as his successor were Minister of Education FW de Klerk, Foreign Minister Pik Botha, Minister of Constitutional Development Gerrit Viljoen and Minister of Finance Barend du Plessis.

The balkanised National Party had also opened the way for discussion on the formation of a new political party, which would consist of members of the PFP, largely a party of English-speaking whites that had not done well in the October elections; and the Independent Party (IP), which was essentially a dissident group that had broken away from the National Party. A merger of the PFP and the IP resulted in the formation of the Democratic Party (DP), in which Denis Worrall, who had been the South African ambassador in London, played a major role. Plans had been well laid for the merger in February 1989, which had the potential for support from at least a third of the white electorate and 30 seats in Parliament. The key principles of the DP would be a democracy with representative government for all citizens in one nation where all cultural groups coexist; a rejection of racism; rooting out corruption within government machinery; and a principled commitment to negotiations.

Zach de Beer, a former director of the Anglo American Corporation, who enjoyed support from all sections of the white South African community, would be the DP leader. The party had developed a 'white system agenda and a black system agenda which must link up'. It would work outside Parliament and planned to set up a negotiation forum that would include everybody, including internal resistance organisations. Above all, the party wanted to demonstrate that negotiations were possible and that a new constitutional dispensation could be worked out. Wimpie de Klerk asked us whether the ANC would accept such a new party and if it would encourage participation in it.

We expressed our appreciation to the Afrikaner group for the frank and candid analysis of political developments within the white community. We informed them, too, that no reformist strategy would work since there was no black leader with any legitimacy who would want to become part of such a process. Such a strategy would only lead to the escalation of tensions and violence, and the securocrats were aware of this reality. The government's strategy was to buy time by making limited concessions to international forces and controlling the internal consequences.

The ANC would not be opposed to the new party working from within the system, but its endorsement would be contingent on its reaction to the ongoing process of unity and the escalating struggle. The party had to be clear about whether its objective was to change the policies of the National Party or act as a 'raft to bring people towards the MDM'. This new party, we argued, should position itself 'not as an agent of change but as a participant in change'. The issue of our endorsement would, therefore, be determined by the way the new party would relate to the MDM and the anti-apartheid struggle and it should, therefore, not be another attempt at modernising apartheid. It had to be a step forward in laying the foundation for a democratic government based on majority rule. However, it was clear to us that they were overly optimistic about the potential of this new white party.

Political prisoners

In our discussions we raised concerns that there had not been any significant progress on the release of political prisoners and starting talks with government officials about their release and the unbanning of the ANC.

The Afrikaner group informed us that the reason for the delay in Mandela's release was because of discussions about whether it would be in 'one step or in several stages', such as the move first to Victor Verster prison. They did, however, report that the government had finally agreed that it would be in several stages and that the new deadline for the final and unconditional release would be in 1989 or after the planned November 1989 elections. As an integral part of the process, it was agreed that the ANC should meet with the NIS, but PW Botha now objected to this because he feared that it 'would be used as propaganda by the ANC and exploited for short-term advantages'.

And yet again we were informed of concerns about Mandela's release. Mandela had recovered from an illness and the government no longer feared that he would die in prison, which would have increased internal and external pressures. The government was, however, concerned about: Mandela's refusal to retire to his 'ancestral' home in the Transkei; the response of the CP to his release; and a possibility of Mandela being assassinated, which could be arranged by the ANC in exile, reflecting divisions within the ANC or the right wing. The government understood that the release of Mandela would have to be followed by the release of other prisoners and the unbanning of the ANC, but that this was problematic because the ANC was responsible for the 'total onslaught' against the country. Moreover, too many security laws would have to be amended to make the unbanning possible, while the ANC's policies precluded it from participating in the political process as conceived and defined by the government. In essence, the Afrikaner group was raising new elements concerning the release of political prisoners, much of which surprised me.

The Afrikaner group also informed us that they had conveyed to the government our view as expressed in the last meeting that the ANC would manage the release and ensure that there was no violence, but the government remained sceptical about whether the ANC could actually deliver on this promise. Mbeki, of course, went on to repeat our previously stated position that Mandela's release would not lead to violence and indicated that if the government did what we had suggested in previous meetings, the release would be orderly. He questioned the view that the government did not have a strategy for releasing political prisoners and asked what the ANC could do to facilitate the release of Mandela and other political prisoners. We even suggested to the group that they convey a message to their principals that a clandestine meeting could be arranged between Thabo Mbeki and Nelson Mandela on Robben Island if this would facilitate the release of political prisoners.

It was suggested, too, that the ANC consider declaring a moratorium on violence. Mbeki informed them that the 1988 January 8th Statement had indicated that once Mandela was released, we would seriously consider all other issues, including the cessation of violence. We had been informed that the reduced 'level and character of our armed actions had been noted positively'. It was therefore surprising that the issue of a moratorium was being raised as an obstacle to the release of political prisoners. Any moratorium would be claimed as a victory by the military, so the continuation of the armed struggle was important for promoting our own political strategy.

Constitutional guidelines

We were briefed about some of the shifts in constitutional thinking in the Afrikaner establishment and related evolving debates. Middle-level structures and the 'left' within the National Party supported the move towards a non-racial constitutional dispensation, recognising that a 'racial federation' solution was not feasible, but group rights had to be the basis of any new dispensation.

We were informed that the ANC's constitutional guidelines had been welcomed as an important initiative and were being discussed by various groups in South Africa. However, it was also argued that the guidelines were 'too static' because the issues of implementation, reconstruction and transition were not dealt with. Other matters of consequence also not dealt with included the interplay of political and economic change. The ANC's constitutional guidelines proposed a sequence of reconstruction in a booming economy and gradual democratisation in order to develop a common set of values. According to the group, the ANC wrongly preferred political democratisation first, to be followed by economic reconstruction. The guidelines, the group maintained, did not deal with language and cultural group rights, which were important to ensure that these rights were constitutionally entrenched.

The group argued that the ANC seemed to be committed to a centralised one-party state and not to a multi-party system. In such a scheme, the state would neglect the role of the judiciary as a balance and check on the Constitution; the guarantee of civil rights would be tied to too many conditions, making it unclear what was being guaranteed; and 'workers' rights' would only be given to ANC-oriented unions and organisations. They told us that a perception persisted that the ANC favoured Soviet-type state economic planning in every aspect of the economy, that this resembled communism and was instinctively anti-Western. We were aware, of course, that such criticisms stemmed from continued mistrust and cynicism towards the ANC, but the Afrikaner group responded that it was necessary to discuss this mistrust and cynicism because they reflected the political problems we were both facing.

It was our opinion, however, that some respondents were mystifying issues by resorting to an 'over abstraction' of arguments. This related especially to the conception of the state, while ignoring the fact that guidelines were shaped by the need to establish a constitutional order that would have to confront issues specific to apartheid South Africa beyond party politics. Our objections were also about the details, since these could only be worked out once a new order had been established.

We agreed that there was a need for more discussion documents on the various sections that would form the basis of a new constitution, especially, for example, the conceptualisation of the state. The guidelines we offered would not be an ANC document cast in stone and we did not have a take-it-or-leave-it attitude. They should serve as a basis for broad discussion with all other interested groupings, but that discussion would have to take place in the spirit of an anti-apartheid context. The objective was to arrive at a 'peoples' document' that was acceptable to all sections of society. The ANC was in favour of a unitary state. We could not accept anything based on the homeland system under apartheid, but the unitary state we envisaged could take various forms. The Bill of Rights and Constitution would have to be very clear about our principled commitment to a multi-party democracy; this could even take the form of a federal system where powers were devolved under the auspices of a central government.

We agreed with the suggestion that we organise a constitutional conference in Zimbabwe or Mozambique. This conference would be part of a broader process of consultations for a much more detailed exchange of views between experts on both sides. The challenge, however, was how to organise such consultations in order to produce a people-centred set of constitutional guidelines that would not be hamstrung by technical issues of implementation and transition.

Regional dynamics

With regard to Angola, it was reported that there were growing South African casualties now that the Cubans had air superiority since taking possession of new Soviet-made MiG-23 jet fighters. The MiG-23s operated at a much shorter range and the South African military brass was clear that their forces on the ground, which were operating in 'a very strange terrain', would now be in much greater danger. The South Africans' response to the Cubans and Angolans receiving MiG-23s was to convert their French mirages into the new Cheetah aircraft, but this was proving to be extremely expensive and was running behind schedule.

The group explained that Angola had never been seen as strategic to South Africa's survival. The actual objectives of going into Angola had been to support Jonas Savimbi's UNITA rebels and to ensure the closure of ANC camps there, but also to keep SWAPO as far as possible from Namibia. They had done this with the encouragement and support of the US. However, the Americans no longer regarded Angola as a terrain on which to fight the Cold War and were lukewarm about their involvement in Angola through South Africa. As a result, the US was increasingly unwilling to provide further legal and diplomatic cover for South Africa's presence in Angola.

The military concluded that, in their own long-term interests, it was better to stop direct military support to UNITA, but to continue with humanitarian aid on the road to finding a negotiated solution. Defence Minister Magnus Malan and some of his generals were not keen on the move, but left the process to be driven by a troika of Neil van Heerden from the Department of Foreign Affairs, Niel Barnard and General Jannie Geldenhuys of the SADF.

In May and July 1988, representatives from South Africa, Angola and Cuba held a series of meetings that drew up 14 principles to secure peace in the territory. The Americans acted as mediators and the Russians were observers. The South African government agreed to implement UN Resolution 435 on Namibia if the Cubans withdrew from Angola. All parties agreed, too, that their territories would 'not be used for acts of war, aggression or violence against other states'. South Africa, Angola and Cuba finally signed the Geneva Protocol on 5 August 1988, which also led to a ceasefire in Namibia and elections in 1989.

The decision to find a solution to the Angolan conflict was difficult and 'angered' PW Botha. Jonas Savimbi had been his ally for many years and had been a guest of honour at his inauguration. He was regarded as 'the kind of black man' that Botha could work with, one who understood Botha's goals, not only for South Africa but for the region. Botha knew that if they did not continue to support Savimbi, UNITA's chances of sustaining the struggle for much longer would be seriously affected.

Pressure on the government also came from Afrikaner parents who felt that they were sending their conscripted sons to die in Angola. They did not understand the significance of Angola for the preservation of white rule in South Africa. We were again warned that one direct consequence of an Angolan solution for the ANC would be that our bases inside Angola would have to be closed as part of the overall agreement. We, however, had already come to that conclusion, and at the previous meeting had informed them that we would be willing to move our camps further north from the Namibian border if it facilitated progress in resolving the crisis in Angola. The Afrikaner group believed that a positive outcome in Angola and Namibia might help to make 'non-racial doves' out of the 'sceptical doves' in South Africa. This would strengthen those internal forces seeking a non-racial constitutional dispensation, but was not a suggestion that they would accept a one-person-one-vote system.

The international situation

Michael Young's analysis was that the US, the UK and Germany's policy towards South Africa was changing. Faced with a DP majority in Congress, the Bush administration, in particular, would not be able to countenance support for the South African government. In the US Congress, a Bill by African-American congressman Ron Dellums was passed to become the Comprehensive Anti-Apartheid Act of 1986, overriding a presidential veto by Ronald Reagan and becoming something of a gold standard in anti-apartheid legislation. This and further legislation would result in greater disinvestment, sanctions and trade restrictions, and put pressure on other Western countries to follow suit. Changes in Soviet foreign policy also had implications for all concerned. In Young's view, the ANC would have to understand that the Soviet Union would not support armed struggle and was looking to normalise relations with the South African government. The Cold War was over and the threat of Soviet expansionism and anti-communism could not be used by the National Party government to justify its policies or to continue garnering support from major Western powers. As an aside, we did question Young on his assessment of the changes in the Soviet's foreign policy and its impact on the ANC (see Chapter 8 for our assessment).

In our view, however, any further escalation of violence and repression by the regime would only intensify the domestic and international campaign for more sanctions. A discussion then ensued about Thatcher's somewhat partisan attitude towards the ruling regime in South Africa. A coalition government led by the conservative Christian Democratic Union under Helmut Kohl was in place in Germany and Kohl was increasingly supportive of a negotiated settlement in South Africa. Prime Minister Margaret Thatcher was also aware that the changes in the US and Germany had isolated her and she, as a result, had to be more cautious about how she dealt with the South African issue, especially in the Commonwealth where she had 'exhausted the patience of its membership'. She had no legitimacy with Africa or black South Africans. The trip to southern Africa by her CP's Africa expert, Lynda Chalker, was meant to prepare for Thatcher's visit in the context of Thatcher becoming impatient with PW Botha. The prime minister believed that he had not properly used the time she had bought for him and she was therefore 'calling in the debt'. There was still no certainty about what role Thatcher would play, but any positive intervention would redound to her advantage at the next UK elections.

These changing positions of South Africa's strongest allies had con-strained Botha's options for destabilising the region. Meanwhile, his inner circle was telling him what he wanted to hear and he thus had no sense of the new political or economic realities; indeed, he continued to remain intransigent even in the face of international pressure. PW Botha's government had clearly been overtaken by events and operated in crisis-management mode. It was time for others to take the initiative.

Thatcher and her advisers persistently asked what they could do to bring the government and the ANC to the negotiating table. The debate among the establishment sections of government, business, religion and academics had shifted from the release of Mandela and reforming elements of the apartheid system to bringing the regime and the ANC to the negotiating table. At issue was identifying the 'building blocks' and guaranteeing all agreements.

A Broederbond conference to discuss South Africa's political future and a statement by the Afrikaanse Handelsinstituut (Afrikaans Business Chamber) calling for talks were good indications of changes in thinking across the Afrikaner establishment.

Given these developments, it was important to examine the 'building blocks' to facilitate this process and also identify countries that could guarantee the process and outcomes. The ANC, however, cautioned that in determining Thatcher's role, we should not underestimate the bonds formed in her long-term friendship with PW Botha and Chief Buthelezi, which had coloured her attitude towards the ANC. It would therefore be necessary not only to change Thatcher's acrimonious attitude towards the ANC, but also her poor understanding of South Africa's fast-changing political dynamics.

This meeting concluded with an agreement on the next steps: organ-ising a seminar on constitutional guidelines with the possibility of Maputo, the capital of Mozambique, as the venue; and informing Downing Street of the ANC's view of what Thatcher's role should be if she were to play a constructive role.

The fifth meeting: Mells Park

This meeting took place from 21 to 24 April 1989. The ANC delegation consisted of Thabo Mbeki, Jacob Zuma, Tony Trew and me; while the Afrikaner group was made up of Willie Esterhuyse, Wimpie de Klerk and Sampie Terreblanche, as well as Louis Kriel from the deciduous fruit industry and Ernst Lombard, a minister from the Dutch Reformed Church.

As we prepared for the fifth meeting, we knew that pressures on the government were intensifying. Not only had there been a ratcheting up of international sanctions, but the decision by the banned UDF and COSATU to form the MDM, which pledged to carry out a campaign of civil disobedience, indicated that momentum continued to move in our favour. The ANC had also declared 1989 as the 'Year of Mass Action to Advance People's Power'.

White politics

We began – as per the format of our previous meetings – by reviewing the domestic political landscape, and in particular discussing the realignments taking place in white politics.

PW Botha had resigned as National Party leader, but retained his presidency. The argument went that as president he could remain above party politics and deal with the long-term concerns of the country. This, however, had caused increasing tensions and division within the Afrikaner establishment about party leadership, since at the time there was wide speculation that the succession battle would be fought between Minister of Constitutional Affairs Chris Heunis, who was regarded as a reformist, and Foreign Minister Pik Botha, whose political star had risen considerably following the Angolan and Namibian settlements, but who did not have much support in the Afrikaner constituency. Finance Minister Barend du Plessis was said to be Botha's favourite but he, too, did not command much support within Afrikaner power structures. Finally, there was FW de Klerk, the Minister of Education, who was regarded as representing the most conservative elements of the National Party, especially in the politically strategic province of Transvaal. (Interestingly, once he assumed the mantle of power, De Klerk took a much more pragmatic approach.)

As it turned out, when the National Party held its own party elections in February 1989, FW de Klerk won the party leadership by eight votes out of the 130 National Party MPs. We were informed that after the leadership change within the National Party, the country's international standing improved and there was a growing body of international opinion that held that De Klerk should be 'given a chance'. The fact that FW de Klerk had become the National Party leader added a new dimension to the presence of his brother, Willem de Klerk, in the group. From all accounts, Wimpie and his brother enjoyed a very close relationship, met regularly, and talked openly and frankly about various issues.

When it came to the forthcoming general election in South Africa, we were told that this was likely to take place on 6 or 13 September 1989. This was a tactical decision because it would precede the elections for a constituent assembly in Namibia that November. The group believed that the expected 60 per cent victory margin by SWAPO would alarm South African white voters and the National Party could lose votes to the conservatives as a result. It appeared that 'better-off whites' – mainly English-speaking – saw FW de Klerk as the best bet to protect their interests and maintain the status quo. However, poorer whites, mainly Afrikaans-speaking, had been badly affected by the economic crisis and were drawn to the right-wing rhetoric of the CP, which had spilt from the National Party. The more liberal DP was attracting 'yuppie' and upwardly mobile Afrikaners and stood to win 24–25 per cent of the votes. The middle- and long-term prospects for the DP were thus strong: it would concentrate its electoral energies on the urban areas and certain constituencies of professionals, women and both sections of the white community who were open to moral persuasion, concerned about international dynamics, and national stability and security. The DP would also target disillusioned National Party supporters who still believed in change from within the system.

The Afrikaner group was of the view that the fight for the National Party leadership in February continued to divide the caucus. De Klerk could thus exploit the situation and project himself as a leader of change by emphasising political reform, recovery of the economy and negotiations. Wimpie informed us that his brother had four options. He could:

- maintain the party's position in a structure based on racial prin-ciples. De Klerk personally opted for this position because this would not 'rock the party boat';

- move to the right, but he recognised that this would be against current trends and would not be practical;

- move a little to the left – that is, initiate some reforms, and commit to negotiations and some vision of the future. This was the course Wimpie believed was the best for his brother since FW understood its inevitability in a pragmatic sense; or

- surprise everyone by moving sharply to the left by rejecting the racially modelled constitution, which had long been the cornerstone of National Party policy. This option was most unlikely since De Klerk was too firm in his belief that some form of race classification was the only cornerstone for a new constitution. He was also aware that his constituency would not accept a 'majoritarian' solution. Even the *verligtes* were not ready to make such a break.

For the National Party it was absolutely vital that PW Botha resign as president of the country before the September general elections because the establishment believed that under Botha's presidential leadership the party majority would be reduced. If FW de Klerk took over as acting president, the chances of the party faring better were stronger. It was thus critical for De Klerk to secure a mandate from his electorate if he was going to take any initiatives within the framework of his available options. The Afrikaner group believed that the best option would be for De Klerk to release Mandela as one of his first acts after taking office. This would not only provide him with international stature, but would also give his presidency tremendous impetus, besides winning him much credibility in the black community. However, they also understood that PW Botha wanted to retain power and the release of Mandela could well become his final act before relinquishing office. They also feared that if Botha imposed conditions on Mandela's release, it would be very difficult for De Klerk to retroactively challenge this since he would be bound by the conditions imposed by Botha.

At that stage it was difficult to predict how international opinion would respond to whatever overtures De Klerk made, but he would certainly have to respond very differently from Botha. A view of one of the members of the Afrikaner group was that De Klerk was not popular with the security establishment and that this could present a 'major problem'. The role and future of the State Security Council would also be important. De Klerk was losing patience with the 'securocrats' who had been so central in the state apparatus: BJ Vorster's inner circle were the police and security police and PW Botha's was the military. It was not clear what and who would comprise De Klerk's inner circle, but the civilian component would be important.

De Klerk's advantage was that he enjoyed a reputation unsullied by corruption in a government that had been tainted by many such scandals. NIS structures and vertical relations remained intact and, since the appointment of Niel Barnard as its head on the basis of a political decision, it was not anticipated that the security establishment would present serious problems for the incoming president. We were told that talk of a military coup that would restore PW Botha to power was exaggerated and should not be given much credence.

There was agreement that De Klerk's administration would be less inclined to resort to force and coercion in responding to any challenges that the state would have to confront and deal with. He was aware that his success or otherwise would be measured by progress in the negotiation process. In what was a marked change of style, we were informed that De Klerk's approach to negotiations would not be co-optive, but would be focused on problem-solving. The ANC, therefore, should signal its position on talks and on what basis it was prepared to participate in such talks. This would go some way in dealing with white fears and strengthen the hands of the *verligtes*.

With regard to other political parties, the Afrikaner group also concluded that CP support had reached its peak and that white-collar workers from the white demographic were increasingly accepting the inevitability of a deal with black South Africans. The DP, which had been launched on 8 April, was facing teething problems. The DP's political philosophy was to seek power through all institutions and talk to everyone, including the ANC. It sought, too, to build relations with all racial groups that accepted or shared its principles on the basis of territorial federalism. Its long-term aim was to consolidate all non-racial constituencies to the left of the National Party, while in the short term it would function in the white political system and, by 1992, it hoped to have significant relations with extraparliamentary groups.

Wimpie's view was that the newly formed DP would replace the CP as the official opposition after the election, and that they would win 25–30 seats. The party's campaigning platform would be to challenge the dismal economic record of the previous government, as well as the corruption that had characterised the National Party. They would campaign for talks with the ANC and other representative groups, but any outcomes would have to be reconciled with the principles of the protection of minority, and religious and language rights.

If the DP successfully replaced the CP as the major opposition, it would be more supportive of Afrikaner interests than the PFP, with its predominantly English-speaking white support base. In fact, the PFP was losing support precisely because it had always represented a very small section of the white community. They believed that the DP was in essence an internal resistance group with a 'leftist' disposition towards the National Party. Wimpie was concerned that a leadership battle between Zach de Beer and Denis Worrall was causing difficulties for the party, but he hoped that this would be resolved before the elections.

So it was that, for the first time since 1948, the National Party was faced with the reality of losing its absolute majority. A hung Parliament would be a prescription for chaos and insecurity, and if the National Party joined forces with the conservatives, the logical consequence would be a move to the right, which would exacerbate confrontation across the country.

Naturally, we expressed some doubt about the estimated strength and influence of the DP, as well as some concern about how the DP saw its role in relation to the MDM, and argued that it should avoid any impression that it was trying to replace or compete with the movement. As such, the DP's focus should be on providing leadership to the many whites looking for a different approach. They should, therefore, avoid trying to manage two strategies at once: seeking power through parliamentary politics while engaging in struggle politics. The DP had to guard against any perception that it curried favour by seeking credibility from the MDM instead of establishing its credentials as a democratic force within the white community, which could then find ways of participating in the struggle led by the MDM.

We indicated that the ANC would be willing to meet with the DP leadership.

Political prisoners

We were again informed that the decision to release Mandela had already been taken. It was now, apparently, simply a matter of timing and whether the release would be conditional or unconditional. PW Botha had told Parliament that the conditions for Mandela's release were unchanged and it was left to Mandela to decide whether he wanted to be released or not. Botha's comment that Mandela could decide if he wanted to play a constructive role after his release was based on the spurious assumption that 'moderate' forces in the ANC were willing to participate in the government's reform process. In fact, it was said, Botha's office had shown Mandela the speech before it was delivered.

The government had concluded that Mandela would agree to help launch the NSC and that this would be an appropriate political role for him. The challenge was how to extricate Botha from a dilemma he had created for himself, namely, by insisting that Mandela renounce violence before he could be released. There were some signs that Botha would release Mandela a few days before he left office, but we agreed that it would be better if Mandela was released under De Klerk's leadership since this would obviate the need for any conditions to be imposed on Mandela. This would allow the 'new person on the block' to take a different approach that would be a basis for finding a real solution. However, before Mandela's release, the nuts and bolts of it – including the actions to be taken to prevent violence and rioting – would have to be worked out in a meeting between the ANC and the NIS.

Negotiation issues

There was some discussion on reviving the EPG concept of the moratorium on violence. We were asked whether the changing situation enabled the ANC to discuss a moratorium, and we responded that the issue of a moratorium had to be seen in the context of our general and stated position on negotiations.

We noted De Klerk's remarks, but he had to demonstrate his resolve by seriously engaging the ANC. In principle, then, we were not opposed to unconditional 'talks about talks'. Both sides had to be confident that the other was resolute and committed to creating a climate conducive for negotiations to take place. The release of Mandela would be a positive signal in demonstrating that the government was serious about 'talks about talks' in line with the assistance we offered and our positive response to the release.

The initial 'talks about talks' would be between the ANC and the government but the actual negotiations would have to involve all democratic forces. It was proposed that we draw up an agenda to discuss preconditions for negotiations and develop the commensurate steps for confidence-building between the parties concerned.

The ANC was asked whether it would take back a message that 'there is openness on the part of the ANC regarding the seriousness with which the new administration might commit itself to negotiations and a willingness to encourage it to do so'. We agreed that such a message could be conveyed, but the new administration should then demonstrate its seriousness through its actions and policy statements.

The regional situation

A commission had been established to investigate the serious military clashes between the SADF, SWAPO and Koevoet, the paramilitary unit created by the South African Police in Namibia for the purpose of fighting local insurgents and SWAPO guerrilla forces. We expressed concern about the clashes, but reiterated that the region remained committed to the peace process. However, it was only later that the problems emerging from the implementation of UN Resolution 435 regarding SWAPO assembly points and its controlling authority became clearer as the driving factor behind the clashes. It was alleged that SWAPO fighters had violated the ceasefire line in the north of the country and, in so doing, had been engaged by the SADF and Koevoet. The South African regime was 'surprised' by SWAPO's military capacity, but believed that the incursion had occurred without the authority of Sam Nujoma, its military and political head.

We explained that regional and international actors were aware at least a day before the clashes that Pik Botha had warned the UN about the presence of SWAPO troops in the north of the country and had asked the UN to deploy its UN Transition Assistance Group (UNTAG) troops, which were responsible for monitoring the peace process and supporting the election preparations in Namibia. The failure of the UN to respond positively – and which resulted in deploying SADF troops against SWAPO – had compromised UNTAG. The SADF intervention again raised questions about the trustworthiness of the South African government.

The Afrikaner group's response was that the South African government wanted the peace process in Namibia to succeed on the basis of respecting the letter and spirit of Resolution 435. They expected SWAPO to get less than two-thirds – that is, around 60 per cent of the vote – which would force them into bargains and striking strategic alliances with other political parties. This would give the South African side valuable time since they were concerned about SWAPO's intention to turn the constituent assembly into a legislature that would ensure SWAPO's domination of parliamentary and political institutions.

The international situation

Michael Young launched the discussion on the role Mrs Thatcher intended or wished to play in the South African process. He stated that although the Foreign Office believed that such a discussion was premature, Downing Street was more positive about her playing a broader role to ensure the release of Mandela.

Thatcher had accepted the advice to be more careful about the language she used when discussing South Africa. After meeting Gorbachev, she was convinced that the Soviet Union wanted the UK to play a leading role in promoting a negotiated solution. She believed that for historical reasons, and because of her own political inclinations, there was pressure on her to play such a role.

However, Young told us that Thatcher had an 'intellectual problem' in meeting with the ANC, a position very similar to her aversion to meeting with the Palestine Liberation Organization (PLO). This, of course, was not a sustainable position for us. The British ambassador in South Africa had provided her with broad input on the changing configuration of forces in the country, but her attitude towards the ANC still rested on strong but negative instincts about ANC violence and communism, compounded by reports of ANC links with the IRA. She had, however, chosen South Africa as 'an issue that will put a cherry on her political cake'. She had also completely written off PW Botha and her new focus was on influencing South African opinion-makers and the new administration. It is in this context that she had welcomed meetings with South African cabinet ministers and was happy that FW de Klerk had accepted her invitation to visit the UK. She believed that this initiative would alleviate the pressures of the sanctions campaign.

On her visit to southern Africa, she encountered little opposition to her position on sanctions and in her meeting with Robert Mugabe she raised the issue of South Africa and the putative role of the international community, including her readiness to play a leading part in finding a negotiated solution. Mugabe was sceptical because he believed that the South African regime could easily manipulate her. She nevertheless relied strongly on the views of Mugabe and Mozambique's President Samora Machel; while they could convey the appropriate messages from Thatcher it would be impolitic for them to act as proxies for the ANC. In this regard, she believed that her approach had the support of the US president.

Mbeki responded that it would be a mistake to believe that the Soviets would want Thatcher as a broker that brought pressure to bear on the ANC. Moreover, the Bush administration regarded overt relations with the ANC as necessary in order to convey a strong message to the South African government, but Thatcher's current stance was not in harmony with US expectations and could create problems for Bush.

Our overall assessment was that Thatcher's project suffered from strategic and tactical flaws and work had to be done to get it more in line with the current realities and the pressing challenges facing South Africa as it entered a critical phase in its history.

If our first five meetings had been exploratory, conceptual and about building the necessary trust and confidence between the parties, the next round of secret meetings in the UK would be much more substantive and extensive in developing the political foundations for the actual negotiation process. It comes as no surprise to me, then, that what was to follow became the very foundation of an entirely new era in the struggle – my own personal one that was determined to see a new dispensation unfold in my lifetime and, more importantly, the broader agenda of the ANC and our comrades worldwide in the quest for freedom and democracy.

Chapter 8

Secret talks in the UK – Towards negotiations

The next phase of our secret meetings in the UK attempted to consolidate the gains we had made in the previous round of discussions. While serious policy and political differences remained, we had indeed made considerable progress in developing sound normative and analytical bases for formal negotiations. In our first five meetings, a sort of dialectical process had emerged where our respective positions could be presented openly and frankly, knowing that, in the nature of the exercise, we were engaged in a historical process that would ultimately help to determine the fate and destiny of the country. The challenge behind this dialectic and the various points of tension, of course, was the extent to which we were prepared to compromise, to make concessions, whether strategic or tactical, and how we could reach a *modus vivendi* on all the key issues that would eventually underpin the actual negotiation process. In this regard, two seminal events that would contribute to shaping the outcome of negotiations took place: the first was the adoption of the Harare Declaration as the ANC's negotiating framework on 21 August 1989; and the second was an emergency meeting of the ANC's NWC in October of the same year.

The Harare Declaration

The adoption of the Harare Declaration represented a watershed in the negotiation process since all future ANC positions would be determined and influenced by it. The Declaration was a product of tireless work by a committee established under Oliver Tambo, who oversaw every step of its evolution, including ensuring widespread consultation with ANC ranks in exile, the Frontline States, our underground structures and selected leaders of the MDM. Tambo was involved day and night in this process, and after a heavy schedule of flights within the southern African region to discuss the draft, in fact suffered a stroke the day the Declaration was adopted.

This was the ultimate price that this outstanding leader would have to pay. It was under his leadership and direction, throughout the years, that we were able to reach this momentous occasion. The Declaration refers to 'a liberation movement' and not 'liberation movements', clearly signalling that the ANC had been recognised as the representative movement of the majority of the people of our country.

The Declaration was guided by the OAU Ad Hoc Committee on Southern Africa, which met in Harare, and at the suggestion of the ANC, it recognised that 'a conjuncture of circumstances exists which, if there is a demonstrable readiness on the part of the Pretoria regime to engage in negotiations genuinely and sincerely, could create the possibility to end apartheid through negotiations'.

The Declaration's preamble referred to the OAU's collective effort to promote peace in Africa and its resolve to end all conflicts on the basis of negotiations. The struggle for liberation in South Africa, coupled with international pressure, had created an atmosphere for fundamental change in South Africa and for the apartheid regime to abandon the abhorrent notions and practices of racial domination. The OAU thus stood ready to assist and support the people of South Africa and the representatives of the oppressed in determining their own destiny in order to achieve the objectives of building a non-racial and democratic society. The OAU also expressed its preference that such objectives be achieved through peaceful means, a position endorsed by the majority of South Africans and their liberation movements. The letter and spirit of the Declaration thus constituted a new challenge to Pretoria to end the system of apartheid. On the basis of a statement of principles, it encouraged the people to negotiate an end to the apartheid system as opposed to simply amending its essential contours and to reach agreement on how the country could be transformed into a non-racial democracy.

These principles, therefore, provided the basis for an internationally acceptable solution that would enable South Africa to take its legitimate place as an equal partner of African nations as well as the world. However, for this to be achieved, the Declaration was very explicit about the prerequisites that had to be met by the regime. It referred in particular to the unconditional release of political prisoners and detainees; the removal of troops from the townships; ending the state of emergency and repealing legislation that circumscribed political activity; and ceasing all political executions.

In order to promote the overall framework of the Declaration, the OAU adopted a Programme of Action that had several aspects. It would, firstly, inform governments and international organisations about the Declaration's intentions and objectives and solicit their support, while assisting the efforts and campaigns of the liberation movement to conform to the Declaration. Secondly, the OAU would intensify the campaign for mandatory and comprehensive sanctions, mobilise against any rescheduling of the regime's foreign debt and press for full oil and arms embargoes. Thirdly, the OAU would ensure that there was no relaxation of measures intended to isolate apartheid South Africa. And finally, with regard to the region, the OAU would ensure the genuine independence of Namibia and extend the necessary assistance to Angola and Mozambique in achieving peace. In this regard, it would assist the Frontline States in withstanding the aggression and destabilisation campaigns by the Pretoria regime.

The Harare Declaration was not only a turning point but, above all, represented a potent political reflection of how the ANC leadership was able to map its own path towards a negotiated settlement. Indeed, it is significant in many ways. It reflected the essence of the discussions held both overtly and covertly in the previous years, starting in the mid-1980s. There were some misgivings within the ANC's own ranks about the wisdom of a negotiated approach and these were compounded by the regime's attempts to sow confusion between the leadership in prison and the leadership in exile. However, ANC leadership rose above this and was able to direct all the relevant processes that would eventually bring about democracy.

The Declaration thus became the basis on which all future discussions with the international community, the apartheid regime and, indeed, the South African population as a whole were conducted. It provided the political and normative framework within which we could conduct all future discussions with the apartheid regime.

The meeting of the National Working Committee

The extended meeting of the NWC on 26 and 27 October 1989 in Lusaka was called because of leaks relating to the secret talks in the UK. The meeting was chaired by Alfred Nzo because Oliver Tambo was ill, and Thabo Mbeki did not attend because he had been instructed to brief the Commonwealth Summit in Kuala Lumpur, Malaysia, about the Harare Declaration.

On Saturday, 30 September 1989, we were informed that the *Sunday Times* was set to publish a 'scoop' the next day that Afrikaners on a 'government Broederbond mission' were meeting secretly with the ANC in the UK and identified the internal participants. On Friday, 29 September, the Afrikaans weekly *Vrye Weekblad* had published a few lines about this and the British press also reported on the secret meetings. The British Foreign Affairs office thus issued a statement that they were aware of the meetings but not their content – although I remained unconvinced that they had not been fully informed.

There was speculation that the leak in *Vrye Weekblad* was a consequence of Security Branch pressure on De Klerk to make a statement about the secret UK meetings, but the more likely scenario was that one of the Afrikaner delegates had inadvertently leaked the story. No details of the venue had, however, been revealed. Naturally, this was a matter of great concern to both sides because it could have derailed the entire process we had so carefully and secretly planned. We knew that both within the government and the ANC there were individuals opposed to any such talks. In fact, FW de Klerk had even publicly criticised Wimpie, and the others for playing into the hands of forces apparently intent on destroying law and order.

To defuse the situation, a report based on a statement issued by Esterhuyse was published in the Afrikaans newspaper *Die Burger*. Esterhuyse indicated that the meeting was part of a series of academic exchanges to find a peaceful solution in South Africa. He clarified that a number of meetings between South African academics and the ANC had taken place over the years, and that participating academics represented neither the government nor the Broederbond. Everybody contributed in their personal capacities and Esterhuyse corrected reports that the principal of Stellenbosch University had attended the meeting. He also denied that he was a member of the Broederbond.

The extended meeting of the NWC was significant because the main item on the agenda was, of course, the secret talks. This proved to be a time of intense debate within our ranks on the way forward, and relations among some of the leadership were quite strained – as were relations among our cadres. The main criticisms and concerns included:

- comrades were not all aware of secret talks and had only learnt about these from the media;
- the President's Committee, established by Tambo to deal with extremely confidential and sensitive issues and which had sanctioned the secret talks, was only an advisory body and was usurping the powers of the NEC;
- the President's Committee had not briefed the NEC;
- rumours about the secret talks were rife and morale among the cadres was low;
- the leadership was chaotic and lacking in cohesion;

- individualism and private agendas had to be curbed;

- there had to be greater accountability at all levels; and

- armed struggle was the only way forward and we therefore had to 'move in' with our MKs.

Clearly, many NWC comrades were not aware of the progress we had made in our secret talks. Many of them still saw the white establishment as a monolithic bloc only interested in minor reforms. They did not fully appreciate that while the ANC's and the government's perspectives on fundamental changes differed, a new terrain of struggle had been opened where the main battleground was how a negotiated settlement would be conducted. We knew that we would continue to face many obstacles and challenges, but these should not deter us from keeping 'our eyes on the ball'.

Some comrades understood that the ANC could not reject negotiations in principle, but they counterposed negotiations with other forms of struggle. Those of us involved in the negotiating process always understood that it was the political, trade union and armed terrains of struggle that made negotiations possible. To suggest that the negotiators were undermining other forms of struggle was surely wrong and self-serving – even dangerous. There were some elements of populism and professed militancy because some believed that conditions were ripe for insurrection. The problem was complicated by the fact that the 'country was burning', the state security apparatus was *de facto* governing the country, and state-orchestrated and black-on-black violence had reached unprecedented levels.

Of course, it frustrated me that I could not disclose details about the secret discussions we were having. I did, however, express the view that conditions had changed dramatically in the country, the region and internationally, and these included major systemic changes, such as the fall of the Berlin Wall and the introduction of Perestroika in the Soviet Union. In the region there was the Nkomati Accord, the agreement on Namibian independence based on UN Resolution 435 and the South African-Cuban-Angolan accord brokered by the US, which led to our forces having to withdraw from Angola and redeploy in Uganda. We could not underestimate the changing balance of forces and neither should we fail to fully understand and take into account the fundamental changes that had taken place in the country's political landscape, including in the structures of white power. Some major powers would seek to impose a negotiated settlement that was not in the interests of either the ANC or the people. These developments – if correctly analysed, I argued – must lead us to conclude that we were in a vastly transformed political environment that demanded more creative responses from ANC leadership. History is riddled with many revolutionary opportunities missed and revolutionary movements destroyed because of the leadership's failure to 'seize the moment'. Subsequently, Jacob Zuma, after having earlier briefed the President's Committee, informed the NWC about his and Mbeki's meetings with NIS operatives in Switzerland (see Chapter 9).

Ironically, the next item on the agenda was the Plan of Action that was to be followed after the release of political prisoners. On 9 October 1989 the President's Committee had been briefed by Thabo Mbeki that we had been informed in the secret UK talks that the release of Sisulu and other Rivonia trialists was imminent. It was therefore necessary for the ANC to make detailed preparations for their release, including discussing the role of the Robben Island leaders vis-à-vis the MDM leadership and the NEC in exile; and the feasibility of some exile leaders travelling to South Africa to meet Mandela. Mandela had suggested that, once released, the leaders should play a 'low-profile role', with the President's Committee agreeing that the leaders should perform an 'unhindered' role. A subcommittee was established to outline the proposals and its report was discussed by the NWC. The MDM did not agree with the proposal that leaders should play a low-profile role and argued strongly that the leaders should be actively involved in the struggle, a view that was subsequently endorsed by the NWC.

We adopted the Harare Declaration, which spoke of the possibility of negotiations, and further discussed details about the release of senior ANC leaders. However, I was surprised that we failed to recognise that the release of Mandela and other prisoners would precipitate a chain reaction that would include the unbanning of the ANC and other organisations, as well as create the climate for negotiations to take place. While we could debate the nature of a negotiated solution sought by the regime, we could not deny that the principle of finding a negotiated settlement was firmly on the agenda.

This was a difficult and trying period for me because I knew that some of us would soon be going back to South Africa to prepare for the return of the rest of our exiled leadership and the first talks between the government and the ANC. As mentioned earlier, after the ANC delegation's visit to Vietnam in 1978, we had concluded that, given the objective conditions in South Africa, the armed struggle had to be based on the political mobilisation and organisation of the people, and the strengthening of our underground political structures. However, because of objective and subjective realities, we were unable to get leaders and cadres involved in the various pillars of our struggle to collectively implement the strategic perspectives and other policy positions related to the supremacy of the political struggle as articulated in the Green Book.

With the formation of the UDF and COSATU and the upsurge of the MDM, we found ourselves in an entirely new situation that was much more favourable to political mobilisation and organisation. It was clear that, unlike in the 1960s, every repressive action gave greater impetus to mass struggle and was thereby forcing the hand of the regime to seek a negotiated solution. Armed propaganda made an invaluable contribution to the militancy and mass mobilisation of the people and we had to grasp the opportunity that had arisen for a negotiated solution.

The next set of secret talks followed a similar format, but took place against the background of ongoing and challenging changes in South Africa's domestic environment and a fast-changing regional and global context – as reflected in FW de Klerk's speech to Parliament on 2 February 1990, which set the stage for final negotiations for a democratic South Africa. However, the Harare Declaration and the extended meeting of the NWC both provided an urgent impetus to inject momentum into our deliberations and to move strategically towards defining the broad architecture and parameters that would enable negotiations towards a political settlement to begin in earnest. It was in this spirit that we again assembled at Mells Park for the sixth meeting.

The sixth meeting: Mells Park

This sixth meeting took place against the backdrop of some major developments at home. On 2 August 1989, the MDM – which had replaced the banned UDF – organised a series of meetings and demonstrations against the segregation of hospitals, beaches and public transport. It had also called a strike against the 6 September all-white elections, a strike in which over three million people participated. The apartheid regime met all these demonstrations and strikes with brutal repression.

Our sixth meeting took place from 29 September to 2 October 1989, with the ANC delegation made up of Jacob Zuma, Tony Trew and me led by Thabo Mbeki; and the Afrikaner group composed of Wimpie de Klerk, Willie Esterhuyse, Sampie Terreblanche, Louis Kriel, Ernst Lombard and Ebbe Dommisse, the soon-to-be editor of *Die Burger*. In one of our informal sessions I was told that FW de Klerk was not opposed in principle to our 'secret talks', but on the eve of his inauguration had sent a top NIS person to convince his brother, Wimpie, to withdraw from the Mells Park initiative.

Reactions to the Harare Declaration

Thabo Mbeki explained the background to the Harare Declaration and the role that the OAU and international community would play in relation to it. The Afrikaner group revealed, however, that there was a significant bloc within the white establishment that believed that the ANC had a hidden agenda by mobilising international support for an internationally imposed settlement. If the UN Security Council adopted the Declaration it would represent a *fait accompli* that whites would have to accept. This would be a problem for them since it would strengthen the position of the right wing, which could argue that a solution was being imposed by outsiders. Another problem, it seemed, was its timing: the Declaration indicated that the armed struggle and sanctions would only end when the process of adopting a new constitution was completed. If that was the case, according to the group, the process was doomed to failure because the economy might collapse. Whites should, therefore, be given some 'carrots', such as the relaxation of external pressures including, for example, the incremental lifting of sanctions.

The ANC explained that, given past experiences in the region, international pressure was necessary to ensure that the government was serious about negotiations and that it would not derail the process. This would induce a greater sense of urgency that would accelerate the process.

Thabo Mbeki also elaborated on the processes leading up to the Harare Declaration and indicated that we did not expect the Security Council to pass a binding resolution that would impose the UN on any negotiation process in South Africa. In fact, the ANC would not support such a move because it would be tantamount to taking the process out of the hands of South Africans and, moreover, could limit what we ourselves could resolve. However, we were indeed mobilising the UN to support the broad guidelines of the Harare Declaration. When the Afrikaner group asked when the armed struggle would be suspended and when we would be prepared to negotiate, Mbeki explained that the armed struggle would end – as distinct from being suspended – after we had agreed to a new constitution. He also indicated that the ANC would work towards ending sanctions as soon as we were satisfied that the negotiation process was irreversible.

We, in turn, asked the Afrikaner group to convey to the government our concerns of who would monitor any agreements through negotiations. This had to be addressed now and debated within the negotiating framework. It was clear that this session was significant in that it was taking place in the context of fundamental changes in white politics, as well as a massive upsurge of black resistance. Increasingly, we were beginning to get a better understanding of our respective positions on the essential issues. We got the impression that the ANC's message that the situation demanded quick and urgent action was now clearly understood by some in the Afrikaner group.

The release of political prisoners and other matters

We were briefed about the progress on the release of political prisoners. The government's dilemma continued to be the role of the political prisoners after they were released. Apparently, Mandela had also sought clarity on this issue. The ANC delegation explained that there was no need for further discussions on the principle of the release. A meeting with government was only necessary to implement the decisions taken on the release of prisoners and the consequences of such decisions, such as integrating them into the political process upon their release.

We were again asked what the status of Mandela was in the ANC. Clearly, they were still trying to determine whether there were differences or tensions between the leadership in exile and those inside the country. Mbeki explained that before Mandela's arrest, he was the president of the Transvaal ANC and that, while Tambo was his senior, Walter Sisulu was senior to both Mandela and Tambo. It was generally expected that Tambo would remain the president of the ANC after Mandela was released – which our interlocutors correctly interpreted to mean that even if a deal was secured with Mandela, such a deal would not be implemented without getting agreement from the ANC as a whole. This was a position that Mandela had confirmed in his discussions with the Commonwealth EPG, as well as with the government's negotiating 'Committee of Four' (see Chapter 9).

For our part, we would be willing and, indeed, had already started the process of withdrawing the majority of MK cadres from inside Angola. Interestingly, we were informed that the South African security apparatus – and therefore the government – was aware of the steps we had taken and that they appreciated the initiative because it indicated the seriousness and the commitment of the ANC leadership to finding negotiated solutions.

The Afrikaner group still believed that 'hardliners' within the ANC would resist negotiations, so we again briefed them about the processes by which the ANC made decisions. We informed them that if there was genuine commitment towards finding a political solution, there would be no 'hardliners' or 'softliners' within the party. Since the inception of the armed struggle, we had made it clear that we had taken up arms because the ANC had been banned and all possibilities of pursuing non-violent resistance had been foreclosed. Therefore we had no doubt that if steps were taken in terms of which we had already discussed on numerous occasions, the people in South Africa would indeed accept the reality of a negotiated solution.

To our surprise, however, the Afrikaner group then asked whether the ANC 'really led the internal resistance' and what the objectives of the Conference for a Democratic Future called by the MDM and religious organisations hoped to achieve. We informed them that the conference was important because it dealt with three crucial issues: negotiations, the role of the international community and a programme of action. Moreover, representatives to the conference were united around strategic issues of non-racialism; lifting the state of emergency; unbanning political parties; and the release of political prisoners. The ANC fully supported the conference and was looking forward to the widest possible participation.

We then discussed their perception of the ANC's reluctance to meet with Chief Buthelezi to discuss black-on-black violence. We gave a very detailed briefing on all our interactions with Chief Buthelezi, including his demand that talks with the ANC be held in London and that there should be equal representation for his organisation, the IFP, while the ANC and the MDM delegations should be treated as a single entity. He also demanded that he be invited personally by Oliver Tambo. We tried to find some accommodation but he made it very difficult for the meeting to take place. We reiterated our commitment to ending black-on-black violence and explained that there were powerful forces fuelling this deadly conflict and sabotaging all efforts to find a solution. Clearly the Afrikaner group was sceptical about our allegations that a third force was fuelling black-on-black violence. Of course, that would later prove to be the case.

Constitutional issues

We explained that the 'ANC Constitutional Guidelines' of 9 October 1987 set out our negotiating principles and had been adopted after discussions within the ANC ranks – and, indeed, much of it later found its way into the Harare Declaration. We indicated that the ANC had initiated a process to achieve the broadest consensus on some crucial issues. The challenge was to determine how the discussions about negotiations would be organised and how the consensus could be tested. In my view, the discussions within the ANC and the broad democratic movement were already taking place in an organised manner and, as such, other groups should initiate discussions within their own ranks so that, at an appropriate time, a broad conference could be arranged to seek final consensus.

Wimpie de Klerk inquired whether the process would move to a negotiating conference where power-sharing would be discussed, and Mbeki responded that we were talking about a broad conference that would agree to final thematic guidelines and where other documents could also be presented.

Sampie Terreblanche suggested that economic guidelines should be elaborated such that there was a distinction between the welfare and developmental functions of the state. He also questioned whether the right to work was appropriate in South Africa where the unemployment rate was 40 per cent. He argued that any guideline document should outline the internal and external conditions necessary for growth and job creation. Redistribution and transformation could not be achieved in a declining economy without generating serious social conflict. What was needed, according to him, was a credible government commitment to guidelines and principles that would facilitate the normalisation of South Africa's international relations and could consequently unlock possibilities for assistance on the scale of a Marshall Aid Plan.

Wimpie, however, welcomed the ANC's Constitutional Guidelines and stated that broad agreement about constitutional matters would not be difficult to achieve in the Afrikaner constituency, but what he did want to know was whether there would be strategic space for compromise, such as addressing white fears regarding a 'unitary majoritarian state'. In line with this imperative for compromise, the Afrikaner group also wanted clarification on the ANC's position with regard to the protection of mineral rights; proportional representation in the transitional phase; appropriate constitutional checks and balances; and veto rights.

Mbeki explained that by the time we reached the transitional phase we would have developed a different consciousness and mentality forged in the mutual struggle to reach this phase. The issues that demanded compromise would be negotiated, but they would probably be different from what seemed to be the burning issues at that moment. To the Afrikaner group's 'surprise', he indicated that the issue of a transitional phase was hardly new. We were well aware, he said, that the process took time and that we had to address white fears, but this had to be in the context of black aspirations. It was therefore important to avoid talking about minority groups because this would be interpreted to mean 'population groups' as defined under apartheid.

We were asked how a principled agreement to hold elections for a constituent assembly would influence the ANC to accept that the present government would stay in place until the assembly was elected and the negotiation process was completed. Mbeki indicated that the ANC had not discussed this issue, but his view was that we would not accept an institution such as the NSC whose deliberations were subject to approval by the regime's structures. The processes that had underpinned the transitional and post-independence experiences in Mozambique, Angola, Zimbabwe and Namibia could serve as examples because the liberation movements there were subjected to external pressures to accept different institutional models and constitutional arrangements that were probably not in the best interests of nation-building.

The Afrikaner group indicated that the ANC's statement was an important leap forward in helping to address 'white fears' in South Africa, and it was agreed that the constitutional guidelines would be discussed further at the next meeting after consultations in South Africa. The discussions proved, therefore, to be good and fruitful, although the group continued to stress the importance of transitional periods that would allow white South Africans to accept the reality of change.

Wimpie believed that the outcomes of the elections opened space for serious negotiations involving 'all parties' to create a new constitution. However, this would have to be based on 'group structures'. He went on to outline what he believed the trajectory of FW de Klerk's process of transition might be. First, there would have to be an agreement through negotiations between the government and the ANC and these negotiations could take at least three years. Then he envisaged a transition to majority rule, to be carried out in the following five years. Our delegation explained that we thought that the process would have to be shorter than outlined. Wimpie accepted that the first step could be much quicker, and indicated that De Klerk had about eight months to move before he would be forced into confrontation with the right wing and isolation from his own support base. He believed that the election had given his brother the initiative and was confident that De Klerk would not 'drop the ball'. He confirmed that the release of Mandela would logically lead to the unbanning of the ANC, because it was clear that upon his release Mandela would immediately continue with his political activities since it was not possible for him to be imprisoned again.

We agreed that this future should revolve around a three-phase political transition. The first would entail establishing an inclusive agenda. This could either result in a cul-de-sac or a breakthrough in the pre-negotiating period, and compromises would have to be made to ensure the latter. The unbanning of the ANC would be a critical pre-negotiation matter. It was salutary for this process that FW de Klerk took important steps in creating a climate for negotiations in his inaugural speech. For its part during this period, the ANC would have to clarify its stance towards participating in pre-negotiations, the armed struggle, the vexing concept of group rights, its links to the SACP and so on.

The success or otherwise of this first period would have far-reaching consequences for the next phases. In the second phase, a new constitution would be negotiated. This would be followed by the third phase, which would involve elections, the inauguration of a new government and the creation of new constitutionally based institutions as a means of phasing out the old apartheid order. The omens were good since discussions would be initiated in the country in order to achieve the broad consensus necessary to decide its future.

The ANC was concerned about the length of time they proposed for these processes – if the necessity of fundamental change had indeed been accepted as an article of faith. We were informed that some obstacles persisted, including fears about loss of control of the process and impending majority rule. There would have to be shifts in decision-making, such that the political centre of gravity would be restored to the Cabinet and Parliament in order to allow FW de Klerk to reposition himself as president. This would allow him to bring structures such as the SSC under his direct control.

The ANC responded that it was not yet clear about the direction De Klerk would take with regard to some contentious issues. For example, he needed to explain his understanding of 'groups' and needed to indicate his attitude towards the ANC proposals for creating a conducive climate for negotiations.

The Afrikaner group explained that De Klerk's view of groups was very different from that of the previous National Party. He was essentially committed to a Bill of Rights that would protect the language, culture and religion of whites, but accepted that there would be majority rule. As could be expected, we regarded the perennial question of 'group structures' as yet another Trojan horse for maintaining apartheid, albeit in a new form. Mbeki indicated that group rights based on racial differences would be completely unacceptable, but if they were defined in terms of a Bill of Rights that guaranteed legitimate cultural, language and religious rights, that would be a matter for further discussions.

Wimpie raised the issue of the links between the ANC and the SACP. We again explained that some members of the NEC were also members of the Communist Party, but we did not see this as an obstacle to any talks. I always believed that they had been briefed fully about who in our delegation were senior members of the SACP, although they never raised the issue of our membership in any of their engagements with us. The Afrikaner group had also hinted at the intense debates within the National Party about unbanning the SACP.

Wimpie then asked whether the ANC would give serious consideration to a power-sharing agreement. We indicated that the matter of power-sharing was something that had to be discussed in Lusaka, but we did not think that there would be a major problem with some form of power-sharing during the transitional period. He, astonishingly, asked whether the ANC would agree to representation of other black parties in the negotiating process. Mbeki responded that as far as the ANC was concerned, Inkatha, the Bantustan leaders, the PAC and indeed any genuine black organisation would be acceptable in the negotiations. The ANC did not claim any monopoly of support from the black constituency and we were therefore prepared to enter into a dialogue, even with all political parties.

Thabo Mbeki then raised three important issues. Firstly, the release of Mandela and the unbanning of political organisations must be a priority. Our understanding was that the government had only about eight months to act. Secondly, the ANC would examine how we could improve the international climate without calling off the campaign for the total isolation of South Africa. And finally, we wanted a better understanding from the Afrikaner group about what they understood by 'group status' and 'protection of minority rights'. This, we understood, was always going to be problematic.

Mbeki also emphasised that the elections had provided FW de Klerk with a fresh mandate for negotiating a new constitution. This process should involve all parties, incorporate a declaration of rights and provide platforms for bringing all groups into state and government structures. Above all, and in a normative and philosophical sense, the election results made it urgent to develop a consensus on a 'Declaration of Intent on a Future South Africa'.

We explained that it was not possible for the apartheid government to control the negotiation process. It was my understanding that the regime and some of the delegations with which we had had discussions were committed to the anachronisms of 'power-sharing and group rights' as distinct from majority rule. They believed that the transition would last as long as they determined. Indeed, their attempt to do this in the CODESA talks bore testimony to this.

We were more confident that, once Mandela was released and the ANC unbanned, the government would not be able to control the process. In fact, events would conspire to push the process in a very different direction. We were quite convinced that the process would fast become irreversible and that the vast majority of people supported the ANC. Even though we did not have military supremacy, we had political supremacy and moral authority to influence the process, the pace of negotiations, as well as the outcomes.

The Afrikaner group welcomed our explanation that once the government took these specific measures, the ANC would declare a moratorium on violence. However, they had to understand that this could not be permanent. There would be a cessation of violence as soon as negotiations started and its continuation would depend on how negotiations proceeded. We had thus reached a stage where both sides understood that we were not placing any preconditions on 'talks about talks'.

The regional situation

In our previous meeting, we had dealt with the very serious military battle that had taken place between SWAPO and the South African forces, resulting in over 300 SWAPO deaths and many civilian casualties. My concern then was whether agent provocateurs had set SWAPO up for this very dangerous but futile offensive. It was clear that the entire Namibian peace process could be wrecked by the massacre; hence, now was not the time to apportion blame but to ensure that the process was successfully concluded.

We informed the Afrikaner group that SWAPO leadership had indicated that, despite crossing swords with the SADF and Koevoet operatives, they remained committed to finding a solution, provided it was genuine and in the context of UN Resolution 435. It was significant that the SWAPO leadership under President Sam Nujoma had received accurate information from other sources rather than what South African and international media were sensationally reporting. This was a lesson we were to draw on during our formal negotiating processes in South Africa. The SWAPO leadership was, therefore, able to come to the conclusion that sad and tragic as this incident was, it should not sabotage the process. As far as the ANC and SWAPO leadership were concerned, the process was irreversible.

The Afrikaner group indicated that PW Botha and Pik Botha had accepted a SWAPO victory as a *fait accompli* and there were no plans for an intervention by the South African government. However, the policies and actions of the SWAPO government would present the real acid test of its credibility and integrity. This took on added significance since the mainly white Democratic Turnhalle Alliance (DTA) in Namibia could prove obstructionist.

We explained that, despite the agreements and the expected SWAPO victory, there was still fear on the part of Namibia's black population and the region that the apartheid regime would intervene to disrupt the process in Namibia. We were aware, too, that the SADF had about 1 500 soldiers and another 1 000 backup troops, together with a skeleton core of officers in Namibia, which could lead to the destabilisation of that country. We also indicated that the SWATF continued to report to its old commanders. There was thus anxiety that they could engineer disorder after a SWAPO victory, which would provide a pretext for the South African Army to intervene under the guise of restoring law and order.

We requested that clear and unequivocal messages be delivered by Wimpie to FW de Klerk in this regard. Among others, these included no further military intervention in the region; the complete demobilisation of the SADF and SWATF in Namibia; allowing the new incoming SWAPO government to play a positive role in regional affairs; and demonstrating goodwill by not obstructing or derailing a political solution in Namibia.

On Mozambique, we argued that RENAMO was a terrorist organisation with no real political perspective, and was hellbent on sowing destruction and mayhem. These 'bandits' were incapable of political direction and control. Hence, the South African regime should seriously consider halting its assistance to RENAMO so that the necessary conditions could be created for democratic elections. Interestingly, both sides agreed that ending support for RENAMO was an important step in any forward-looking exercise to promote peace and democratic governance in Mozambique. We informed them that the American administration had a similar understanding of RENAMO.

Our group was told, too, that there was evidence that some Portuguese South Africans were still funding and supporting RENAMO. Because these Portuguese were in key marginal seats, the National Party could not afford to antagonise them and, therefore, could not take any action to stop such financial support.

We were also informed that major South African business interests over a period of time had been paying protection money to RENAMO to safeguard their stakes in Mozambique. Clearly, the profit motive here trumped any ethical consideration. This was an interesting revelation, as I had always believed that RENAMO's support came from the apartheid military and had never seriously thought that the South African business sector was supporting it. How our business community, given regional and international developments, could have such a skewed interpretation of developments in Mozambique is inexplicable – although the same is probably true for the region and Africa.

Young informed us that, in a meeting in Namibia, Thatcher had 'severely reprimanded' Pik Botha for South Africa's continuing support for RENAMO in Mozambique. She also warned him that if the SADF 'went out of control', South Africa would lose support in terms of playing a constructive role in Namibia with regard to the implementation of Resolution 435, and this in turn could lead to an intensifying of the sanctions campaign.

The international situation

Michael Young's view was that President George Bush, unlike Ronald Reagan, would be much more reluctant to veto the imposition of sanctions by the US Congress. Also, the black caucus within Congress was more united and had become more militant on the issue of congressional sanctions. Young stressed that the US administration, which had many other challenges at this stage, was not willing to fight Congress over sanctions. The South African government accepted, too, that Thatcher needed some sign of flexibility on its part if she was to have any impact on ameliorating the impact of international sanctions. The Russians were in favour of negotiations in South Africa and would be less willing to support the armed struggle in view of fast-changing geo-strategic dynamics. Given this, the Americans were taking a more moderate view of the conflict and did not see the struggle in South Africa as part of its broader national interest.

It would be useful to reflect here on the Soviet Union's posture towards the ANC and negotiations. Much has been written about the changing attitude of the Gorbachev administration and Foreign Minister Eduard Shevardnadze and whether they pressured us to negotiate. It is true that foreign policy under Gorbachev was based on new thinking, an element of which was the need to find common ground with major Western powers on the basis of 'human values', as well as removing ideological considerations from state-to-state relations. Shevardnadze's Foreign Ministry was given extensive powers to pursue this course. South Africa and Africa generally were not priorities, but the new policy resulted in increased meetings with South African academics about the situation in the country and the region – without discussing or consulting with the ANC. There was even a failure on the part of the Soviets to respond to Mandela's proposal that the first country he wished to visit outside Africa would be the Soviet Union. All of this was, therefore, taking place without consulting or informing the ANC and the real problem was that the Soviets' new policy was not properly explained to the ANC or other relevant players in the Soviet Union.

However, a proper analysis will show that the impact of the Gorbachev administration's policy on the ANC's tactical and strategic approach was grossly exaggerated. Notwithstanding Shevardnadze's attempt to limit the influence of the Soviet Communist Party (SCP) on foreign relations, he could not do so completely. We were aware that the powerful Soviet Afro-Asian Peoples' Solidarity Committee (AAPSC) – the traditional mechanism through which the ANC interacted with previous USSR governments – had good contacts with the international department of the SCP, with the KGB, the Ministry of Defence and the Institute for African Studies of the USSR Academy of Sciences. All of these influenced the positions of the party's

Central Committee, which continued to exercise a measure of influence over Soviet foreign policy.

The Foreign Ministry's approach was short-sighted since an increasing number of Western governments were developing a better understanding of the importance of the ANC and, indeed, were having increasing contact with us. In 1990, Shevardnadze had to acknowledge that the 'main' task of Soviet policy towards South Africa was to 'contribute as fully as possible to the process of liquidating the apartheid system and settling the conflict through political means'. He went on to say: 'In solution of that task, we rely primarily on our traditional friendly relations with such democratic organisations as the ANC and their allies.' In helping to find a political settlement, they had to deal with other South African forces, including the government of FW de Klerk. Shevardnadze explained that after the ANC had moved its headquarters back to South Africa, contact with the ANC had been affected because the Soviet Union had no representation in South Africa at the time. They were, however, receiving ANC delegations in his Ministry and extensive discussions were being held.

Returning to the issue of Margaret Thatcher, her position on sanctions was well documented. The British boycotted the Canberra Commonwealth meeting of foreign ministers because the latter had produced a paper calling for increased financial sanctions against South Africa. According to Michael Young, there was no real domestic pressure on Thatcher to change her position. In rolling over South Africa's loans, only two British banks were involved in the rescheduling exercise and their objective was really to recover their money rather than to help relieve the fiscal pressures on the South African government. Young reported that Thatcher continued to harbour strong antipathy towards the ANC, but that her opposition to talking to it might change if the ANC expressed an unequivocal commitment to peace.

Decisive pressure would be exerted on all sides in South Africa to seek a negotiated solution. Young's interpretation was that, on one hand, the ANC was no longer assured of unlimited support from the Soviet Union, which now wanted peace; on the other, whites could no longer depend on the support of the Americans. He went on to suggest that the Cold War had ended and the major powers that had previously sought to divide South Africans in pursuit of their own parochial ends were now seeking a political solution. The positions of the two superpowers meant that the peace process would be given some impetus during this period. What Young was basically suggesting was that the South African government and the ANC would be subject to strong international pressure to negotiate.

These international dynamics could certainly not be ignored by FW de

Klerk and if he did ignore them, it would – in Young's view – mark 'the beginning of the end'. There was a window of opportunity of six to nine months for De Klerk to make irrevocable changes.

We discussed Young's input, and despite some important differences when it came to his analysis, we agreed that the changing international paradigm opened the possibilities for peaceful solutions to conflicts generally, and the South African conflict specifically. When the meeting ended we all concluded that we had, after several discussions, laid the foundations for a decisive breakthrough in the negotiations process.

The seventh meeting: Mells Park

This meeting took place from 10 to 13 February 1990 in the immediate aftermath of FW de Klerk's historic speech at the opening of Parliament in Cape Town on 2 February 1990. Whether for extra effect or other considerations, De Klerk addressed negotiations in the final part of his speech among other topical issues. He recognised that negotiations were critical to establishing a new dispensation based on reconciliation and peace and was prepared to address any obstacles that stood in the way of making this possible. In order to create such a climate, he announced several steps. Primary among these were lifting the ban on the ANC, the PAC and the SACP and releasing all political prisoners associated with them, including Mandela. Other ancillary steps included abolishing emergency regulations controlling the media and lifting emergency regulations that restricted 33 other organisations, including the UDF.

De Klerk's speech also focused on other critical thematic issues that had an impact on the negotiation process. There was reference to the changed international situation since the fall of the Berlin Wall; the importance of embedding human rights in the new dispensation; the need to rescind the death penalty; and the imperative of ensuring a stable and growing economy by introducing certain reform measures. He also indicated his willingness to negotiate with all political parties in order to create a new national constitution. He was not, however, prepared to lift the state of emergency or sanction the withdrawal of troops from the townships.

For me, nevertheless, it was a very exciting, emotional and satisfying moment. The scenario unfolding, although at a slower pace than antici-pated, went exactly according to what we had discussed in our secret UK talks and, as we were later to learn, also the Mandela discussions in prison. Of course, I realised that while De Klerk committed himself to 'power-sharing' with blacks, he did not go as far as accepting majority rule. Thus, while De Klerk's announcements were a watershed, we also understood that we had to remain vigilant. It was important to ensure that our people and the international community did not conclude that the struggle was over. In an article in *The New York Times* on 4 February 1990, Mbeki wrote: 'The oppressed have a duty to continue the struggle, with arms if necessary, until we achieve freedom ... To save lives the ANC proposes a mutual suspension of armed conflict, even before negotiations begin. It is only after a constitution was in place could hostilities, by both sides, be terminated permanently.'

Thus we entered our seventh meeting fully armed with the knowledge and dramatic impact of De Klerk's speech and acutely aware of our role in the unfolding historical process. We were also aware that the Afrikaner group would have important representatives of the Afrikaner business community. Besides Esterhuyse, the group included Mof Terreblanche, the brother of Sampie Terreblanche and one of De Klerk's closest associates; Attie du Plessis, a leading Afrikaner businessman and the brother of Finance Minister Barend du Plessis, who had been a presidential candidate; Marinus Daling, the head of Sankorp and Sanlam, two influential Afrikaner-led companies; Willem Pretorius, Chairman of Metropolitan Life Limited; Gert Marais, editor of *Finance Week;* and Fanie Cloete, a political scientist. Wimpie de Klerk apologised for not attending. Thabo Mbeki, Joe Nhlanhla, Henry Makgothi, Tony Trew and I made up the ANC delegation.

There was a general feeling and overwhelming sense of achievement. For over 18 months we had been meeting to discuss various issues of great complexity that would impact on the future of our country. And over the course of time we had gotten to know one another well – in fact, some of us had become friends. On Friday night, we enjoyed a wonderful dinner and sat around a log fire socialising and informally discussing issues till late in the evening.

One of the issues raised was that of the British rebel cricket tour to South Africa led by Mike Gatting, which had provoked major demonstrations and boycotts organised by the MDM. The atmosphere in South Africa was very tense, and some members of the Afrikaner group were concerned that the protest actions could impact negatively on the possibilities of talks between the ANC and government. After a long and thorough discussion about the reasons and importance of the sports boycott, it was agreed that more important events were transpiring and that the tour should not interrupt the opportunities that had presented themselves during this process. We thus advised that if the tour was stopped we would get a message to our people in the country to cease the boycott. As it turned out, the response of the Afrikaner interlocutors was that they had the power to stop the tour – because they were the ones paying for the tour. And so an agreement was reached that evening that the Afrikaners would stop financing the tour and that, at most, the rebel team would be allowed one more game, and in return the ANC would demobilise. That message would be conveyed to Ali Bacher, and I was asked to contact Sam Ramsamy and inform him about our discussions and request him to convey our positions to Krish Naidoo and the MDM, which he did. The significance of this anecdote is that it shows the level of influence our interlocutors had with the Afrikaner establishment. Although they were miles away, they had the power to influence decision-makers in the country. It also demonstrates the stature of the ANC – that they could inform the people of South Africa to call off the boycott.

Reactions to De Klerk's speech

The Afrikaner group explained that De Klerk's speech was a historic compromise for the National Party and this time they had indeed crossed the Rubicon. De Klerk had dealt with some of the obstacles to negotiations. The speech was really a call to all concerned South Africans to come to the negotiating table. It reflected De Klerk's awareness that the National Party and the ANC had different views on broad political goals and procedures, but advocated a process by which we could reach consensus on overcoming fundamental differences.

A few days after the speech, Gerrit Viljoen stated that in five years' time the National Party would not be the sole governing party, although it would still play a significant and influential role. All these were positive indications that the government was not simply 'shuffling the deck chairs on the *Titanic*'. The speech signalled a final break with the right wing and sent a clear message to DP members that they could either go to the left or return to the National Party. The National Party was also responding to the post-Cold War situation where new ways were being sought to resolve conflicts.

Thabo Mbeki responded that De Klerk's speech was positive and courageous, confirming the ANC's position that it was a genuine move and not one intended to play games. We noted that De Klerk had committed himself to deal expeditiously with outstanding issues, especially the definition of political prisoners. (Mbeki informed the meeting that the ANC was aware that this issue had been discussed with Mandela in December 1989.) One participant asked whether we could find a mutually acceptable definition of political prisoners that was different from that of both the National Party and the ANC, and Mbeki went on to explain that the government had already released prisoners who fell into the 'excluded category', but the ANC was willing to discuss any issues De Klerk might have that prevented him from accepting our definition. And if the government accepted that the

ANC also had legitimate problems with a narrow definition that excluded some political prisoners, then a solution would indeed be possible.

On the issue of Mandela's security after his release, we had consistently and publicly indicated that this was not only a problem for De Klerk's government. Given the violent activities of the extreme right wing, the concerns also related to the security of all ANC leaders, as well as De Klerk and his colleagues. It was therefore necessary for the government and the ANC to meet urgently to discuss mechanisms that would ensure the security of both sides of our leadership. We were told that this matter would be raised with the government and would be discussed further after that.

Thabo Mbeki stated that we had to accept that there was a legacy of mistrust and suspicion between the two parties and our constituencies, and it was thus important that we did not undermine each other, knowingly or otherwise. We were advised that De Klerk had taken the high ground domestically and internationally, and if the ANC wanted to maintain support, it was important for it to convince the white population that it was genuinely committed to negotiations, to publicly welcome De Klerk's speech and to make some concessions, such as proposing a moratorium on violence and the lifting of sanctions. The ANC should also give a clearer indication of its economic policies, and make public its thinking on transitional arrangements, such as a Bill of Rights and the protection of individual and minority rights.

Thabo Mbeki responded that we had immediately and positively responded to the speech. We could not make another statement that repeated the same message. Any new statement, he said, had to address the implications of the unbanning of the ANC, suspending the armed struggle and the joint ANC-government responsibility to manage Mandela's security after his release. Both sides had to be cautious about expectations; the release of right-wingers, like the assassin Barend Strydom, must be in the context of the release of all political prisoners. Furthermore, the ANC constituency still questioned the commitment of the government to negotiations and was strongly opposed to ending the armed struggle and lifting sanctions. This constituency would not be convinced by one statement. It had to see real progress in the removal of obstacles to negotiations and the transitional arrangements would have to be viewed in the context of constitutional principles and the role, if any, of the international community.

Once there was agreement on these issues, there would have to be a structure representing all parties in the negotiation process. The ANC had publicly committed itself to a Bill of Rights and our commitment to the protection of language, religious and cultural rights was unequivocal.

In his speech, De Klerk had made a statement on the role of Bantustan leaders and urban councillors in the negotiations process based on an assumption that they would support a solution based on group rights. But a meeting of the Bantustans' leaders a few weeks later would indicate that they had very different perspectives. The ANC had also been informed by important local councillors that they expected to have a local administrative role, but did not expect to be involved in the national negotiating process. Even the coloured Labour Party would dissolve itself. The government therefore had to accept that separate-development institutions and group rights were not going to be the building blocks in the process of negotiations and in a new constitution.

The Afrikaner group responded that an ANC statement on language, cultural and religious rights would meet with a positive reaction from the Afrikaans community. They further informed us that the government strategy envisaged four stages: a climate-creating phase in which the government would act unilaterally; initial confidential discussions between the government and the ANC about identifying and removing obstacles; discussions with many groups to get a broad consensus about the fundamentals of a new dispensation and the process; and negotiating a new constitution. We accepted that this would be an acceptable roadmap in principle.

On the economy, we once again dispelled any notions of being committed to a 'Soviet-type state-controlled' economy and massive nationalisation or expropriation. We explained that while nationalisation did indeed feature in the Freedom Charter, it was a matter to be discussed once negotiations had started. Only an ANC conference could change clauses of the Charter, but we reiterated our position that the ANC was committed to an economy that had both a private sector and state-owned enterprises. However, if democracy was to be consolidated in future, it was imperative that the new government address control of the economy and the gross discrepancy between the 'haves' and the 'have-nots'. On the issue of poverty, we argued very strongly that black poverty was largely a result of the system of apartheid. It was interesting to see that some of our interlocutors readily accepted this argument.

The issue of law and order always proved to be one where differences arose. We were again quite emphatic in our view that black-on-black violence was being instigated, supported and indeed organised through a third force, and that elements of the white security forces were assisting elements of the Inkatha movement to carry out acts of violence. The Afrikaner group listened, but was not fully convinced of our arguments on the role of agent provocateurs – although later, when they returned to South Africa, they found that our information about the third force was indeed correct. I believe that this was important, because even those who did not fully trust us during these talks realised that we were candidly sharing detailed information about developments in South Africa and that we were identifying the root causes of some problems. This convinced them that we had solid and reliable information about developments in South Africa and were familiar with the internal situation. Also, and most importantly, I hoped that they would raise our concerns with De Klerk and other members of the government so that they could take appropriate measures to stop the violence. As events turned out, the black-on-black violence continued for many years, even after the unbanning of the ANC and our return to the country. It remained a great source of tension between Mandela and De Klerk during the post-1990s.

Mandela's release and other matters

Later that day members of the Afrikaner group received a message informing them that Mandela was to be released the following day. They told us that Mandela had refused to be released on 10 February because he had insisted that De Klerk give a clear indication that all ANC political prisoners would be released as well. He wanted a delay of at least a week, but eventually agreed to be released from Victor Verster prison on 11 February 1990.

I have to confess that I was surprised that we were informed by the Afrikaner group about Mandela's release. We had been told by the NIS that we would be given fair warning about his release so as to make appropriate preparations, and the agreement was that the NIS would call Thabo Mbeki at his home in Lusaka and relay a coded message. However, by the time the NIS called the Mbeki house, Thabo had already left Lusaka for London. In a moment of historical satire, it was Thabo's wife, Zanele, who received the message in Lusaka but, unaware of its coded content and hence its significance, delayed relaying the message to us via Anne Davis, my partner at the time. Eventually, when Anne received the message she also delayed conveying it to us. This delay meant that the leadership in Lusaka did not, in fact, have ample warning about Mandela's release!

Esterhuyse informed us that while we were at Mells Park, he had received a call from a British television network inquiring as to his and Thabo Mbeki's whereabouts and requesting an interview on the subject of Mandela's release. It was thus decided that, after our celebrations, we should leave Mells Park and return to London where Mbeki and Esterhuyse would appear on the TV talk show. Esterhuyse was fond of telling the story about how he and his two sons returned to London in a large limousine sent by the TV network while Mbeki, the 'future leader of a democratic

South Africa', had to travel by train to London. I, of course, also proceeded to Trafalgar Square where huge celebrations were already taking place. It was a fantastic occasion, with thousands of anti-apartheid activists – many of whom I had worked with for decades – joyously celebrating the release of a man who had become an icon of the South African struggle.

An overall assessment of the talks

We agreed that progress in the overall negotiations would not have been achieved if the Mandela meetings in prison and the secret UK meetings had not taken place. These were richly complemented later by the ANC meetings with the NIS in Switzerland. We finally agreed that we ought to continue maintaining the friendships and contacts we had developed and to lend our experience to any problems that would inevitably arise during the negotiating process. As it happened, however, the negotiation process had taken on its own dynamics, and parallel meetings such as the Mells Park talks could no longer be sustained. But we decided that whatever the circumstances in South Africa might be, we would return to Mells Park for another, perhaps final meeting (see Chapter 10).

Our Mells Park meetings were nevertheless not without controversy in the ANC. These meetings had provided cannon fodder for some of our comrades to castigate the negotiators and to advance their arguments for the 'all-round intensification of the struggle and the seizure of power'. It appeared to me that these comrades had lost the plot and could derail what I considered to be an irreversible step forward. Fortunately, the ANC President's Committee had grasped this historic opportunity and encouraged our Steering Committee, which had been established to facilitate the return of exiles, to guide our participation in the negotiation process and to address any obstacles in this regard. After temporary indemnities were finally granted, the full NEC was able to return to South Africa in April 1990.

The UK secret talks, as well as the more openly public engagements with the captains of industry in Lusaka and the Dakar, Paris, and Leverkusen meetings, the Harare Children's Conference, and the various other meetings that took place across Africa and Europe, all taught us a simple lesson that Mbeki had tried to inculcate in us: that the most important lesson of warfare was to know your enemy. We had to always probe and ask certain questions: What was the thinking of the ruling group? How could the Afrikaners be saved from themselves? And how could we better exploit the internal contradictions that were arising in South Africa? And we also had to better understand and appreciate Afrikaners' fears. In Mbeki's view, once we began to answer such questions, the breakthrough would be much easier than many expected.

In meetings we had with people from many Afrikaner groups, Mbeki was always fond of saying that Afrikaners were like Africans in that they had nowhere else to go. Unlike English-speaking South Africans, they did not have conflicted loyalties and the only homeland that the vast majority of them knew was South Africa. In the end, therefore, once they understood that their destiny was inextricably interwoven with that of the majority of South Africans, they would be able to adjust to the changing realities. I also recall that when I was young, my father would often tell us that in the end Afrikaners would be more willing than English-speaking South Africans to make compromises and accept change. I was always doubtful.

Many of our comrades were sceptical of this sort of thinking, but those of us who had interacted so intensively with Afrikaans-speaking South Africans understood exactly what Mbeki was trying to convey. We were fully cognisant that Afrikaners really wanted to be understood and, indeed, be accepted by Africa and the world. In time, they would realise that this would not be possible unless they made fundamental changes to the oppressive political environment that existed in the country.

We were always conscious that our Afrikaner interlocutors, wherever we met, came to the meetings nervous that we would be rigid and dogmatic, that we would go on the offensive and be confrontational. They were thus surprised, it seemed, that the ANC delegations could be accommodating and avoid dealing with issues in an adversarial or combative manner. We did not condemn them as racists; neither did we castigate them for practising racism and being complicit in supporting the policies of apartheid. We understood that we had to start from where they were and, as we built their trust and confidence, we began to discuss the disastrous impact of the apartheid system, even on them.

In the discussions we indicated that we were conscious that they feared for the future of Afrikaners as a distinct and differentiated people, compounded by apprehension that the Afrikaans language and culture could be 'lost' and that Afrikaners would not be able to have their own schools. We were at pains to indicate to them that we understood their fears. Of course, such fears were irrational, but that did not mean that they did not exercise a powerful resonance among the Afrikaner people. Together we therefore had to answer the question about what we would do about such fears, but at the same time they had to understand that the black majority also had legitimate aspirations.

When I conducted my own review of all these discussions, I confidently concluded that as barrier after barrier of fear was removed, we began to get the Afrikaners to understand that our destinies were interlinked. We were able to get them to accept that change would not endanger their future, and that their religion, culture, language and heritage would not be under any threat in a future existence that would be predicated on a non-racial democracy. In short, we had to sink or swim together.

The Afrikaners, in turn, were surprised and impressed by the fact that we never treated them as the hated and mortal enemy, and that we were neither vengeful nor vindictive. In the end, they accepted that we were fighting a repugnant system and not white people per se; and that we were genuinely committed to finding a common understanding of the way forward. We understood their yearnings to be accepted as 'proud Afrikaners' who were also Africans. In fact, our meetings also had moments of levity. In one of them, Louis Kriel brought some South African grapes and wine. As we enjoyed the wine, Louis boisterously joked about the contradiction that we were breaking sanctions. I reminded Louis that since he was the arch-conspirator he would not be able to use this against us and that next time he should bring more wine and less grapes.

I got a sense that for years our Afrikaner compatriots had been comfortably ensconced in their laager, but now were finally breaking out of that suffocating environment. They wanted 'understanding' and 'acceptance'. Their pariah status had effectively cut them off from almost all economic, political, cultural, sporting and religious contact with the world. The sports sanctions, especially in rugby and cricket, weighed heavily on their morale and psyche. They could not be welcomed publicly and had to carry a burden of being constantly confronted about the apartheid system, even by their 'friends'. This must have had a profound and lasting effect on the elite who had become wealthy and had worked diligently to expand their contacts and interests internationally. The crisis of apartheid also impacted on their financial and economic interests. Moreover, a new generation of Afrikaner youth was starting to question the morality of the system that the UN had declared a Crime Against Humanity.

We were all convinced that these meetings had been invaluable. In Willie Esterhuyse's view, 'they helped create the conditions for negotiations'. For him, our discussions amounted to 'a dress rehearsal for the peace talks' and represented one of many initiatives designed to uncover the 'bottom lines' of various parties. As a key player, he summed it up cogently when he said: 'It was the most liberating experience of my life'. Our intense and wide-ranging talks had helped him to get a better understanding of ANC politics. He was persuaded about our perspective that South Africa 'belonged to all who live in it, black and white' and that our commitment to 'unity in diversity' was not tactical opportunism but stemmed from ANC policy since our formation in 1912.

The Afrikaner group also understood that our rejection of 'group rights' and 'reforms' did not stem from engendering a one-party state that would essentially replace 'white apartheid' with 'black apartheid'. In their schools, universities and churches they had been brainwashed to accept that only Afrikaners could be leaders capable of determining the future of South Africa. The Mells Park encounters provided eloquent testimony that other South Africans, not defined by colour, also had the capacity to lead and govern.

I believe that at that stage our Mells Park discussions and other secret meetings were much more than just 'one of many initiatives', as Esterhuyse would have it. Until then there had been no direct contact between people close to the establishment, on one hand, who then went to report back to their principals, and people close to the ANC leadership, on the other, reporting back to their leadership. FW de Klerk commented in his memoirs that he had been briefed about the secret UK talks and had 'taken note of the impressions of the ANC and its intentions'.

Delegation views about the talks

A sampling of the views and impressions of participants in our talks opens a window not only into shared sentiments, but also into the strategic and path-breaking nature of our discussions and debates.

Mof Terreblanche considered the discussions important because he was able to get a better sense of what 'these people' really wanted. He refers to the unreal experience in his first conversation with the ANC and goes on to say:

> To me Mbeki was just another ANC person. I thought of the ANC as tough people, but he impressed me from the first day. It was strange to be meeting at an English-type dinner with silver – the real stuff. As South Africans we were keen to get a solution. It was important because we had to see what these people really wanted. The meeting ended with us all drinking whiskey around a fireplace until 4 a.m. the next morning. We got really acquainted with one another in a personal capacity; the masks came off. After the meeting though, I felt there was something wrong – hell, the ANC couldn't be this positive, they must be bullshitting! So when I flew back to the next meeting, I said to my colleagues, 'This time we won't be taken in, we must be tough.' I guess they felt the same. For the first half hour, we were tough with each other. Then we realised that the dispute between us was not that big. As with a lot of things, common sense is a most wonderful thing to reach understanding. Previously there had been no common sense at all.

Attie du Plessis' view was that:

> it was not a peace process, we had no mandate on either side, but these meetings were very important for us to get to know our future governors ... the two sides were sounding each other out in considerable depth on all the major issues – economic, constitution, military that were to be the subject of direct negotiations after 1990.

Ebbe Dommisse, the editor of the influential *Die Burger*, said:

> I was an observer, a *verkenner*, a reconnaissance scout, out in front of the lines to see what was going on. There is no doubt that the ANC was very important. The ANC would not have embarked on negotiations if communications had not been established. It was a crucial moment.

In his diary, Wimpie de Klerk captured what I thought was the essence of the talks for the Afrikaner establishment interlocutors:

> For me personally, the talks meant a great deal. The luxury trips and accommodation, the experience of sitting close to the fire and engaging in political breakthrough work to bring the National Party and the ANC to dialogue, the bonds of friendship that had developed between Thabo, Aziz, Jacob Zuma and myself, the access to direct confidential information, the position of intermediary because from the beginning until now I have conveyed secret messages from the ANC to FW, and even the other way around, but FW was and is very cautious. Our agendas are very concrete and direct; on Mandela's release and ANC undertakings in that connection, on the armed struggle and the possible suspension of it by the ANC, on the various steps that must be taken before pre-negotiation talks with the government can take place, on constitutional issues such as a transitional government, minority safeguards and the economic system, etc., on concrete stumbling blocks and exploration of compromises to get out of deadlocks, on sanctions, on the ANC's thinking on all kinds of South African political issues, and on government thinking on those self-same issues.

He went on to say:

> I am convinced that the discussions had greatly increased mutual understanding, created a positive climate of expectations, brought a mutual moderation and realism to our politics, sending important

messages to Lusaka and Pretoria, and even included the germs of certain transactions. In general, therefore, a bridge-building exercise between NP Afrikaners and the ANC. Our little group's unique contribution has been that we engaged in extremely private discussions that were taken seriously by both sides, and that exposed Thabo, Aziz and Jacob to Afrikaners for the first time, and that they found an affinity with us and so with the group we represent.

Wimpie told us that he fully briefed the Broederbond about our discussions. He had told them that the National Party could do business with the ANC who were not 'radical' and were willing to negotiate and make the necessary compromises. He also briefed them on the ANC's positions on the economy in a future democratic South Africa.

The Mells Park talks would have clearly indicated to the apartheid regime that their tactics of secretly talking to Mandela in order to detach him from the rest of the ANC could not succeed. When they compared notes of our discussions in the UK and their talks with Mandela, they realised that even after so many years in prison Mandela's views did not substantially differ from the views of the ANC leadership in exile. It was therefore better that the regime coordinate its positions so that any agreement reached with Mandela would be acceptable to the ANC in exile. I believe that, in the process, we were even better able to coordinate our interaction with the regime, both through Mandela and through the Mells talks. And, indeed, the informal talks allowed us to convey a lot of important messages to key players on both sides. Mbeki informed me that Esterhuyse would privately raise issues to which Niel Barnard wanted a response; and he took back questions from Mbeki to Barnard. There is no doubt in my mind that some messages were even conveyed to Mandela through this channel.

It was interesting that all the participants in the Mells Park initiative were Afrikaners. I was informed that when some names of potential English-speaking participants were proposed, they were rejected by the NIS. The participation of top Afrikaans-speaking business people such as Marinus Daling, Attie du Plessis, Louis Kriel and Mof Terreblanche, who were also in the Broederbond, was significant. They had direct links to PW Botha and FW de Klerk and I am certain that they would have briefed them about our discussions. This was also a time of important regional developments, inter alia, when following the defeat of the South African military in Cuito Cuanavale, the regime was forced to start negotiations with the Angolans to end South African support for UNITA. Progress was also made to impose a solution based on UN Resolution 435 in Namibia, the independence of Mozambique was consolidated and, with the defeat of Abel Muzorewa's third force, a free and democratic Zimbabwe under a ZANU government was established. We had focused on regional issues in every UK meeting and were therefore well acquainted with one another's thinking.

The end of the Mells Park process inaugurated an emotional turning point for those of us in exile and who were set to return home after so many decades. The talks themselves mirrored perfectly the metaphor of memoir-biography within the broader context of the struggle, weaving the personal with the grander scheme of things. That was certainly the case for me. What had taken off as an uncertain secret exercise with many imponderables and unknowns had developed into an important platform for discussion, debate and thought concerning the future of our country. Above all, we had been both agents and participants in an unfolding drama that would launch South Africa irrevocably into a new social and political order.

Chapter 9

The secret Mandela talks and other covert meetings

Dr Niel Barnard, the head of the NIS, who I got to know well over the years, perhaps best captured the fundamental objective of our challenge in shaping a new future for South Africa when he said: 'Negotiations about a people's future is about passion and you [the ANC] have passion on your side. We have to negotiate to hand over power, and you have to negotiate to take over power.' Barnard, perhaps subliminally, was expressing a core concern about the historic nature of building an appropriately solid edifice on which that future could rest, but underlying the passion, the ANC and the government were also aware of the intense political differences, the divergent strategic interests and the separate ideological world views represented by both sides in their direct engagements with each other. This helped to explain the importance of our secret talks in trying to find the necessary common ground and the grand compromises that would over time help to shape the edifice of a future South Africa.

The many private and secret talks managed by Barnard as the regime's chief interlocutor with Nelson Mandela were an important contribution to the negotiation process. (According to Barnard, there were 48 such meetings between 1987 and 1989 – the time during which Mandela was moved from Pollsmoor to Victor Verster prison.) However, it was necessary that there be synergy between the secret talks with Mandela *and* an engagement and agreement with the ANC in exile about their main themes, something the NIS insisted on. This was how I became involved in the secret talks, along with Thabo Mbeki, in Switzerland where the government was represented by two senior NIS operatives with direct links to Barnard, who in turn enjoyed the confidence of PW Botha.

It is interesting to note that the secret talks between Mandela and the government in South Africa on one hand, and between the ANC and the NIS in Switzerland on the other, were taking place almost concurrently with the secret talks in the UK. The logic of all these talks were well expressed by the straight-talking Niel Barnard when he said to Mandela, 'if you want the [Afrikaners] to negotiate with you ... [and] I am warning you beforehand and I will advise PW – do not bring in a third party.' He went on to correctly observe that 'we did not have a consulting firm or the UN to do the negotiations for us'.

All these different sets of talks, both overt and covert, should therefore be seen as tributaries of one main stream: to avert a looming disaster and, through a negotiated settlement, put South Africa irrevocably on the path towards a non-racial and democratic future. Barnard himself indicated that time was not on the side of the regime: the longer it delayed, the stronger the hand of the ANC became – and hence the urgency to use all appropriate channels to set the negotiating process in motion in the face of what appeared to be insurmountable difficulties. The secret talks were thus a key component in the larger construction of an edifice for a new South Africa.

The Mandela talks

In Barnard's often sceptical turn of mind, the secret talks with Mandela and the ANC were the 'real McCoy'. For him and the NIS, no settlement would have been possible 'without finding a kind of understanding with Mandela himself', while aware too that agreement with the ANC leadership in exile was essential. This change of mindset is particularly poignant in view of some historical antecedents.

For many years the National Party government had offered to release Mandela if he agreed to move to the Transkei Bantustan – a suggestion he had consistently rejected with the disdain it deserved. In 1982, after more than 18 years on Robben Island, Mandela and other Rivonia trialists were moved to Pollsmoor Prison on the mainland, but by this point it was increasingly clear that the international campaign for the release of Mandela and other prisoners was becoming more strident, and even South Africa's major Western supporters joined the clamour. In fact, a similar campaign was launched in South Africa. To the consternation of many, however, during a parliamentary debate in January 1985, PW Botha offered to release political prisoners if they 'unconditionally rejected violence as a political instrument'. In what must rank as one of his most specious utterances, he went on to say: 'It is therefore not the South African government which now stands in the way of Mandela's freedom. It is he himself.'

In his autobiography, Mandela recalled writing a letter to Foreign Minister Pik Botha rejecting the offer. He did this because 'PW Botha's offer was an attempt to drive a wedge between me and my colleagues by tempting me to accept the policy which the ANC rejected. I wanted to reassure the ANC in general and Oliver Tambo in particular that my loyalty to the organisation was beyond question. I also wished to send a message to the government that while I rejected its offer because of the conditions attached to it, I nevertheless thought that negotiation, not war, was the path to a solution.'

Then Mandela's daughter, Zindzi, read out a message from Mandela at a mass UDF rally in Soweto that again expressed his rejection of the government's conditions. The message eloquently laid out his perspectives on his release. However, he was also responding to concerns among the ANC ranks in Lusaka and the MDM about his talking to the regime and the possibility that the regime's strategy of divide and rule might succeed.

The first real contact between Mandela and the government began while he was being treated in hospital for a lung infection and he was visited by Kobie Coetsee, the Minister of Justice and later Prisons. In his post-medical treatment, Mandela was isolated from the other prisoners in Pollsmoor. Later that year when he met the EPG, he indicated in his own capacity that he believed the time for negotiations had arrived. In June 1986, after Mandela had to return to hospital for further medical treatment, Kobie Coetsee paid him a courtesy visit.

However, it was only in 1987 that Coetsee resumed contact with Mandela. After several meetings, Coetsee informed Mandela that PW Botha had established a Committee of Four to hold discussions with him. The committee consisted of himself as chair; Johan Willemse, the Commissioner of Prisons; Fanie van der Merwe, the Director-General of the Prisons Department; and Niel Barnard, head of the NIS. It later emerged that Barnard played a central role in facilitating the 48 meetings that took place with Mandela between 1987 and 1990.

In Mandela's autobiography, he revealed that after agreeing to meet with PW Botha's committee members, he requested to see the other Rivonia trialists. Permission to see them collectively was refused and he had to meet with them individually. He thus informed each of them in turn about the talks, but not about the committee. While Walter Sisulu was not opposed to negotiations in principle, he expressed concern about capitulating, yet still gave the talks his 'lukewarm' support. Raymond Mhlaba and Andrew Mlangeni were more supportive, but Kathy Kathrada's response was said to be 'negative'. While not opposed to negotiations in principle, Kathrada strongly believed that Mandela was capitulating but indicated – in Mandela's words – that he 'would not stand in my way'. In Lusaka, Tambo had also received information about the talks and sent

Mandela a message expressing his concern, but wanted to know more details.

Mandela replied in a terse letter: 'I was talking to the government about ... a meeting between the Executive of the ANC and the South African government. I would not spell out the details because I did not trust the confidentiality of the communication. I simply said the time had come for such talks and that I would not compromise the ANC in any way.'

The first meeting between Mandela and PW Botha's committee took place in May 1988. The 48 meetings referred to above covered the same thematic and substantive ground as the EPG meetings, the meeting with the captains of industry in Zambia, and the other overt meetings with the IDASA delegations in Dakar, Paris and Leverkusen. These included issues related to the armed struggle, the SACP, majority rule, group rights and nationalisation – in short, the same matters we dealt with in the secret UK talks with the Afrikaner group.

The committee members' strategy with Mandela was to probe whether they could convince the ANC to change its positions on these matters; but they were also trying to find strategic and political differences among us that could be exploited in order to sow divisions in the ANC. It remains a remarkable matter of principle that, while there might have been dif-ferences in emphasis and tactical approaches, fundamental policies on negotiations could not be changed outside the leadership collective, something Mandela understood all too well.

The Mandela-PW Botha meeting

Mandela had, over the years, requested a meeting with PW Botha and became even more persistent in view of Botha's failing health. According to Barnard, Mandela had requested such a meeting based on their own interactions and long meetings about trying to define a common frame-work, and the NIS's belief that South Africa's problems stemmed from a 'political system which cannot hold'. Mandela believed that a meeting with Botha would be auspicious in trying to deepen this common framework. It was also important that this interaction be maintained in the utmost secrecy. As Barnard would have it, not even FW de Klerk or Botha's cabinet knew that they were talking to Mandela about the future of the country without their knowledge. In Barnard's view, if PW Botha had made his cabinet aware of these secret discussions with Mandela 'we would not be close to where we are today'. For him, therefore, the meetings with Mandela were an important part of laying the foundation for future negotiations.

Finally, after much advice from Barnard to PW Botha, on the morning of 5 July 1989 Mandela met with PW Botha at his official office, Tuynhuys, a meeting that Willie Esterhuyse described as a 'historic miracle'. The trip from Victor Verster prison was planned with great security precision and only a few 'trusted persons' had any knowledge of it. They were afraid that if news of the meeting leaked, the possibilities of an assassination attempt on Mandela were very real. Even the driver of the car that transported him and the other drivers accompanying his car had to be handpicked.

Mandela entered the premises under the guise of a visiting leader from Africa. The guards were obviously familiar with such visitors and paid no special attention to this one. Mandela was immaculately dressed in a tailored suit and the warder had to assist him to put on a tie, a skill he had forgotten since going to prison. Botha was accompanied by Kobie Coetsee, Johan Willemse and Niel Barnard.

According to Mandela, the hour-long meeting was 'friendly and breezy', and 'like two old men' they talked about family matters and other social issues until the last moment when Mandela raised the issue of the unconditional release of himself, Walter Sisulu and other prisoners, which suddenly made the secret encounter uncomfortable. As Barnard recalled on their way to Botha's office, he advised Mandela especially not to raise the issue of Sisulu's release since Botha would refuse and the risks were too high. Now, Botha rather instructed Barnard to attend to the matter of Sisulu's release. The meeting nevertheless ended on a cordial note with a group photo being taken. However, on their way back to the prison, Barnard exchanged words with Mandela over their different understandings of PW Botha's instruction concerning Sisulu's release.

According to Barnard, Mandela asked him: 'Now, Dr [Barnard], when are you going to release Walter? You are a civil servant [and] the President has given you an instruction to carry out.' To which Barnard replied: 'You and I apparently understood it wrongly or differently. He did not say release; he said discuss it with Barnard. This means I have to use my judgement now.' Barnard then relayed how he went on to give a visibly shaken Mandela some advice: 'Some time from now you will be President of this country. Please appoint civil servants around you who will tell you the truth ... I am telling you, regardless of what the President [Botha] said, it is not possible [to release Sisulu].' Presumably, Barnard based his judgement on what they perceived to be a problematic and inflammatory aftermath following the release of Govan Mbeki.

After the meeting between Botha and Mandela took place and the news broke, Barnard's informants in London conveyed to him that the ANC ranks were 'concerned'. They were asking, 'What did the *boere* do to mesmerise Mandela? He is completely in their power now, possibly they have bought him.' Barnard had apparently received similar reports about reactions to the meeting in Lusaka and elsewhere. I knew that in London there were discussions about the secret talks with Mandela, but I think Barnard's sources were 'spicing' up reactions in the ANC ranks.

Clearly there was a perception that there were serious differences between Mandela and the ANC in exile. It appeared that the senior regime officials had not studied the EPG reports, which would have helped them understand that while there might be some differences on fundamental policy issues, ultimately the ANC and the MDM sang from the 'same song book'.

Talking with the ANC was still considered treasonous and unacceptable to 'conservative' sections of the National Party and the securocrats. Barnard told me that during a hunting trip with key securocrats, PW Botha showed them a photograph of his secret meeting with Mandela. This caused tremendous anger and outrage, but Botha stood his ground. A senior general reportedly said, 'We are dying fighting terrorists and you are talking to their leader.'

Later in our secret talks in the UK, we were informed that there were four principal goals and objectives for PW Botha's meeting with Mandela. He wanted, firstly, to demonstrate to the UK and the US that a serious effort was underway to expedite the prisoner release process. Secondly, it would be impossible to make progress in the extraparliamentary talks without going through Mandela or getting his endorsement and support. Then, thirdly, Botha wanted to do something 'positive' before he left office as part of securing his legacy. Finally, the meeting had in fact been planned the year before. It had been linked to separating the presidency from the office of the prime minister, which would thus allow the new president to function above sectional and parochial politics in promoting a new constitutional dispensation. The meeting with Mandela was seen as a key step in launching this process of a 'Great Indaba'.

There was no detailed information about the secret talks that would enable us to deal with the persistent rumours that Mandela had agreed to participate in the NSC and call for the suspension of the armed struggle before the necessary progress had been made in the negotiating process. However, history will acknowledge that Botha's decision to meet Mandela and initiate a process of dialogue with him was a courageous and important step. Even though PW Botha died an embittered man, I was not surprised that Thabo Mbeki, when he was president, attended Botha's funeral. Most people who knew PW Botha told me that he could be very short tempered and aggressive, but that he was a good listener and welcomed alternative views.

In retrospect, Botha's meeting with Mandela was significant since it *de facto* represented an acceptance of Mandela and, therefore, the incontrovertible reality that the ANC could not be ignored. Moreover, it was confirmation of the inevitability of reaching a negotiated settlement if the country was to have a peaceful future.

Secret talks in Switzerland

Increasingly, as the NIS received reports – including those about the 'Mells talks', and other meetings that had taken place between South Africans and the ANC – it concluded that any decisions reached with Mandela in prison or any internal organisation would not be implemented if the ANC exile leadership did not accept those decisions. Barnard was aware, therefore, that it was essential to talk to the external ANC leadership. This was in recognition of certain facts: we controlled the armed struggle; we had significant contacts with the MDM; we had developed substantial relations with many governments; and we had the support of a powerful and globally significant anti-apartheid movement.

This helps to explain why on several occasions Barnard told Mandela that the NIS 'needed to talk with Thabo and others overseas'. However, according to Barnard, Mandela was not happy about any form of direct contact between the NIS and the ANC in exile. Mandela was of the view that the government had ulterior motives and was trying to divide the exile leadership from him in prison. This had a ring of truth to it, actually, because a July 1989 document of StratCom, the regime's psychological warfare and 'dirty tricks' department, outlined a plan to create divisions between the hardliners and moderates in the ANC. Mandela rather suggested that the NIS bring Thabo Mbeki secretly into South Africa to meet with him – Mandela – in prison, which Barnard believed was a trick. (This was an interesting coincidence since we had made a similar suggestion in our Mells Park talks.)

Barnard did not inform Mandela that the NIS had much earlier sent a message with Esterhuyse that they wanted someone from the NIS to join the UK secret talks, a suggestion that never materialised. Barnard eventually decided to make arrangements to meet with the exile leadership without informing Mandela. However, he believed that Mandela had later become aware of the NIS meetings with the ANC in Switzerland but never raised this issue.

Barnard asked Willie Esterhuyse to make contact with Thabo Mbeki to set up a meeting with Intelligence services. In April 1989 Esterhuyse came to London and met Mbeki in Michael Young's Consolidated Goldfields office. While waiting for Young, Esterhuyse wrote a note to Mbeki indicating that they should not talk about the proposed secret meeting with the NIS in Young's office because the office could be bugged and suggested that they meet later in a nearby pub. So when Young joined them, they instead discussed the next secret meeting in the UK with the Afrikaner delegation.

Later in the pub, Esterhuyse informed Mbeki that Maritz Spaarwater, an NIS operative, would call a safe phone in Lusaka, introduce himself as John Campbell and set up a meeting in Switzerland. Spaarwater's task was also to make all the necessary security arrangements for the NIS delegation. Confidentiality and secrecy were at a premium and absolutely vital. It was pivotal that knowledge of these meetings was never leaked because, according to the NIS, 'both sides had forces opposed to negotiations' and there was great potential for any 'talks to be sabotaged'. Also, the NIS delegation would be travelling under false documentation which, if exposed, could lead to 'difficulties' with the Swiss government. It was necessary as well to keep the meeting secret from other intelligence services, including the CIA, British Intelligence, the KGB and the French, German and Swiss services because they wanted no outside interference which coincided with our view.

The beginning of talks

The Swiss operation was labelled 'Operation Flair', and it took three months of conversations between Pretoria and Lusaka before the meeting date could be finalised. Thabo Mbeki's code name was John Simelane and Jacob Zuma's was Jack Simelane.

I learnt that Esterhuyse would alert Mbeki if he suspected that a 'trap' was being planned. He had also written a comprehensive report of the Mells Park talks and his role in setting up the meeting between the ANC and the NIS in Switzerland. He deposited these in a bank so that, should there be any 'foul play', the documents would be made public.

Initially, the Afrikaner group informed us that the direct talks between the ANC and the NIS had been stalled because of PW Botha's intransigence. We were told that because of his illness, Botha had not given Barnard permission to start such discussions. Barnard, in turn, did not want to seek authorisation because of Botha's illness, especially given that Botha had apparently become very 'erratic and aggressive' and it was likely that he would veto such a meeting. However, we were informed that Barnard did manage to get the necessary authorisation from De Klerk within the first week of his acting presidency by couching the request in broad terms.

During the informal discussions in Switzerland, we learnt that the day after FW de Klerk was sworn in as acting president on 15 August 1989, Barnard had sent him a 'very cleverly' worded proposal to allow the NIS to meet with the ANC in exile. This was tabled at a meeting of the SSC. The proposal argued: 'It is necessary that more information should be obtained and processed concerning the ANC, and [to better understand] the aims, alliances, and approachability of its different leaders and groupings. To enable this to be done, special additional direct action will be necessary, particularly with the help of the National Intelligence Services functionaries.'

Barnard correctly calculated that De Klerk, in the excitement and mayhem of his first week as acting president, would sign off on the proposal without 'due consideration', let alone appreciate its implications.

Eventually it was decided that the meeting should take place in the luxurious Palace Hotel in Lucerne, southwest of Zurich, on 12 September 1989. Spaarwater was accompanied by then NIS deputy director, Mike Louw, both travelling under false passports, with the aliases Jakobus Maritz and Michael James respectively. They were accompanied by three NIS field agents. We were informed that Switzerland had been chosen for the meeting because South Africans did not require entry visas, and they believed that it would be easier to enter Switzerland and meet with the ANC rather than to do so in London. I, however, suspected that they were convinced that British intelligence services had better capacity to detect any such secret meetings.

Spaarwater and Louw were nervous because this was their first ever meeting with the ANC and, in their opinion, they were taking 'serious chances' if there were leaks. The NIS was aware that Mbeki and Zuma would fly to Geneva from Zimbabwe, and would travel by road to Lucerne. All their movements in Zimbabwe were monitored by an NIS agent who informed Louw and Spaarwater that the plane from Zimbabwe had been delayed for a day because of technical problems. Three field agents then followed Mbeki and Zuma from Geneva to Lucerne. They told us later that they were suspicious that the ANC could set a trap and wanted to determine whether Mbeki and Zuma were bringing 'support staff' – by which they really meant hitmen!

Mike Louw often repeated the story that, as they were anxiously waiting for Mbeki and Zuma to arrive, he said to Spaarwater, 'How can we expect these guys to trust us? We could have been sitting with AK-47s and the moment they entered, we could have just blown them away.'

They therefore decided to keep the door open so that they would be in full view of Mbeki and Zuma and went on to recall that, as the two walked in, Mbeki said, 'So here we are, bloody terrorists, and for all you know, fucking communists as well.' It was the first time I had heard of Thabo Mbeki using expletives, but this story was told to me on many occasions and I have no reason to doubt it. Everybody accepted that this light-hearted interlude helped break the ice and everyone relaxed.

Since the two delegations were not really negotiating, the meeting proceeded informally in the evening and continued until 3 a.m. the following morning. The discussions covered all the issues raised in the UK secret talks: the imprisonment of Nelson Mandela; the continued banning of the ANC, the PAC and other organisations in South Africa; the ANC's alliance to the Communist Party; and the armed struggle. Louw believed that he left that meeting with a clear indication from the delegation that the ANC was 'willing to negotiate' and that this message had to be conveyed to FW de Klerk. The meeting also provided an opportunity to discuss the type of concrete arrangements to be made in order to get the negotiation process started.

Mbeki and Zuma were driven on the long journey to Lucerne by an ANC member, Trevor Abrahams, who lived in Switzerland. As far as Abrahams was concerned, they were on a fundraising mission and were in Switzerland to meet business people keen to assist. After he dropped Mbeki and Zuma at the meeting venue, he went off to the cinema, leaving a note to the effect on the windscreen of the car; but when Abrahams returned, he could find no sign of either of them and the car had disappeared – only to be found later in a different spot. As it turned out, the security operatives who were the 'backups' for the NIS team had seen the car parked for a while and had become suspicious. They informed the local police, who then removed the car.

However, the meeting took so long that, at one stage, fearing that Mbeki and Zuma had been kidnapped, Abrahams considered whether he should contact the ANC in London to alert us. Fortunately, reason prevailed and Abrahams did not lose his head as that would have been a disastrous exposure of a meeting we wanted to keep secret. Nevertheless, six months after this meeting between two 'enemies', Mandela was released, the ban on the ANC and other organisations was lifted and the negotiation process started in earnest.

We were later informed that when Louw and Spaarwater were reporting back to De Klerk on 17 September 1989, three days before his inauguration, he interrupted them and asked who had given them permission to 'negotiate' with the ANC. Louw, with a mischievous smile and a glass of whiskey, told us that he always made sure he carried with him a copy of the SSC resolution, which he was able to give to De Klerk. They thus informed him that, as the resolution stated, they had participated in an 'investigative meeting' and not a 'negotiating meeting'.

Louw believed that De Klerk was concerned, not because he had any objections to the idea of an investigative mission, but because he had the feeling that he was not being fully briefed about what was happening and that his involvement was peripheral at that stage. However, according to Louw, after reading the council resolution, De Klerk quickly realised that theirs was no 'Mickey Mouse' operation by the security services and wanted to know more about what had transpired. From that moment, De Klerk became fully involved in the process of negotiations with the ANC in exile. He was basking in the accolades of support and congratulations he was receiving from many countries and understood that he could not stop the process that had already started and, as a pragmatic politician, now had to try to manage the process.

Quite importantly, it was through our contacts with the NIS that we were informed about the essential contents of De Klerk's dramatic speech of 2 February 1990. Barnard recalled that two days before the speech there was 'heated debate in top government circles whether the SACP should be unbanned'. The argument was won by those who stated that Mandela and the ANC would not accept any situation in which the SACP remained banned. I was convinced that events in Eastern Europe, the fall of the Berlin Wall and the 'thawing' of the Cold War made it very difficult for the hardliners to continue exploiting the notion of the 'red bogey'. All conversations with the ANC, both overt and covert, ought to have sent an unambiguous message that we would never accept conditional unbanning.

Moving to substance

Five months later, on 6 February 1990, Louw and Spaarwater returned to Lucerne to meet the ANC. This was four days after De Klerk had made his historic presidential speech in Parliament where he outlined major changes in the political landscape of South Africa. Jacob Zuma did not attend this meeting because of other commitments so I accompanied Thabo Mbeki. As usual, strict precautionary measures had to be taken by the NIS because the South African agents were again travelling on false passports and identities and feared violent right-wing reprisals. They again used their European contacts to deal with the logistics and security arrangements, and remained anxious about possible leaks, constantly reminding us about the utmost importance of keeping these meetings secret.

According to Spaarwater, the atmosphere at the second meeting was more 'substantial, congenial and fun'. He added, 'Aziz could be a truly entertaining man.' He often referred to my 'enthusiasm and witticism' while drinking 'halaal' alcohol, which made us all more relaxed and comfortable while we continued our informal discussions until the early hours of the morning. While these sessions had an air of levity, we remained aware that we were dealing with crucial issues that would have an impact on the future of the country, and had to deal with the issues on the agenda as concretely and in as much detail as possible. It was at these sessions where I would repeatedly use the phrase 'What is to be done?' and Spaarwater and Louw found it hilarious that I was using the title of Lenin's 1902 book. However, and on a more serious note, their observation reconfirmed my understanding that the NIS and Military Intelligence were well versed in Marxism-Leninism because they believed such knowledge was important for breaching the top levels of the ANC.

We indicated that this meeting had to resolve the consequences of the burning issue of the unbanning of the ANC, the PAC, the Communist Party and other organisations. More specifically, we asked, 'After the unbanning, how do we get the ANC and SACP leaders and cadres back into the country?' There were several concerns in this regard: their security apparatus was trained to shoot our leadership on sight; the regime's propaganda had also created a deep enmity towards the ANC among the majority of white South Africans; we were aware that black-on-black violence was escalating and this could be used as a smokescreen to eliminate our leadership; and most of the exiles, including the leadership, had defied many of the security and apartheid laws that were still in the statute books and were therefore liable to arrest and prosecution.

The NIS delegation explained that for the exiles to return, the issue of indemnity had to be resolved. This was a reflection of what became a consistent theme: the apartheid regime's security establishment and even the political establishment were always arguing that everything had to be done by the rule of law and the Constitution. It was ironic, then, that a regime that had blatantly violated every international and human rights law and had presided over such an inhumane system always took a legalistic approach. I began to get a better understanding of the psychology of the Afrikaners and realised that this explained why so many laws were passed to provide the legal justification for the apartheid system. Doing things 'by the law' was the rationale for the system and complemented their belief that their actions were sanctioned by biblical teachings.

We discussed the reality that there were some within the ANC leadership who believed that the regime was duping the negotiators in the ANC into 'a false sense of security'. According to some of our comrades, the regime was simply using the negotiators to circumvent its international isolation, but more importantly, was cunningly trying to get us to stabilise the volatile situation in the country.

Because of the sensitivity and secrecy of the talks, our membership was not fully briefed and indeed magazines like *Africa Confidential* ran a number of articles about 'Mbeki and other negotiators being agents of Western interests who were not negotiating for fundamental change in

South Africa but for apartheid in new guises'. Many of our comrades, even in the camps, looked forward to getting copies of *Africa Confidential* and this, coupled with other 'black' propaganda initiatives by the apartheid regime, had confused some of our cadres, who began to believe that our initiatives were no more than attempts to sell out the struggle. 'Black propaganda' was similarly used to create confusion in the ranks of liberation movements such as SWAPO, ZANU and ZAPU.

Our discussions were, however, frank and open and we had to elaborate on the suspicions and paranoia that we were being 'duped' into coming back home where we would all be arrested and, once again, that the liberation movement would be seriously weakened. On the issue of the release of political prisoners, we again discussed the definition of a political prisoner. We also talked about the processes that would kick off the negotiations. We were aware that there would have to be an initial period when there would be 'talks about talks' to decide on participants in the direct negotiations, what form the discussions would take and what would constitute the agenda.

It was quite evident that the secret Mells talks, the Mandela talks in prison, and the first meeting between the intelligence services and the ANC all came together to lead to a much better understanding of one another's positions on fundamental issues and to concretely map the 'way forward'.

Following intense discussions, we identified some priorities: the release of Mandela, the return of exiles, including members of MK and the release of other political prisoners. We also wanted greater clarity on our demands for indemnity, including exiles, against possible prosecution under the many security laws still in place. We concretely discussed the structures that needed to be established and all the arrangements that had to be made for the return of the ANC leadership to South Africa, which would then be followed by the rest of the ANC cadres in exile. We agreed that our discussions would be presented to our principals and we would recommend that working committees be established to deal with each of these points and propose the way forward.

We started the process of setting up specialised committees to deal with priority issues under specific code names: Mandela's release was code named Group Alpha; the release of detainees was Bravo; maintaining contact between the NIS and the ANC intelligence agency was called Delta; and the process of setting up political discussions was code-named Charlie. In this process, we were beginning to build close personal relationships. The meeting went on till late into the night and I kept falling asleep. Mbeki kicked me and said, 'Aziz, wake up – don't leave me alone with these *boers*,' and everybody laughed uproariously. This became a standard joke over the years.

Our meeting, however, had to terminate unexpectedly – and we often laughed about this in later meetings. Our interlocutors informed us that while they were sightseeing they realised that they were under surveillance, most probably by the Swiss Intelligence Services. This was done 'openly' to 'send a message to them' and they informed us that they had to depart urgently. We had no evidence of any surveillance, but had no reason to question their suspicions.

Two weeks later, in late February 1990, we had a third meeting in Switzerland, this time at the luxurious Bellevue Paris hotel in Berne. It was a beautiful building that overlooked the majestic Aar River. The NIS delegation believed that since many South Africans travelled to the capital for financial transactions and since Berne was larger than Lucerne, the chances of exposure would be diminished in the Swiss capital.

The NIS delegation was strengthened by the presence of Niel Barnard and Fanie van der Merwe, Director-General of the Department of Prisons. As mentioned, both were on the Committee of Four that had been meeting with Mandela in prison. Mike Louw was also present. Our delegation was composed of Thabo Mbeki, Joe Nhlanhla (the ANC's head of intelligence) and me. This was my first encounter with Niel Barnard. I had read a lot about him and had studied his background and rise to the position of Director-General of the NIS. It was also the first time that we met with Fanie van der Merwe. Initially, it was again a period of 'getting to know one another'. It was clear that Barnard had been fully briefed about the meetings in Lusaka between the business community and the ANC, and many other such meetings, including the secret meetings in the UK, as well as the overt meetings in Senegal, France and West Germany. He would have also been privy to reports from agents who had infiltrated the Alliance structures.

Of course, the presence of Barnard took the strategic and political content of the meeting to a higher level. As head of the NIS, he was in direct contact with De Klerk, which – as he himself indicated – made him much more vulnerable than anybody else and he therefore had to be very careful.

The third meeting lasted longer than the previous two, mostly because we had to deal in greater detail with the establishment of the planned working committees we had discussed at the last meeting. We talked about the return of the exiles in greater detail and started making logistical preparations for the first meeting in South Africa between the government and the NEC of the ANC. This was quite a delicate operation because at the meeting before we had already discussed fears and suspicions, and the fact that many of our people did not trust the process and suspected that we were 'being led' into a trap. Given these realities, we perforce had to be detailed and meticulous about everything we discussed.

Our discussions dealt with the fact that Mandela's release would result in mass celebrations and even demonstrations, and that there would be a lot of 'toyi-toying'. We wanted assurances that such activities would not be repressed or banned. Barnard, in turn, wanted assurances that the ANC would be prepared to control the situation and did not have a 'hidden agenda' to exploit the release to prepare for insurrectionary activity. It was particularly during our informal sessions that the NIS gave us the distinct impression that they had infiltrated the ANC and the MDM at the highest level and were aware that some 'comrades' were intent on insurrection. All my attempts, especially during the more relaxed informal sessions, failed to get the names of their agents, and I had to concede that the NIS was very good at what it was doing to penetrate our Alliance structures. At no time were any names revealed, even after 1994, and Barnard always argued that no intelligence agency would be respected or would survive if it ever exposed its agents and sources.

When we discussed the composition of the ANC delegation for the first meeting with the government, the issue of Joe Slovo, General-Secretary of the SACP, who was also a member of the ANC NEC, was raised. Barnard informed us that the most difficult section of De Klerk's 2 February speech was the unbanning of the SACP because so many government and security people were strongly opposed. They would accept a 'nationalist ANC' but not one controlled by communists. Barnard went to great lengths to explain that it would be very difficult for the government to countenance 'one of the most hated adversaries' as part of the ANC delegation. Since the scheduled meeting was already 'highly sensitive', the presence of Slovo in the ANC delegation could lead to a backlash within the white community, the cabinet and the security apparatus.

Mbeki explained that Slovo was a leader of both the ANC and the SACP, and had been part of many of the major decisions of both organisations, as well as a key player in the armed struggle. He was heading Special Operations at that time. Consequently, it was important that no restrictions be placed on the ANC delegation; in similar fashion, neither would there be any restrictions or conditions placed on the government delegation. The meeting was then adjourned to allow Barnard to phone De Klerk.

When Barnard returned he informed us that the president was 'shocked' and categorically vetoed any idea of Slovo being part of the delegation. He had indicated that it was inconceivable, as president of South Africa, for him to welcome the leader of the Communist Party into the country for that crucial first meeting. Barnard had told him that the ANC delegation had made it clear that there should be no interference with the composition of each other's delegations and that government had no alternative but to accept Slovo should the ANC decide to include him in its group. The ANC had also made it clear that this was not negotiable – but De Klerk remained adamant that Slovo could not be part of the ANC delegation. This, of course, meant many more hours of intense consultation.

Barnard gave us more detailed explanations of what appeared to the ANC to be 'a simple matter of representation' in our respective delegations. This was a fundamental issue for the government, and indeed, for white South Africans as a whole. They had been completely brainwashed against communism. For them to have agreed to the unbanning of the SACP and now to accept its General-Secretary as part of the ANC delegation was a very difficult pill to swallow.

Eventually, it was agreed that Barnard would once again phone De Klerk, even though he was not at all confident that the president would change his mind. We were all greatly relieved when he came back and informed us that De Klerk had agreed that each side would determine the composition of their respective delegations and, moreover, that the issue of delegations should not delay further progress in preparing for the first ever meeting between the government and the NEC of the ANC. Barnard's understanding of the nuances of our position, coupled with his strong powers of persuasion, had convinced De Klerk that the ANC would not budge on Slovo's exclusion as a matter of principle. Barnard is, in fact, fond of telling the story of how, in those early morning hours, after De Klerk had agreed, he had bought the most expensive whiskey available to celebrate this breakthrough and how the finance officer spent much time and effort to reclaim the money because it was 'unauthorised expenditure'.

Another issue that saw very heated debate was the integration of the intelligence services. Joe Nhlanhla was extremely agitated and angered by the NIS perspectives of the comparatively small size and calibre of our intelligence cadres and operations. Fortunately, Mbeki helped calm things down and we concluded that this matter would be revisited once the relevant working committees had been established and were functioning. When this thorny matter was resolved, we continued to discuss the work of the other working committees and made substantial progress. By the end of the meeting, we were confident that the process was irreversible and we had firmly established measures that would make it possible for the negotiation process to start in South Africa.

However, it was again in the informal discussions that we began to discuss in greater detail not only personal matters, but also broader political dynamics and the concrete measures that had to be taken for the exiles to return to South Africa. In these conversations, both formal and informal, we were actually making concrete decisions that had far-reaching implications.

I was curious to understand the dynamics that convinced senior members of the NIS to support a negotiated solution. Mike Louw recalls that, as 'a strong supporter of change', he was disillusioned by the mid-1980s when he realised that there was no leadership within the National Party to deal with tectonic shifts in the international, African and domestic situations. The constitutional chess game by PW Botha to 'reform' rather than radically change apartheid did not bode well for the future. He concluded by 1985 that Botha had no real solutions or answers to the country's challenges, and that while he had extended cosmetic 'power-sharing' arrangements to Indians and coloureds, he was not really prepared to go any further. Louw's view was that Botha sincerely believed that he could maintain the status quo and that by bringing some blacks into government, in one form or another, this objective would be achieved. In other words, Botha was not ready to begin to consider the inevitable reality of majority rule.

The international isolation campaign also made an impact on Mike Louw and his family. His children were growing up conscious that the 'whole world hated' them and that they were not welcome anywhere outside the country. They were also growing up realising that Afrikaners were being stigmatised. By the mid-1980s, he had concluded that it was time for Afrikaners to deal with the perceptions that they were 'barbarians' and that they had to take concrete action to disprove them. He, with others, concluded that it was time to talk to the ANC and that they had to work out some arrangement that everybody could live with. He was convinced that minority domination could not be sustained and that the only path to a stable future South Africa would be to negotiate and to plan for one that would take into consideration the diversity of our nation.

I was convinced that an important influence was that, following the call by the ANC to make the country ungovernable, all attempts to ameliorate the conditions of the people were being challenged at every level of society. The Afrikaner ruling class was constantly confronted by the reality that all their efforts to discuss change and to improve the lives of the people were met with statements such as 'Why should we negotiate about such things when we do not have the vote and we are not a free people?' Much of this was revealed in private conversations with Louw during our meetings in Switzerland.

Barnard also, especially when we were relaxing, talked about the misconceptions that the ANC and the international community had about Afrikaners. He argued that they were a pragmatic people and not Old Testament Calvinistic-type conservatives; as such, they were capable of adapting and adjusting to changed circumstances if required. He liked repeating the Afrikaans saying, *'n Boer maak 'n plan'* (an Afrikaner makes a plan). He insisted that by the 1980s he and others were willing to accept real change. I, on the other hand, am not entirely sure if at that stage this was necessarily correct: they wanted change, but was this fundamental enough to lead to majority rule?

As we returned to our respective destinations, I had a sense of fulfilment and excitement. For the first time, I realised that rather sooner than later the other exiles and I would be returning to South Africa. Since I was a boy I used to shout the slogan 'Freedom in our lifetime', and after so many decades in exile, I began to think that there would be no freedom in my lifetime. Now the optimism of my youth was becoming a living reality.

However, this was also a period of reflection: how were we going to convince those of our leaders and cadres who had not been part of the process? Despite the obstacles, difficulties and challenges that would inevitably emerge, we still had to keep 'our eye on the ball'. We would have to make tough decisions to ensure that the process that I believed was irreversible would not be sabotaged by elements on both sides.

During our discussions in Switzerland the NIS people went to great lengths to let us know that they were aware of 'the sharp differences within the ANC leadership about the negotiation process', and there were suggestions that they were also cognisant of the ANC's decision to intensify armed activities and were particularly concerned about the continuing infiltration of arms and cadres into South Africa. They suggested that they were monitoring such activities. I, of course, tried to probe for more details, but these were not forthcoming.

We parted, agreeing that in two weeks we would once again meet in Geneva, but this time at the Noga Hilton hotel. At the fourth meeting with the NIS, in early March 1990, we decided to establish a joint Steering Committee that would deal with the minute details of the return of exiles and make preparations for the first formal meeting between the government and the ANC on South African territory. We discussed how members of the Steering Committee could enter South Africa secretly and sought assurances that they would not be arrested. All our comrades were wanted for defying apartheid laws which, as mentioned, were still in the statute books. We were given firm assurances about all such concerns, as well as the safety and security of members of the Steering Committee: Jacob Zuma, Penuell Maduna, Joe Nhlanhla and me.

The talks in Switzerland were extremely important in terms of key substantive issues and concerns, helping both sides to deal with and find answers to some difficult but pressing practical matters. Despite the nature of the intelligence services' world of intrigue, deception and subterfuge, we had managed to build very good relations with the NIS operatives – to the extent that we became good friends with Barnard, Louw and Spaarwater. Our Swiss talks were perhaps a harbinger of what was to come and had served as a microcosm for what could be achieved through honest negotiations, trust and tactical compromises on the larger political stage we South Africans were about to enter.

Chapter 10

'Coming Home' and crossing the final hurdles

In March 1990 – as agreed with the NIS in the secret meetings in Switzerland – an advance ANC team led by Jacob Zuma, and including Penuell
Maduna and Mathews Phosa, returned to South Africa. A few weeks later,
Joe Nhlanhla and I joined the advance team. My brother, Essop, returned in
July and started full-time work for the SACP. We were all given temporary
immunity to enable our return. When I had gone into exile in 1964 my
concerns were about leaving South Africa, compounded by my own sense
of alienation from the society I had grown up in and coping with the
London weather. But 26 years later, my concerns about coming home were
more about my safety and security, and some friends even warned me that
we were walking into a trap. Our advance team's brief, based on the secret
meetings, was to finalise outstanding issues so as to enable the rest of the
ANC leadership and cadres to return to South Africa to start the process of
talks with the government. However, I was also aware that some powerful
forces in government and the extreme white right wing were vehemently
opposed to any negotiated solution, while black-on-black violence had
also intensified.

Nhlanhla and I cleared immigration without a problem, and as we stepped
into the arrivals hall I was overjoyed to see my father and many members
of my family and friends. After years in exile I began to fear that I would
never see 'freedom in my lifetime', but now I was finally back home with
comrades, family and friends. It was bewildering, noisy, chaotic and exciting.
Emotions ran high and there was much hugging and shedding of tears. My
joy, happiness and excitement were tempered with sadness, however, that
my mother and so many comrades who had made the ultimate sacrifice
were not with us at the dawn of what promised to be a new democratic
South Africa. These included some of my best friends, such as Ahmed Timol,
who was murdered in John Vorster Square at the tender age of 29.

Another source of grief for me was linked to my partner, Anne Davis, whom I had been living with for several years. Anne shared my political commitment and was extremely tolerant and understanding about my frequent and prolonged absences. She was intelligent, kind and generous, and a dedicated educationalist: an anti-racist activist fighting to build a system that would cease to reproduce historical inequalities across race, class and gender. She was looking forward to continuing her work back in South Africa, and we had planned to return together. We invited my son, Sam, to join us for a holiday in December 1990, and it was agreed that Sam and Anne would travel together with Essop's wife, Meg, and their children, Amina and Govan, who were also coming to South Africa at that time to join Essop. Sadly, before we could make this journey home, Anne was diagnosed with cancer, which was already far advanced and untreatable. So my joy at returning from exile was blighted by Anne's illness, followed by her untimely and tragic death.

My return, however, was not without joy. I was quite taken aback at the level of development in white South Africa, including the very impressive infrastructure and transport system, as well as the fact that some aspects of the apartheid structure had already been abolished, such as separate amenities, public facilities and residential areas. However, unlike myself, many of the comrades who would be returning to South Africa would not have the privilege of being met by family and friends and, moreover, had very little means of survival or family support.

I went to my brother Ismail's home for a welcome-back celebration. My last recollection of Ismail's home was of a small flat in Kholvad House, Ferreirastown. Now I returned to find him living in a large residence in the previously 'whites-only' area of Mayfair. I was aware, nonetheless, that my 'coming home' would be another step in an arduous journey that still had to be travelled before we reached our ultimate objective of creating the conditions in which a new South Africa could emerge. The difficulties we had to face in the negotiating process often seemed intractable, especially in view of a deteriorating political environment, punctuated by violence and serious breaches of trust and confidence between the government and the ANC. As we approached this phase of our struggle, our resolve, commitment and leadership mettle would be tested every step of the way.

Resuming discussions

Every morning we were driven to Pretoria by a police official, a Mr Oost-huizen, to meet with the government team on the Steering Committee. Our discussions centred on the definitions of political prisoners, the terms of indemnity, the return of exiles and the release of political prisoners.

The government position was that prisoners who had been convicted for being members of a banned organisation or because of offences they had committed as members of a banned organisation would be granted amnesty. This did not, however, include those convicted of offences such as 'murder, terrorism or arson', even if for political reasons. The definition of 'political offence' determined guidelines for deciding who was or was not eligible for amnesty. The government wanted the guidelines to be based solely on those prepared by the Danish legal expert Carl Norgaard for the Namibian negotiations. Norgaard argued that there was no universally agreed-upon definition of a 'political offence', but that there was some international consensus on what constituted a 'politically offensive' act. He identified six factors that should be considered: motivation; circumstances; the nature of the political offence; the legal and factual nature of the offence, including its gravity; the target of the offence, such as government personnel, state property or private citizens; and the relationship between the offence and political objective, including the proportionality between the offence and the objective.

The government interpreted the Norgaard principles as meaning that violent crimes, such as cold-blooded murder and assassination, should under no circumstances be allowed to go unpunished, irrespective of who had committed them. This implied that those responsible for MK actions, such as the Ellis Park bombing and Robert McBride's bombing of the Magoo's Bar in Durban, would not be granted amnesty. The government failed or refused to understand that MK comrades operated under the rubric of our political policies, which prohibited civilian targets; however, in any conflict civilian targets were unavoidable. There was steadfast resistance to any counter-arguments suggesting that this particular interpretation of the Norgaard principles could apply to the thousands of security personnel who were just as guilty of such actions. Not surprisingly, we rejected the government's interpretation and demanded the release of all political prisoners, regardless of the severity of the offence and how this might be interpreted. This was clearly defined in the Harare Declaration and the refusal of the government to accept this aroused much suspicion and anger in our ranks.

The bitter irony in not resolving these differences meant that the remaining ANC leadership in exile could not return to the country to start the negotiating process. This again raised the spectre of suspicion and distrust among some comrades about the government's commitment to a negotiated solution. As a result, there were unrealistic calls for abandoning all talks and the clamour for intensifying preparations for an armed uprising became even louder.

The advance team consistently raised the need for unequivocal answers to a range of concerns that bedevilled the return of exiles and the release of political prisoners. The issues we raised with our government interlocutors included:

- why individuals had to seek indemnity as opposed to there being a general amnesty;

- what constituted a political offence;

- whether it was a political offence to be a member of the ANC;

- whether our leaders would also have to complete indemnity forms;

- why regime personnel would be exempt from seeking indemnity;

- what guarantees we had that information provided to justify indemnity would not be used in a court of law;

- whether security laws would be repealed without which we could not guarantee the safety of our members who returned from exile or participated in ANC/SACP activities in South Africa; and

- the cessation of all political trials that were continuing despite an earlier agreement.

The Lusaka leadership was concerned at our 'slow progress' in resolving these issues, which continued to remain a source of contention – as reflected in negotiating frameworks of the Groote Schuur talks, the Pretoria Minute, the DF Malan Accord and later in the CODESA talks. We also could not ignore the ferocity of black-on-black violence and the armed activities of the extreme white groups, which threatened to engulf the country in a civil war with dangerous tribal and racial undertones.

Mandela accused FW de Klerk of having a double agenda, of 'talking peace but fueling violence' and held the government responsible for the mounting killings. De Klerk had set up the Harms Judicial Commission in January 1990 to investigate the causes and consequences of the violence, but its efforts had been sabotaged by the Civil Co-Operation Bureau (CCB), established in 1986 as part of the SADF's Special Forces to cause maximum disruption in the 'enemy ranks'. The ANC was a special target of the CCB, which resorted to murder, infiltration, bribery and blackmail in their operations. Their sinister activities also included targeted assassinations. Among the many people they killed, the cold-blooded killing of anti-apartheid activist and academic David Webster in May 1989 was probably one of the most high profile. Harms concluded that the CCB had 'contaminated the whole security arm of the state', but De Klerk and senior SADF leaders denied any knowledge of the workings of the CCB.

The ANC's concerns were subsequently justified when, in mid-1990, the *Weekly Mail* exposed how the government had given the IFP financial support. The money had come from the Department of Foreign Affairs' secret slush fund and the department explained, albeit unconvincingly, that the money was being used to counter the sanctions campaign. Further exposés revealed that about 200 KwaZulu police had received military training in Namibia's Caprivi Strip. The country was teetering on the brink of a catastrophe and it was difficult to understand why the government, despite the Harms Commission's report and the new exposé, continued to deny that third-force elements were largely responsible for the violence.

Our discussions with our government interlocutors thus proceeded in an atmosphere of great tension between their leadership and ours. Fortunately, we had developed a good understanding among ourselves and tried to find solutions that were in everyone's interest. The advance team's main objective was to get the negotiating process started. I still believed that any negotiated solution would need some compromises, but this should not be at the expense of majority rule and, of course, taking account of white fears and black aspirations.

Soon after his release from prison, Mandela and senior members of the MDM travelled to Sweden to meet with Oliver Tambo and the leadership of the NEC in exile. I was part of the NEC delegation. This was the first meeting between the two leaders in decades. Tambo, who was at the time recuperating in a Swedish hospital, was transferred to a Swedish castle. Thus our meeting took place in luxurious surroundings, reminiscent of the Mells Park setting. The emotional reunion between Mandela and Tambo was a remarkable and unforgettable experience. We had intensive discussions about the continuing obstacles to starting the negotiating process, and there was a strong view that the black-on-black violence was allowing extremists to sabotage the negotiations process.

In March 1990 we were informed that the first meeting between the government and the ANC would take place in Cape Town on 11 April. However, shortly after this announcement, on 26 March 1990, the police opened fire on a group of protestors in the Sebokeng township, killing several protestors and wounding close to 400. Outraged by the massacre, the ANC cancelled its meeting with the government. De Klerk expressed concern that the ANC had suspended a meeting that was to discuss negotiations to end the violence, but the truth was that black-on-black violence was escalating. By 1990, a total of 3 699 political deaths were recorded, and many ANC leaders and cadres suspected that the government was aware of third-force activities and yet was doing nothing about it. Subsequently, on Mandela's return to the country, he and De Klerk held an informal meeting and De Klerk agreed to establish the Goldstone Commission to investigate the Sebokeng killings. It was agreed further that the formal talks would resume on 2 May.

To enable the first talks between the ANC and the government, temporary indemnity was given to some ANC leaders in exile. In this way, Thabo Mbeki, Alfred Nzo, Joe Slovo, Ruth Mompati and Joe Modise arrived from Lusaka on 28 April 1990 in a plane provided by President Kenneth Kaunda. We travelled to Cape Town to welcome them. Given that many in this senior leadership group were also returning home after 30 or more years in exile, the reunion was very touching and emotional. The leadership was driven to the Lord Charles Hotel in Somerset West, where they would stay, and providing a somewhat surreal experience in that it was in a previously whites-only luxury hotel that our leaders were being protected by members of the SADF. Over celebratory drinks, we joked that we could be killed in our beds. Given the right-wing threats and black-on-black violence, such fears were not without justification. Fortunately, our light-hearted humour helped ease an otherwise tense homecoming.

With the arrival of the leadership from exile, the first official talks between the ANC and the government could now begin. We suspected that the Lord Charles Hotel was bugged, so talks in preparation for this first meeting were held at a comrade's house in Cape Town and on other days at the Vergelegen wine estate owned by Anglo American.

The Groote Schuur Minute

The first meeting of the 'enemies' took place at Groote Schuur from 2 to 4 May 1990, the objective being to clear away the obstacles to negotiations. The ANC delegation was led by Nelson Mandela and included Joe Modise, Thabo Mbeki, Joe Slovo, Alfred Nzo, Ruth Mompati and Cheryl Carolus, and I was a member of the support team. The government fielded a large delegation. It was headed by De Klerk himself, and included Pik Botha (Minister of Foreign Affairs), Gerrit Viljoen (Minister of Constitutional Development), Barend du Plessis (Minister of Finance), Adriaan Vlok (Minister of Law and Order), Kobie Coetsee (Minister of Justice), Stoffel van der Merwe (Minister of Education and Development Aid), Dawie de Villiers (Minister of Mineral and Energy Affairs and Public Enterprises) and Roelf Meyer (Deputy Minister of Constitutional Development).

The atmosphere was cordial and both sides used the opportunity to mingle and to get to know one another. Mandela began the meeting by giving an extensive analysis of the Anglo-Boer War, the detention camps, and the humiliation and poverty the Afrikaners suffered under British rule. He asked why Afrikaners did not seek an alliance with the similarly oppressed black majority. I remembered our first secret meeting with the Afrikaner group in the UK where we posed the same question! The rest of the meeting dealt with the issues that we in the advance team had been discussing with our government interlocutors. After extensive discussions, the Groote Schuur Minute was signed on 4 May 1990. The Minute represented an ensemble of several important agreements integral to starting the process of negotiations:

- It was agreed to establish a Working Group to make recommendations on the definition of political offences; to discuss time scales; and to advise on norms and mechanisms for dealing with the release of political prisoners and the granting of immunity in respect of political offences committed inside and outside the country. Offences that would receive immediate attention included leaving the country without a valid travel document and any others related to organisations previously prohibited. This work had to be completed before 21 May 1990.

- Temporary immunity from prosecution for political offences committed before 4 May 1990 would be considered on an urgent basis for members of the NEC and other selected members of the ANC from outside the country. This would enable them to help with the promotion and management of political activities, assist in bringing violence to an end and allow them to take part in peaceful political negotiations.

- The government would review existing security legislation in order to ensure free and normal political activities.

- The government reiterated its commitment to work towards lifting the state of emergency.

- Efficient channels of communication would be established to curb violence and intimidation from whatever quarter.

As we were trying to make progress with these steps – and in the wake of increasing black-on-black violence – in early July 1990 the police in Durban 'uncovered' Operation Vula, which they sensationally alleged was a SACP plot to overthrow the government and was being orchestrated under the 'smokescreen of negotiations'. They further alleged that weapons, ammunition and computers were found at two safe houses, which revealed that more advanced weapons would be smuggled into the country. They linked the 'Vula plot' to a SACP consultative conference held in Tongaat on 7 May 1990, which supposedly agreed that there was great uncertainty about the negotiations and that secret work should be intensified to prepare for a national uprising. Soon afterwards, Mac Maharaj, Siphiwe Nyanda and six other comrades were arrested and charged with attempting to overthrow the state by force.

I had some knowledge about Operation Vula, which was launched in 1987. At that time it was necessary for the ANC and SACP to strengthen their collective political and military capacity in the country and this was the essential rationale of Vula. However, by 1990 I believed that Vula-related activities had stopped, although cadres remained underground with their weapons, and that the ANC leadership was working on the challenges of maintaining underground structures after the ANC had been legalised and was involved in negotiations. However, the slow progress in implementing the Groote Schuur agreement and the 'Vula plot' intersected to push the negotiation process into a serious crisis. Naturally, the right wing conveniently exploited the Vula incident to mobilise whites against a negotiated solution, while extreme-right elements intensified their violent activities. Meanwhile, some Vula cadres, supported by other comrades, expressed their anger by suggesting that the leadership was 'selling out' and not doing enough to secure the release of the arrested Vula comrades.

Following the Vula incident there were further intense discussions in the NEC about how to respond. These took on added urgency since many comrades did not know of the existence of Vula and were surprised at the allegations that an insurrection was being planned. After heated discussions, the government agreed to grant indemnity to Maharaj, Nyanda and the other Vula-accused and all charges were dropped. As a tactical gesture, the ANC announced suspension of 'armed activities' so as to give momentum to the negotiation process.

The Pretoria Minute

The second major meeting between the ANC and government was held on 6 August 1990, at which the Pretoria Minute was signed. The agreements and decisions at this meeting had great significance for injecting new energy into the negotiations.

The Working Group on political prisoners was instructed to 'draw up a plan for the release of ANC-related prisoners and the granting of indemnity to people in a phased manner', and to submit a report before the end of August. The further release of prisoners that could be dealt with 'administratively' would start on 1 September, such that by 14 September

125 prisoners would be released. Indemnity would be dealt with in terms of categories of persons and not individuals, and would start on 1 October and be completed by the end of 1990. Where there were grey areas, these were not included in the deadline but would be dealt with on their own merits and expeditiously.

For its part, the ANC would suspend all armed activities with immediate effect and no further armed actions and related activities would take place.

Both delegations expressed serious concern about the general level of violence, intimidation and unrest, especially in Natal, and both parties committed themselves to undertake steps and measures to normalise and stabilise the situation. The government thus undertook to consider the lifting of the state of emergency in Natal as early as possible. It further agreed to give immediate consideration to repealing all provisions of the Internal Security Act, including any reference to communism and the furtherance of its aims. There was also agreement on lifting the prohibition on publishing statements and writings of certain individuals. The relevant amendments to give effect to these would be passed at the following session of Parliament.

In order to make the process more participatory and inclusive, the two parties acknowledged that they were not the only parties involved in creating a new South Africa and called on all other parties to fully commit themselves to peaceful negotiations.

The parties to the Pretoria Minute concluded that 'the way is now open to proceed towards negotiations on a new constitution'. However, we were aware that many of our cadres and people were not happy with the negotiation process, as well as our decision to suspend the armed struggle. We thus developed a 'Report Back to the People of South Africa', which appeared in most of the media and in which we explained the decisions of the Pretoria Minute and indicated that our basic demands remained. These included the arrest and prosecution of warlords who continued to foment violence, the lifting of the state of emergency, and disbanding the KwaZulu police and dissolving the KwaZulu Bantustan. For our part, we had not abandoned the armed struggle and nor had we forfeited the right to self-defence. Mass resistance would continue and our suspension of the armed struggle was conditional on the behaviour of the police and army. As the obstacles were removed and the government demonstrated greater goodwill, exploratory talks on the drawing up of a democratic constitution could begin. We also explained that there had to be an interim government to supervise the transitional process and that a constituent assembly – elected on a basis of one-person-one-vote on a common voters' roll – would draw up a new constitution.

The ANC and the government, however, differed in their respective interpretations of the Minute. This included failure to agree on the definition of a political offence; the slow pace of repealing the provisions of the Internal Security Act; indemnity and the release of political prisoners; and the return of exiles.

The release of political prisoners started in September 1990, but by the end of February 1991, only 270 had been released and a further 760 applications were at an advanced stage of being processed. By the end of April, 933 prisoners had been released. The government asserted that fewer than 200 prisoners still had to be released, but we insisted that about 800 political prisoners remained in detention, including prisoners arrested for 'provoking unrest'. Such differences caused major and heated arguments between De Klerk and Mandela, and the situation was made more fraught by Pik Botha who, speaking in Germany, alleged that the ANC and SACP had violated the Pretoria Minute and other agreements.

More ominously and despite the agreements, black-on-black carnage was spiralling out of control. This continued to be engineered by third forces or was carried out by elements that were controlled by neither side. In 1990, white extremists carried out 52 acts of violence, resulting in many black casualties, and from early 1991 to the end of 1993, it was conservatively estimated that the white extremists were responsible for 40 shooting sprees where black people were their main targets. In response to these right-wing assaults and black-on-black violence, the ANC launched a campaign of militant mass action. Its basic objective was to fast-track negotiations and to strengthen our hand at the negotiating table. More than 10 000 related actions took place as a response to the campaign. Most were spontaneous, but included organised protests on education issues and consumer boycotts relating to rents and services. As a result, tensions between Mandela and De Klerk escalated and their relationship continued to deteriorate.

In May 1991, the NEC met and decided to suspend all talks with the government because of the continuing violence. Once again, I believed that there were powerful elements bent on sabotaging the negotiating process. Paradoxically, by suspending negotiations we would be enhancing the ability of those very same elements who were determined to undermine the pace and agenda of the negotiating process.

Rising tensions in the Alliance and growing distortions

In 1990, the ANC held its first National Consultative Conference inside the country since its banning in 1961. While delegates to the conference were concerned about the strategic implications of the negotiating process, these concerns were exaggerated by some media and analysts who quoted undisclosed sources. 'Concern' was also expressed about the hierarchical 'top-down leadership' and rising tensions between the exiles and internal cadres. The then Secretary-General of the ANC, Alfred Nzo, warned delegates that we lacked 'enterprise, creativity and initiative' and that 'we appear to be very happy to remain pigeonholed within the confines of popular rhetoric'. The leadership had correctly and frankly identified the complexity of the challenges facing our movement at this stage of the struggle and acknowledged that we were learning lessons as we entered this new terrain and period. It was thus pointless to discuss whether the negotiating process was irreversible or not. The fact of the matter was that we had already entered the negotiating process, which did not proceed in a linear straight line that would be favourable to the ANC.

During this period, analysts and sections of the media were writing extensively about what they perceived as problems and sharp divisions within the ANC and SACP – effectively the same divide-and-rule tactics that had been used against other liberation movements in Africa, as well as other anti-colonial and anti-imperialist movements internationally. In this context, there was an orchestrated campaign to demonise Thabo Mbeki and other leaders from exile. Even in our ranks, they were criticised for being soft on the enemy, opposed to mass-militant action and therefore out of touch.

In May 1990, at Johannesburg's Carlton Hotel, an ANC delegation that included Mandela, Mbeki, Zuma, Ramaphosa and I met with the major white captains of industry. The meeting was organised by the Consultative Business Movement (CBM), a corporate social-responsibility arm funded by big corporations. At that time Thabo Mbeki had no accommodation and the CBM arranged for him to stay in a suite at the Carlton. This was convenient for the many meetings he would need to attend. The arrangement by white capital gave rise to media reports from sources critical of Mbeki as 'selling out'. Essentially, the argument was that he was more comfortable with the captains of industry and the rich and was therefore neglecting his constituency work and not addressing mass rallies.

Comrades were dangerously abusing the calculus of mass action, setting it up against the important work of trying to build a strong ANC foundation for the negotiating process and those post-apartheid political and economic challenges this would pose. In the NEC and in other discussions, some of us argued in support of the importance of mass action, but cautioned against brinkmanship and the mistaken belief that mass action would result in regime change or that it mutually excluded a systematic approach to negotiations. Our strategic objective was to prioritise creating

241

an environment for free and fair elections based on universal franchise. We were confident that a democratic election would result in an ANC victory and that this, in turn, would enable us to transform the political, economic and social architecture of South Africa.

The first ANC National Conference (as distinct from the Consultative Conference) on South African soil took place in the shadows of black-on-black violence and the slow progress in implementing the Groote Schuur and Pretoria Minutes, which only served to heighten many comrades' fears and distrust of the De Klerk government. The conference was convened at the University of Durban-Westville (now part of the University of KwaZulu-Natal) in July 1991, with over 2 000 delegates attending. A new NEC was elected, with Oliver Tambo and Nelson Mandela unanimously elected national chairman and president respectively. Thabo Mbeki had been nominated for the position of deputy president by seven of the 14 ANC regions, as well as by the ANC Youth League. Chris Hani had not been nominated, but there was nevertheless a push to nominate him from the floor. Fearing that Mbeki and Hani both being nominated could create divisions within the organisation, Joe Modise advised Mbeki to withdraw, which he did. Hani, likewise, agreed not to accept a nomination. Modise then advised Walter Sisulu to stand – resulting in Sisulu being elected deputy president of the ANC. Cyril Ramaphosa was then elected ANC Secretary-General, replacing Alfred Nzo. I was elated to be re-elected to the NEC, but disappointed that many comrades – including Joe Jele, Jackie Selebi and Penuell Maduna – had not been elected.

I recall the evening after the NEC elections when Thabo Mbeki, Sydney Mufamadi and I, as well as a few other ANC comrades, had drinks at the Durban hotel at which we were staying. Mbeki asked Ramaphosa to join us at the hotel and 'informal' discussions centred on the very important role of the Secretary-General. All previous Secretary-Generals had been members of the ANC for many years and were well schooled in the ANC's struggle history and politics, which enabled them to deal with the many complex challenges faced by the Alliance. They had to be well versed in the ANC 'Strategy and Tactics' document; had to understand the characterisation of South Africa as 'colonialism of a special type', and the relationship between the national and class struggles that underpinned the relationship between the ANC and the SACP; and had to understand African and international dynamics within which the ANC had to work historically and up to the present.

Comrades cautioned that Ramaphosa had little experience in working in ANC structures, having cut his teeth in the trade union movement. Given his very different experiences and modus operandi, it was therefore

242

essential that he get to know the ANC better to ensure that he successfully fulfilled his responsibilities as Secretary-General. His primary task was to build a strong and united ANC. Mbeki explained to Ramaphosa that the ANC wanted him – Ramaphosa – to succeed as Secretary-General of the ANC and therefore to think of comrades such as Alfred Nzo, himself (Mbeki) and other senior leaders as resources who stood ready to support and assist him in whichever way necessary. The atmosphere was comradely and the discussions intense but constructive, with Ramaphosa participating fully. I mention this incident because, not for the first time, sections of the media and other 'experts' had a field day analysing divisions between the exiles and internals, and the battle between militants and moderates as the reasons for the sharp divisions in the Alliance.

In August 1991, while Mandela was on a trip to Cuba, and Mbeki and Zuma were attending a conference in Cambridge, England, the ANC's NWC decided that Mosiuoa (Terror) Lekota should replace Zuma as head of Intelligence and Cyril Ramaphosa should replace Mbeki as head of the negotiating team. The decision troubled us, especially as the reasons were never explained. Many of us did not understand. In fact, on his return, Mandela demanded to know why such important decisions were taken by the NWC, which was not a full committee since many of its key members were not present. It was not a decision of the NEC, and one that otherwise may have had a very different conclusion.

Of course, analysts and the media had a field day speculating about this turn of events. Even I to this day fail to appreciate why Mbeki and Zuma were replaced, especially since both had been actively involved in every critical phase leading up to the official negotiations. This included their role in the formulation of the Harare Declaration and our secret talks in the UK and Switzerland. Moreover, in the post-1990 period, both Mbeki and Zuma played a crucial role in creating the conditions for the negotiations process to start.

Soon afterwards, the NWC decided that Zuma should be the chairperson of the ANC's Negotiating Commission, tasked with overseeing the work of the various negotiation structures but not directly involved in the negotiations. Thabo Mbeki remained a member of the negotiation team and continued to play an important role in the negotiating process. There was a view that provoked wide public debate that the emerging power struggles were symptomatic of growing cleavages between internal members of the MDM and the ANC in exile, as well as perceived ideological rifts between nationalists and communists within the Alliance.

I was concerned that we might be experiencing dangerous factionalist tendencies in our Alliance structures within a surprisingly short time since our unbanning. The fundamental question was: who was engineering these tendencies and how would we be able to combat them? I also wondered whether our communications strategy was inadequate or whether we were victims of a deliberate destabilisation campaign that was successful because the ground was fertile for it.

The challenge of escalating violence

Whatever the case, it seemed that there were elements who were intent on sabotaging progress in the negotiating process and who seemed to be succeeding in creating a more volatile and violent political milieu. As such, an urgent response was required to avert what appeared to be a looming disaster.

Consequently, a third preparatory meeting between the government and the ANC took place on 12 February 1991, which resulted in the DF Malan Accord (named as such since the meeting took place at the eponymous airport outside Cape Town). Here the ANC confirmed our commitment to ceasing forthwith with any armed attacks or threats of armed attacks; the infiltration of men and material and creating underground structures; statements inciting violence; and military training in the country. While the Accord ruled against private armies, it was agreed that MK should continue to function so as to ensure that no armed actions or related activities were carried out.

As the violence increased and the reported death toll reached alarming proportions, it appeared that the government seemed unwilling to inter-vene. Mandela did not spare De Klerk his vitriol and his attacks became more strident, but De Klerk's response was that they had intelligence reports implicating the ANC in the violence and he called for a multi-party conference to discuss the matter. The ANC rejected this on the grounds that the government knew who the third forces were and needed to take decisive action against them once and for all.

On 16 November 1992 there was an exposé of serious criminal beha-viour on the part of senior army officials aimed at aborting the transition. A Mozambican, João Cuna, revealed to the *Vrye Weekblad* that he had been recruited to attack ANC activists in the Pietermaritzburg area. Further evidence surfaced after De Klerk had instituted the Goldstone Commission of Inquiry into the Prevention of Public Violence in October 1991. The commission submitted 47 reports to De Klerk and one of these was based on its investigators raiding the offices of 'Africa Risk Analysis Consultancy in Pretoria. This turned out to be a front organisation for the awkwardly named Directorate of Covert Collections, a section of Military Intelligence. Many of its operatives were formerly with the CCB, which had been disbanded on De Klerk's instructions – although his orders that no CCB members should be re-employed in any security structure were conveniently ignored.

De Klerk was aware of the dangers and risks of alienating the SADF and rumours of an impending coup persisted. Notwithstanding this potential threat, he appointed Lieutenant-General Pierre Steyn and gave him a wide mandate to investigate all illegal activities carried out by the military. Steyn was further given overall command of the SADF's intelligence operations with a brief to develop an effective division of responsibilities between the SADF, the police and the NIS.

In December 1992, Steyn's preliminary report found that rogue elements were operating outside the political and military command structure and some were still involved in illegal and unauthorised activities that could be 'prejudicial to the security and wellbeing' of the state. The report also referred to other activities: some units had been illegally stockpiling weapons in the country and abroad; they had provided arms and assistance to IFP warlords; they were involved in the instigation and perpetration of violence; and they were also carrying out an extensive campaign to discredit the ANC and sabotage the negotiating process. The findings of the report resulted in the demotions of Minister of Defence Magnus Malan and Minister of Law and Order Adriaan Vlok.

But the report also had wider ramifications. On the 'Night of the Generals' 22 officers, including two generals and four brigadiers, were forced to retire or placed on leave pending further investigations, although no evidence was forthcoming to charge any of the accused. Some, like Major-General CRJ Thirion, the deputy head of Military Intelligence, continued to insist that he was innocent and later the TRC found no evidence against him. He sued De Klerk and the matter was settled out of court. Magnus Malan, in turn, criticised De Klerk for making an error of judgement and also insisted that there was no wrongdoing when he was head of the SADF. He failed, however, to explain the exposés behind the activities of the CCB and the Directorate of Covert Collections. In February 1994, Justice Goldstone informed Malan that the disbanded but infamous third-force Vlakplaas Unit was still operating.

Years later, ANC allegations that third-force elements had engineered and supported the violence were confirmed when Military Intelligence operatives testified to the TRC that they were involved in activities to sabotage the negotiating process. In return for amnesty, Vlok gave evidence that he had sanctioned illegal activities against the ANC and other opponents of apartheid. In the TRC hearings, De Klerk took political responsibility, but vehemently denied that he was aware of any illegal activities carried out by his security forces.

Notwithstanding the fact that some ANC cadres were responsible for violence and that some violence was carried out by criminal and other uncontrollable elements, the government had to accept responsibility for failing to act decisively and expeditiously to stop the violence engineered by rogue third-force elements from the military and the police.

The National Peace Committee

There was a growing concern in our ranks that the government's strategy was to delay negotiations for as long as possible in order to exploit ANC 'divisions and weaknesses' and to form an anti-ANC alliance with moderate African and other minority parties and so-called leaders.

In September 1991, and after many consultations, the National Peace Accord was signed by 29 political parties and organisations, including the National Party, the ANC, the IFP and COSATU. Those who did not sign the Accord included the PAC, AZAPO, the CP and the right-wing paramilitary organisation, the AWB.

The Accord established a broad framework of norms for ensuring peace. All signatories were required to abide by the Code of Conduct and there was also a code of conduct for the police. The code provided guidelines for reconstruction and development, and dispute resolution committees at regional and local levels were established to work under the National Peace Committee (NPC). Businessman John Hall was the first chairman of the NPC and I served as one of its ANC representatives, which gave me valuable insight into the root causes of the violence and the extent of third-force activity. The Goldstone Commission was an important part of this process and its findings exposed many forces involved in the dirty-tricks campaign. In a rather colourful turn of phrase, De Klerk even commented that the commission had helped all parties to 'escape from the miasma of unfounded allegations, accusations, disinformation and propaganda'.

It was in this promising but highly volatile environment, where great hope collided with utter despair, that we decided to return to Mells Park. We needed time away from the country to reflect on some critical issues that had the potential to subvert the many gains we had made in moving the country towards reaching a negotiated settlement.

Return to Mells Park

And so, as we returned to Mells Park from 28 to 30 June 1990 for an eighth meeting, we were aware that the state of emergency had been lifted throughout the country, except for the then province of Natal. The reason given was that black-on-black violence there did not allow for the state of emergency to be lifted. We were also aware that there were major differences between the two sides on constitutional negotiations. The ANC was arguing for the establishment of an interim government that would oversee the transition to elections for a constituent assembly, while the government wanted the existing system to be changed to allow for black majority rule, while maintaining a form of white veto over legislation.

This last meeting at Mells Park was significant because, for the first time, a senior government minister formed part of the Afrikaner group. He was Dawie de Villiers, Minister of Mineral and Energy Affairs and Public Enterprises, as well as National Party leader of the Cape Province. The other members of the delegation were Wimpie de Klerk, Willie Esterhuyse, Attie du Plessis, Mof Terreblanche and Marinus Wiechers. On our side, the delegation was made up of Thabo Mbeki, Joe Nhlanhla, Tony Trew and me.

The domestic situation

The meeting started with Wimpie complaining that Mandela had been criticising FW de Klerk for delaying the negotiating processes, while in reality it was Mandela's heavy overseas travel schedule that was responsible for impending progress in promoting peace. Wimpie's view was that the ANC was ineffectual when it came to dealing with the spiralling violence. In addition, he held that the ANC had failed to respond to the reports of the Working Groups (established as per the Pretoria Minute Agreement), and was unwilling to convince its supporters about the need for compromise.

He motivated to put in place a Working Group that would have direct access to De Klerk and Mandela and which could monitor day-to-day processes. He also argued that a joint security secretariat had to be established to deal with the growing violence and also assist the ANC to control Natal as the worst affected region of the country.

He further explained that the government supported the participation of the ANC in a transitional government with the National Party – an important step in meeting our demands for a joint mechanism to oversee the transitional phase and elections. He also suggested that the government was of the view that the ANC was not willing to confront its youth and its left wing and called on the party to be more serious about cooperation with whites. He indicated that the government had to confront its own set of problems emanating from the right wing.

Wimpie explained that Mandela's constant criticisms about whites dragging their feet were 'ridiculous'. He thought that our delaying tactics were due to a power struggle within the ANC and it was becoming increasingly difficult for the ANC to restrain what he referred to as the 'hotheads' who were advocating an immediate overthrow of the South African state.

This discussion took some time because many of our white interlocutors joined in and further emphasised the points made by Wimpie, with Mof insisting on 'tough-talking'. We were told that they also had to deal with the reactions of their constituencies to Winnie Mandela's statement made in Harlem, New York, about returning to the bush to fight the whites. There was a marked increase, too, in crime and concern was growing about what the 'new South Africa' portended. They therefore called on the ANC to promote mutual respect and trust by improving the style and content of its language, rhetoric and communications.

The ANC delegation expressed surprise at the issues analysed in the document presented by the group, as well as the subsequent concerns they had raised. It was our view that the issues raised had to be symptoms of something else – and that 'something else' needed an explanation. We argued that we should not be too concerned about the perception behind the lack of progress. Our own view was that President FW de Klerk had also been travelling and he had already indicated that he would wait until Mandela returned before starting the talks. We explained that our leadership was also taking some risks to achieve peace, and referred to the meeting at which Mandela had been heckled by our own supporters when he called for a solution to the violence in Natal by telling them 'to throw their guns and pangas into the sea' and for suggesting that he was willing to share a platform with Chief Buthelezi. This was indicative of the mood of our people. The ANC would have to convince its supporters of the need for compromise, but we were also mindful, on the positive side, that the government had shown more commitment in seeking a negotiated solution. The ANC, like the government, wanted to see speedy progress in the peace process. Whites should understand, however, that black expectations were high and any delay would breed greater distrust, nervousness and instability.

The question of violence

The ANC was committed to dealing with the issue of violence and had reached agreements with other groups, such as the PAC and AZAPO on how to end it. However, we all had to understand that many of our younger supporters and even non-supporters had not been to school or received an education since the 1976 uprisings. We appreciated that unemployment was rife and indeed, given the great expectations, the potential for violence was very serious. Draconian security legislation had to be repealed with great urgency so that the ANC would have the space to set up its own structures, which would then enable us to deal more effectively with the violence.

We thus called for a joint approach to deal with the violence and suggested that we consider setting up a monitoring group to deal with it. We went on to explain that neither the ANC nor the National Party had anything to gain from the violence. It was taking place in specific areas of the country and was part of strategic alliances between Zulu and Afrikaner groups, or between Inkatha and the National Party, all of which were intended to undermine the legitimacy of the ANC.

The police knew that the provocateurs of violence recruited into Inkatha were the warlords, and yet, instead of arresting them, they armed them. The root causes of the violence had to be addressed and effectively tackled, which explained why the government had resisted instituting a judicial commission of inquiry into the violence as it feared exposure of the facts on the ground that they would also reveal its complicity. In the interim, both sides could initiate a major public offensive to counter the black-on-black violence that was raging in Natal and in some sections of the Transvaal.

Constitutional matters

One of the Afrikaner members led a discussion based on a paper written by Fanie Cloete, the political scientist who had attended the previous meeting. The paper was informed by a book written by Cloete's American-based counterparts, Guillermo O'Donnell and Philippe Schmitter, titled *Transitions from Authoritarian Rule: Tentative Conclusions about Uncertain Democracies*, published in 1986. The points Cloete drew from the book, and its relevance for our discussions, focused on the extent to which transitions from authoritarian rule present great uncertainty as well as difficult choices and ethical dilemmas. Such transitions typically have to deal with the lack of structural and behavioural parameters that can guide the passage to an irreversible and preferably democratic outcome.

Transitions thus did not follow a linear logic but were accident-prone and very unpredictable. Critical and strategic decisions had to be made in the absence of adequate information; the main protagonists had to face unforeseen political conundrums and ideological ambiguities, as well as dramatic turning points in the transition process, whose future significance was not always clear or easily understood.

The authors, therefore, emphasised critical imperatives that could help drive the transition process. These included the 'opening up' of the authoritarian regime; negotiating the transitional phase on the basis of pacts; giving civil society its rightful place in the process; and putting in place electoral mechanisms through which political parties could emerge in an open and transparent contest for power.

This analytical framework proved to be useful for our discussion.

We were reminded that while the National Party formally rejected the notion of setting up a clearing house for legislation before it was put to Parliament, a National Party Congress resolution in 1986 (which was later incorporated into its manifesto) had mooted the idea of a Council of State. This was potentially an embryonic transitional government. There was a principled acceptance of cooperation between the government and the ANC, but in the pre-negotiations phase this could not be made public because of opposition within the National Party.

The government would not accept the idea of an elected Constitutive Assembly for several reasons, and here the example of Namibia's transition was instructive. Firstly, unlike Namibia, South Africa had an elected government and was an independent and sovereign state. Secondly – and again unlike Namibia – there was no third-party mediation or involvement necessary in South Africa. Thirdly, in Namibia the South African Admini-strator-General continued to administer the territory during the negotiation process without being part of that process, but this would not be the case in South Africa. Finally, in Namibia the elections and Constituent Assembly were the result of negotiations, but in South Africa's case a Constituent Assembly based on universal suffrage was still a matter that had to be subjected to intense negotiations and thus was not a *fait accompli.*

The ANC responded that it and the government had agreed to meet to discuss the new constitution, which would include the broad principles as well as the nature of the constitution-making body. However, the government's argument that any new constitution had to be passed through a vote by the present electorate was unacceptable, since we were informed that the government was consulting with many other role players whose endorsement was required for any new constitutional dispensation.

The National Party would not agree to the government being replaced by a transitional authority. However, the ANC delegation argued that FW de Klerk, as leader of his party, could lead the negotiations but that he could not stay on as the head of government. It would be grossly unfair for one party to remain the exclusive governing party during negotiations unless all other parties agreed to this arrangement.

The discussion then focused on constitutional matters, with Mbeki arguing for a constituent assembly because it was our view that no new constitution could be drawn up and ratified by the existing white government on its own. Our interlocutors averred that a constituent assembly was not suitable for South Africa. They strongly argued that South Africa was an independent country with a standing constitution, whereas in Namibia three countries had been involved in drafting the

Constitution. The South African government would regard a constituent assembly as an insult to its own sovereignty.

We then suggested the possibility of a Council of State, which would share power with the main opposition parties, including the IFP and the PAC, but that we should guard against too many so-called leaders who claimed that they had supporters or a constituency. This would simply overwhelm the process and affect its credibility and potential to deliver and be effective. We stressed that the argument that elections based on a new constitution should be supervised by an independent body was reasonable and should not be seen as a major obstacle.

Marinus Wiechers, the constitutional expert responsible for the drafting of the Namibian Constitution, indicated that the prime element of a constitutional settlement should be a Bill of Rights; the main organs of state must be defined through a separation of powers; local authorities and subsidiary interests should be established; and transitional arrangements for a new constitution should be put in place.

During the discussions three other key elements were identified: affirmative action in favour of blacks, particularly over property rights; the authority of the courts; and the need for measures to protect the rights of the white minority. There was a good discussion on the issue of the Bill of Rights. It was generally accepted that a Bill of Rights was necessary to avoid a repetition of past injustices but, quite importantly, it would help protect the interests of minorities. On the issue of the judiciary, we argued that a constitutional court should reflect social justice. We also argued that the judiciary was too white and too male-dominated and that it would be absolutely necessary for women and black judges to be appointed.

We proposed that the new Parliament consist of two chambers. The second chamber could have constitutional checks to represent broad minority rights, not only of the white minority's but of all minority groups. It was also our view that the South African situation demanded an electoral system based on proportional representation. We would also be favourable to a Bill of Rights that contained provisions for referenda.

In the informal discussions, the SABC was discussed. The ANC's firm belief was that this institution had been a propaganda arm of the apartheid regime for many decades and, therefore, needed complete restructuring and reorganisation. In the context of the SABC, we discussed Radio Truth, a radio station used by the defence forces to beam anti-ZANU propaganda into Zimbabwe. There was agreement that Radio Truth should be shut down.

Economic matters

The economy was another major issue under discussion. Dawie de Villiers argued that the government was committed to long-term growth without which it could not deal with broader objectives and, in particular, redressing inequalities and the wide discrepancies in social expenditure. From the government's perspective, growth had to be driven by the private sector. He indicated that South Africa's record was historically one of state intervention, which had resulted in the profound neglect of the private sector. The intention was to reduce government control in the market place, which would also allow those previously excluded to enter the economy.

Another critical element of policy was commercialisation. Statutory objectives, such as providing services, determined the activities of many companies and corporations, and this prevented the most efficient use of scarce resources. Companies and corporations constituted about a third of the country's economic resources and their inefficiencies had a major impact on the productivity and price competitiveness of the rest of the economy. More prudent policies and better managed commercialisation would make companies and corporations more efficient and productive. However, and according to De Villiers, the privatisation of railways, telecommunications and electricity sectors was not an option at that moment. The government was not ideologically committed to privatisation or regulation, but in a mixed economy such as South Africa the challenge was to determine the appropriate mix.

De Villiers then raised the question of the ANC's position on socialism and nationalisation. His view was that nationalisation would only deepen the economic crisis and lead to greater unemployment, and expressed surprise at our explanation about nationalisation, indicating that as early as May, Mandela had insisted in a speech to 300 business leaders that there would have to be some measure of state intervention. This was because fewer than 10 companies controlled 90 per cent of the Johannesburg Stock Exchange, a situation which, according to Mandela, was patently unacceptable and could only be dealt with through the process of nationalisation.

Mbeki explained that the ANC was deeply concerned about the state of the economy and the quality of life of all South Africans. The ANC was committed to a mixed economy, but again the type of mix posed the real challenge. The ANC fully understood that the economy had to survive – this was in all our best interests – and we were conscious that if economic issues were not resolved, then no political resolution would work. Mbeki made it clear that the ANC was examining a British-type 'monopolies-and-mergers' commission to curb unfair competition, and that participation and planning had now become an important element of our discourse.

We cautioned that the government not make any major economic decisions that would have a negative impact on the new dispensation. We also discussed some challenges arising from the SACP's decision to become a mass party and how it was beginning to organise itself for mass action in the promotion of 'Socialism Now'. We agreed that the economy needed capital and an educated population. Mbeki, for the first time, introduced the concept of black empowerment and referred to the 226 000 shortfall in middle-management and the demand for technical skills that needed to be addressed.

The Afrikaner group also firmly argued for the lifting of sanctions since this would assist FW de Klerk to take further steps in accelerating the negotiating process, and De Villiers acknowledged that the government would have to make some concessions in return.

Our delegation indicated that the issue of international investment was consistently raised by the ANC in all its international discussions, and when Mandela returned to South Africa on 18 July, he would raise the issue of sanctions. We had to ensure that when we supported the lifting of sanctions, we had the understanding and backing of our people. In this regard, the government's response was important in helping us to convince our supporters. This meant that if there was substantial progress in the negotiations, then sanctions could be lifted that year.

Following what was to be our last meeting at Mells Park, we returned to South Africa in a much more optimistic and buoyant mood and for what were to be the final phases of the negotiating process. However, little could we anticipate some of the dramatic countervailing forces that would not only take the country close to the brink of a civil war, but also prove instrumental in providing the impetus for hammering out a new constitutional dispensation.

The ups and downs of the CODESA talks

The work of the NPC proved to be very important in creating a climate conducive to convening CODESA, which was the formal negotiating platform for facilitating a new constitutional dispensation for a post-apartheid South Africa. In late October 1991, and as a critical prelude to CODESA, 92 organisations assembled in Durban to form the Patriotic Front to discuss negotiating modalities and to examine mechanisms and technicalities for a political transition and an interim government. There was broad agreement that a non-partisan approach was necessary to take control of the security forces, manage electoral processes, define areas of the budget and finance, reintegrate the country into international affairs and elect a constituent assembly on the basis of 'one man one vote', and which, in turn, would draft a democratic constitution.

These matters formed the basis of discussions in the CODESA process, which began on 21 December 1991 at the World Trade Centre in Kempton Park, outside Johannesburg, where about 230 delegates representing 19 political parties showed their commitment to the negotiating process by signing a Declaration of Intent. The PAC had withdrawn a few days before since it believed that an external party such as the UN or the OAU should be a steward of the process. The IFP, AZAPO and the CP also did not attend. Nevertheless, this beginning, known as CODESA I, laid an important foundation by setting up five Working Groups with distinct mandates: the new constitution; the setting up of an interim government; the future of the homeland system; the time period to implement the transition; and the nature of the electoral system.

A major problem arose, however, when the ruling National Party felt that CODESA had usurped its role and function, with De Klerk having to allay Afrikaner fears by reassuring his members at the opening of Parliament in February 1992 that his party still held power. On 19 February, the white South African establishment was shocked when the right wing decisively defeated the National Party in a by-election in Potchefstroom, which had historically been a safe seat for the party. There was wide speculation that this was a clear warning to the National Party that the majority of whites opposed a negotiated solution and so, the day after the by-election, FW de Klerk called for an all-white referendum to be held on 17 March 1992. Voters had a simple binary choice to vote yes or no to the question: 'Do you support the continuation of the reform process that the State President started on the 2 February 1990 and which is aimed at a new constitution through negotiations?'

The National Party campaigned on a ticket of constitutional change but not majority rule, and businesses, religious leaders and other influential sectors of white society exercised immense pressure to secure a 'yes' vote. The ANC and many other black organisations expressed concerns about an all-white referendum, but still encouraged a 'yes' vote. In the end, 86 per cent of the white electorate participated and 68 per cent voted in favour of a negotiated solution.

We found that, because of the outcome of the referendum, the National Party's delegation was more aggressive and less willing to compromise. Each side thus ended up attacking and accusing the other of playing 'hardball'.

And then, while CODESA was still in progress, a brutal incident took place in the township of Boipatong near Vanderbijlpark when 46 residents of this informal settlement were massacred by IFP-affiliated hostel-dwellers. Observers believed that the massacre was intended to undermine the CODESA process and it certainly succeeded in poisoning the atmosphere of negotiations, with the ANC holding the De Klerk government and its security forces liable for this mad moment of popular violence. A livid Nelson Mandela was unsparing when he said: 'I am convinced we are no longer dealing with human beings but animals ... We will not forget what Mr de Klerk, the National Party and the IFP have done to our people. I have never seen such cruelty.' The Goldstone Commission subsequently brought in a British criminologist, Dr Peter Waddington, to investigate the attack and, while his report noted no police complicity, he criticised them for lacking proper investigative procedures that would identify the perpetrators for purposes of convicting them.

This was the foul mood that pervaded the second sitting, known as CODESA II, which began on 15 May 1992 amid two controversial issues between the ANC and the government: the disbanding of MK on one hand, and the future role of the SABC as the public broadcaster and its history as a propaganda tool of the ruling regime on the other. The ANC viewed the disbanding of MK with suspicion, especially the government's insistence that arms be surrendered to its security forces. With regard to the SABC, the ANC argued for its restructuring so as to ensure more neutral coverage of political developments and the negotiating process.

But the problems for CODESA II were compounded even further by lack of consensus on two other major issues, this time relating to the interim government and the constitution. The ANC had proposed an interim government with a cabinet composed of various parties that would last no more than 18 months. The National Party, however, insisted on a minority veto within such an interim set-up, which the ANC rejected. On the constitution, the National Party proposed a 70 per cent majority for a constituent assembly to take decisions and 75 per cent on major constitutional issues, such as a Bill of Rights; the ANC thought that 66 per cent, or two thirds, was sufficient for all constitutional matters. And so a deadlock ensued. As the ANC had entered the negotiations on the understanding that 'nothing is agreed until everything is agreed', and even though there was agreement on most issues, the consequence of deadlock on these issues resulted in the ANC not agreeing to anything. This is in fact what stalled the negotiations.

The breakdown of CODESA II in December 1992 caused great consternation both within the country and abroad. CODESA II was, however, not an unmitigated failure since some very constructive discussions and critical decisions had ensued from that phase. The most important was the matter of 'sunset clauses' and their implications for both sides. According to several accounts, a meeting took place in Cape Town in early 1992 between ANC and National Party representatives. The ANC delegation was made up of Cyril Ramaphosa, Joe Slovo, Thabo Mbeki, Penuell Maduna and Joe Modise, while the National Party contingent included Kobie Coetsee, Dawie de Villiers, Barend du Plessis and Roelf Meyer. Mbeki had briefed Ramaphosa that he was going to raise the idea of power-sharing in a transitional phase and clarified at the meeting that this reflected his own thinking and not that of the ANC. Barend du Plessis responded that Mbeki's proposal represented what was technically known as 'sunset clauses'.

After these discussions, some ANC cadres – including Joel Netshitenzhe – started raising the idea of sunset clauses within our own ranks. Mbhazima 'Sam' Shilowa, who later became COSATU's General-Secretary and Premier of Gauteng, raised the subject in an ANC preparatory meeting with the National Party. Joe Slovo, however, opposed it – but after the ANC accepted the idea at an informal meeting of the ANC Negotiations Committee, he asked Joel to develop a paper on sunset clauses. Joel's paper formed the basis of an article written by Slovo for *The African Communist* in September 1992, in which he argued that we were not dealing with a defeated enemy and, therefore, unconditional surrender was not an option. In an almost 'Road to Damascus' turnaround, Slovo then proposed sunset clauses for the new constitution. It included provisions for compulsory power-sharing for a fixed number of years, but very importantly and in order to ensure a smooth transition, the clauses also guaranteed security of tenure for all existing civil servants, including those in the Bantustans – although those who wished to leave voluntarily would be compensated for early retirement.

Even though the sunset clauses provided some relief, we had to acknowledge that overall, and in terms of its great promise and potential, CODESA II had not been successful. It was this acknowledgement that led Mandela and De Klerk to make fresh attempts to resolve the outstanding issues through a Multi-Party Negotiation Process (MPNP) – the successor to CODESA II.

With the collapse of the CODESA talks and the dark cloud of continuing violence hanging over the country, the UN Security Council organised a special sitting to discuss the crisis. The outcome of the session was the adoption of Resolution 765, which called on all parties to cooperate to end the violence and resume negotiations. Cyrus Vance, the former US Secretary of State, was appointed as a special representative with a brief to visit South Africa and assist with implementing the letter and spirit of the resolution.

Vance had extensive discussions with the main parties on the failure to agree on a definition of amnesty, but could not resolve the issue. This had been a perennial issue that had been discussed since the preparations for talks began, but the government refused to change its position. It seemed that they were using this issue as a bargaining chip and refused to accept that it was causing serious tension and having a negative impact on trust and progress in the negotiations.

Finally, however, good sense prevailed, and at a press conference on 13 August 1992, Kobie Coetsee and Pik Botha announced that the government had accepted Vance's proposal that a team of 30 UN observers be allowed to come to South Africa to work with the NPC and the Goldstone Commission so that a mutually acceptable amnesty package with a definitive cut-off date could be worked out. These developments provided an important impulse for the MPNP.

The Multi-Party Negotiation Process

The breakdown of CODESA still inspires contentious discussion, but, from a technical point of view, it was just unwieldy and unworkable, with its five Working Groups of 80 representatives per group a recipe for deadlock and compromise fatigue.

Fortunately, important lessons had been learnt to ensure that the MPNP was a relative success. This represented a new platform after the ANC and the National Party met on 2 and 3 March 1993 to freshly appraise the prospect of resuming negotiations and resolved that the MPNP had to be as inclusive and transparent as possible. And so it was that 26 parties and organisations attended the first meeting of the MPNP at the World Trade Centre in Kempton Park from 1 to 2 April 1993. A hierarchy of seven technical committees was established to govern the manner in which negotiations proceeded, while a Planning Committee ran the day-to-day operations of the talks. However – and in an important departure from CODESA – the most critical component of the MPNP was its Negotiating Council, whose deliberations were open to the public, the media and international observers.

Another critical moment arose when the MPNP was almost derailed on that fateful day of 10 April 1993 when South Africa once again teetered on an abyss after two white extremists, Janusz Walus' and Clive Derby-Lewis, assassinated SACP leader Chris Hani outside his home in Boksburg. Rioting and looting broke out and at least 70 people were killed, with an estimated 90 per cent of the black workforce embarking on a strike. In fact, Hani's assassination had a rippling effect and led to plummeting investor confidence and an increase in white emigration. On the day of the assassination itself, however, Nelson Mandela – in a televised appeal to the nation for calm – said:

> What has happened is a national tragedy that has touched millions of people, across the political and colour divide ... Now is the time for all South Africans to stand together against those who, from any quarter, wish to destroy what Chris Hani gave his life for ... this is a watershed moment for all of us.

At Hani's funeral in Soweto, Mandela again called for calm and reiterated the ANC's commitment to a negotiated solution, demanding that the process be accelerated. Hani's assassination, rather than causing a collapse of the negotiating process, had the opposite effect: the MPNP was accelerated. Once again, outstanding leadership by all parties and the response of our people had prevented us from toppling into the abyss.

Very sadly for the movement, Hani's assassination was followed shortly by the passing of our great and inspirational leader: on 18 April 1993 we mourned the death of Oliver Tambo.

The troubling right wing

However, several other troubling developments kept cropping up – and these had the potential to undermine the MPNP. Firstly, during this period General Tienie Groenewald, a retired director of Military Intelligence in the SADF, and several former military leaders, including General Constand Viljoen, established the Committee of Generals. Their purpose was to support the establishment of an Afrikaner homeland and to this end they formed a political party, the Afrikaner Volksfront (AVF). The generals soon became far more successful than other right-wing parties in uniting Afrikaners and they posed distinct challenges for what was already a highly polarised society. Viljoen, Buthelezi and other homeland leaders had formed the Concerned South Africans Group (COSAG), which argued for a federalist model that would allow them significant autonomy in governing their own territories. In June 1993, bolstered by the CP and the homeland governments of Bophuthatswana, KwaZulu and Ciskei in their ranks, COSAG walked out of the MPNP and refused to return unless their demands were met. An extremely dangerous situation was developing: the nightmare of thousands of armed Afrikaners, reinforced by the IFP and other homeland supporters resorting to violence to prevent the emergence of a democratic South Africa, was becoming a reality.

While we were still coming to terms with Hani's violent demise, in a dramatic show of opposition to the negotiations on 25 June 1993, the right-wingers of the AWB – led by their charismatic leader, the late Eugéne Terre'Blanche – stormed the World Trade Centre and tried to disrupt the negotiating process. This posed another challenge for derailing the negotiations and the Negotiating Council pressed for an agreement on two important issues, namely agreement on a date for the first non-racial democratic election and the establishment of the Transitional Executive Council (TEC), where I subsequently became a member of its International Relations Sub-Council.

In May 1993 Jürgen Kogl, a business consultant closely involved in Namibia's peace process and with contacts among senior SADF generals as well as the right wing, organised a meeting between Mbeki, Zuma, General Viljoen and two other generals. They discussed the growing violence and Mbeki and Zuma warned them that their activities would lead to a bitter conflict that could destroy the country and that they would lose everything. The generals were beginning to understand the necessity of mutual dependency.

Soon after this meeting, Viljoen and his Committee of Generals met with Mandela who conveyed the same message. Mandela instructed Mbeki and Zuma to help bring 'Viljoen and his men in from the cold', and so the two again met with Viljoen and his delegation in Waterkloof, Pretoria. The Afrikaners insisted on their own self-governing homeland, a so-called Volkstaat, but could not provide answers to basic questions, such as where this homeland would be located, who would be allowed to live there, what would constitute its economic base, how viable a social and political entity it would be and so on.

Between August and December 1993, Mbeki and Viljoen – supported by their two delegations – met six times. These meetings were co-facilitated by Kogl and Braam Viljoen (General Viljoen's twin brother). Mandela was briefed about the meetings. In the end, Braam Viljoen expressed appreciation that at least Mandela and the Mbeki team listened to their views, 'unlike the ANC negotiators who dismissed him out of hand'. Viljoen, however, continued to argue for a Volkstaat, but the problem remained that they had no clear understanding of what they meant by 'self-determination'.

Finally, a major compromise was reached on 21 December when the AVF agreed to the 'development of a non-racial democracy', while we agreed that the idea of a Volkstaat would have to be addressed. A Joint Working Group would be established to look at the viability of a Volkstaat, and if both sides came to agreement, the AVF would participate in the elections scheduled for April 1994. Mandela agreed to the proposal and a press conference was scheduled at the Carlton Centre to announce the decision. Then, at the last minute Ferdi Hartzenberg, another AVF leader, informed

Viljoen that he would not sign – which then forced Viljoen to withdraw. Some comrades in the ANC criticised the Mbeki team for exceeding our mandate and, surprisingly, Mandela publicly announced that there would never be a Volkstaat in South Africa. The generals then openly started talking about resorting to war and communication between the two sides ceased.

Given the volatile and fractious environment that was fast emerging, and at a request from Mbeki, Kogl organised another meeting in January 1994. At this meeting Viljoen warned ominously that if war did break out, the SADF would be divided and the ANC would not be able to govern. Zuma proposed that Viljoen accept the December accord as an unsigned agreement, which would allow both sides to look at the viability of a Volkstaat. After further discussion, Mbeki proposed that the April elections serve as a referendum for a Volkstaat. Support for it could be expressed through the ballot rather than through war – although his suggestion that there could be a separate ballot for a referendum was later rejected by the government delegation. Mbeki then suggested that votes for Viljoen's party would be counted as an endorsement of a Volkstaat, which could be further investigated by a proposed statutory body, the Volkstaat Council.

There seemed some positive response to this idea, but confirmation of its acceptance remained elusive – until the Mmabatho incident on 11 March 1994. Mmabatho was the capital of the Bophuthatswana homeland and its head, Lucas Mangope, had appealed to his allies in their right-wing Freedom Alliance (FA) to help him deal with a planned mass action by the ANC Alliance that demanded the reincorporation of Bophuthatswana into South Africa. Based on his involvement in the FA, Viljoen arranged for the training of Bophuthatswana soldiers to resist such reincorporation. As it happened, on that day in March, ignorant and gun-happy 'cowboys' from the AWB stormed into Mmabatho, indiscriminately hurling grenades and shooting at any black person they saw.

In retaliation, the Bophuthatswana army mutinied and, in full public glare, executed three of their AWB 'liberators'. This widely televised incident shocked the country and was a tragic reminder of the carnage that would follow any attempt to stop the democratic process by military means. That same day, Viljoen registered his party to participate in the coming elections. However, it was only after five more weeks of negotiations, and an ANC commitment that a clause on self-determination would be included in the transitional/interim constitution, that the 'Accord on Afrikaner Self-determination' was signed on 23 April 1994 – four days before the elections – and Viljoen accepted the proposal that the elections serve as an indicator of support for a Volkstaat.

As it turned out, the successor of the AVF, the Freedom Front, went on to win over 400 000 votes and had nine members in the first democratic Parliament. Even though the Volkstaat Council was convened, there was still no consensus on what it should be. In fact, the appetite for such an entity diminished considerably and the idea ultimately died.

Mbeki correctly understood the situation that we had at all costs to avoid our militaries going up against each other. He therefore quietly kept working with Zuma, Nhlanhla, Phosa, Maduna and me. Our approach was based on the imperative that we had to keep talking to and engaging all sections of the Afrikaner community. The right wing in general was not the main threat – but the security forces were. Since the National Party had lost control of the security forces, it was necessary to negotiate with them separately.

Once again, I recalled the outcomes of our secret talks in the UK and Switzerland and the many open talks between the ANC and Afrikaner groupings. Those discussions had led to a building of trust and understanding that we were not enemies, but simply reflected the fears and aspirations of our respective constituencies. The challenge was how we could make difficult yet necessary compromises in the interests of the country. Years later, in our discussions with Viljoen and his generals, we conveyed the same message.

Buthelezi and the IFP dilemma

As if the MPNP did not have enough on its negotiating plate, in July 1993 the IFP walked out of negotiations and threatened war. Unfortunately, at this time the concept of 'sufficient consensus' was being narrowly interpreted by some ANC and National Party negotiators to dismiss elements like the right-wing Afrikaners, the PAC, Buthelezi and other homeland leaders.

As background to the issue at hand, Mandela had given a public commitment to the IFP that the election date would remain as agreed and that there would be international mediation, before this matter could be discussed with the ANC. Mbeki and other ANC leaders then met to discuss how to give effect to Mandela's commitment to international mediation. These meetings were attended by Buthelezi's adviser and later IFP Member of Parliament, the late Mario Oriani-Ambrosini. One of the IFP demands was that the elections should be postponed in order to allow international mediation to run its course. From the IFP perspective, Mandela's agreement to international mediation was interpreted to mean that mediation should be concluded before the election and elections, therefore, had to be postponed. By contrast, the ANC held firm that the election date could not be changed and that it was the ANC's responsibility to ensure that mediation was concluded before the election date. The IFP continued to argue, however, that this understanding was flawed – and, as such, elections could not take place and neither could international mediation. In the end, and on the very last day of negotiations, Oriani-Ambrosini informed the meeting that he needed to call Buthelezi. He then left the boardroom and, after a few minutes, returned and asked Penuell Maduna to accompany him. When the two returned they reported that Buthelezi had accepted that international mediation can go ahead. It turned out that Oriani-Ambrosini had asked Maduna to accompany him to ensure that there could be no mistake that he (Oriani-Ambrosini) reported back correctly on Buthelezi's response.

Thus in March 1993 Mandela met Buthelezi and convinced him to register the IFP provisionally pending the intervention of international mediation on the constitutional debate. The ANC and IFP agreed that Henry Kissinger (former US Secretary of State) and Lord Peter Carrington (British Foreign Secretary), nominated by the ANC, should lead a team of mediators to help resolve the IFP's concerns. The problem, however, was to get agreement on the terms of reference that the mediators would follow. The IFP wanted the mediators to postpone the election due date by three weeks. This, however, would cause serious political and technical problems and the ANC rejected the demand.

At a meeting on 10 April 1993, the ANC delegation led by Mbeki agreed that the ANC would remain 'silent' on the IFP's insistence that the mediators deal with the election date. The ANC NWC, however, came to the incorrect understanding that the election date was to be postponed, the consequence of which was the ANC subsequently turning against international mediation. The collapse of international mediation once more took the country to the edge of chaos and instability. With Kissinger and Carrington already gone, one member of their mediation team stayed behind. He was a little-known Kenyan, Washington Okumu, who knew Buthelezi very well. And so, with the assistance of Colin Coleman of the CBM and Michael Spicer from Anglo American, Okumu convinced Buthelezi that since the date for the elections had already been set, it would go ahead irrespective and it was in the IFP's best interest to participate. And so it was that, after a series of discussions, on 19 April Mandela, Buthelezi and De Klerk signed a Memorandum of Agreement for Reconciliation and Peace that ensured the IFP's participation in the historic elections, which were then more than a week away. We saw the last of Buthelezi's brinkmanship when on 25 April 1994 Parliament held a special legislative session that allowed the late registration of the IFP as a participating party in the elections.

Some analysts have concluded that both Buthelezi and Viljoen later believed that they were tricked into joining the negotiations process and participating in the elections – although there is no substantive or convincing evidence to substantiate such conclusions. I am convinced that, given the stark reality that South Africa was inexorably sliding towards a racially and tribally inspired civil war, all parties had no alternative but to participate in the process and ultimately the elections. In hindsight, Viljoen had much greater potential than Buthelezi to destabilise the process, but the question was always at what cost.

Towards the grand finalé

The arduous and demanding work of the MPNP, and all those hundreds of South Africans who participated in it with such conviction and commitment, set the stage for our hard-won transition to democracy. And, as I have chronicled here, this took place in the face of many insurmountable odds, serious impediments and political rivalries. It was only in the final six months of 1993 that the final pieces of the transition puzzle began to fall into place. Quite importantly, in August and September, the Negotiating Council tabled four bills which, as irony would have it, were passed by the apartheid Parliament establishing the Transition Executive Council, the Independent Electoral Commission, the Independent Media Commission and the Independent Broadcasting Authority. Then, between 25 and 28 October, the ANC and the National Party met intensively to finalise the interim constitution for South Africa.

In another crucial development, Mandela, De Klerk, Ramaphosa and Meyer met on 16 November to iron out our differences on all outstanding issues. This resulted in the 'six-pack deal', which included cabinet not having veto power; a Government of National Unity lasting for five years; using a single ballot for the April elections; a Constitutional Assembly adopting a new constitution by a 60 per cent majority should deadlock arise; provisions relating to provinces and their constitutional status and authority; and the final constitution having to be certified by the Constitutional Court. All this proved highly instrumental for ensuring that preparations for the April 1994 elections could begin in earnest in December, including the appointment of electoral commissioners under the leadership of Judge Johann Kriegler.

This did not mean, though, that we would be without any further high drama. Indeed, on 24 April, three days before the elections, right-wingers set off a massive car bomb in downtown Johannesburg, with more than a dozen similar bombings being reported elsewhere on the eve of the elections. We, however, would not be deterred, and this did not prevent me and millions of other South Africans from casting our first ballots for a democratic South Africa on 27 April 1994, a day that will forever be memorialised in South Africa's post-apartheid history.

I took great comfort in the fact that, finally, the birth of a free and democratic South Africa was a vindication of all our efforts and those of so many other comrades and ANC leaders who had dedicated their lives to the struggle. And so it was that on 10 May 1994 I was privileged, along with South Africa and the world, to witness Nelson Mandela being inaugurated as the first president of a free and democratic South Africa, with Thabo Mbeki sworn in as his first deputy president and FW de Klerk as his second deputy president.

Postscript

The awarding of the joint Nobel Peace Prize to Nelson Mandela and FW de Klerk symbolised a victory for the negotiated settlement as the genesis of a new democratic dispensation.

After Nelson Mandela formed the Government of National Unity in 1994 on the basis of the negotiated settlement, I was honoured to be appointed as Deputy Foreign Minister, a position I held until 2008. This gave me the opportunity to become closely involved in the realignment of South Africa's foreign policy and international relations, as well as our reintegration into the comity of nations.

South Africa's transition to democracy represented the culmination of one stage of my life as an insurgent diplomat, and the beginning of another at the hard coalface of international relations and global politics. My life in the ANC and the SACP straddled the worlds of progressive activism and the difficult art of negotiation. Within the boundaries of human frailties, I tried to stay committed to the essential principles and practices that underpinned our struggle for liberation in South Africa. And when President Mandela took the oath of office at the Union Buildings in Pretoria on that sunny afternoon in May 1994, he embodied a new social contract with the people of South Africa.

In this book I have attempted to demonstrate the resilient power of dialogue and the necessity of building trust and confidence with our adversaries. If we did not pursue the path of negotiations with ingenuity and flexibility, the ingredients of a potent brew of civil conflict would have been all too palpable and real. Ours was a historic task because, after all, we were involved in changing the very foundations of an apartheid state that drew its logic from racial divisions and group identity, where a minority had absolute control of the state and where white interests prevailed over those of the majority of South Africans. Moreover, the end of the Cold

War added another catalytic dimension to South Africa's transition and exposed the spurious illusions of a communist threat.

A triumphant ANC had thus emerged from the trenches of liberation to govern an extremely complex society with formidable social and economic challenges. We have been able to revolutionise the South African polity, but transforming its society and economy remain persistent challenges – as liberation movements elsewhere in our region have discovered. The country has made great strides in consolidating the benefits of democracy, with a strong focus on people-centred growth and development, but there are many morbid symptoms that conspire against our ability to address the deeply embedded legacies of poverty, inequality and unemployment. There are growing levels of corruption, alienation, political and tribal factionalism and demagoguery in our movement that threaten our already delicate social fabric and require urgent redress. In short, we need to reclaim the ideological and political centres of gravity that have shaped the Congress Movement and, in this regard, we must continue to strive to develop politically literate and ideologically committed cadres.

The great lesson we can take away from my reflections here is the need for the ANC as a ruling party to constantly renew and regenerate itself from within in order to promote a uniquely South African patriotism and a shared sense of nationhood. Deputy President Thabo Mbeki spoke cogently in Parliament in 1998 about South Africa representing a country of two nations: one white and prosperous and the other black and poor. He argued very forcefully that until we confront the divisive and debilitating reality of these two nations, it would be difficult to promote reconciliation, a new patriotism and a common national agenda. This is a key requirement, not only for sustaining our hard-won democratic freedoms, but also for ensuring that real and tangible social and economic benefits flow to the majority of South Africa's citizens. History is replete with the tragic consequences of progressive political parties that failed to respond to the needs and demands of ordinary people. Ultimately, we are servants of the people and we must be honest and sincere in the face of our manifest failures as stewards of this country's democracy. Our core values must include an acknowledgement that our destiny is inextricably interwoven with that of the African continent and its people. A progressive pan-Africanism is called for to combat the divisive forces of imperialism that continue to impede our larger endeavour of integration.

President Mandela best captured the progressive and revolutionary ideals of the ANC when he concluded his inauguration address by saying: 'Never, never again shall it be that this beautiful land will again experience the oppression of one by another and suffer the indignity of being the skunk of the world. Let freedom reign. The sun shall never set on so glorious a human achievement.'

Acronyms

AAM	Anti-Apartheid Movement
AAPSC	Afro-Asian Peoples' Solidarity Committee
AMWU	African Mine Workers' Union
ANC	African National Congress
ANC YSS	ANC Youth and Student Section
AVF	Afrikaner Volksfront
AWB	Afrikaner Weerstandsbeweging
AZAPO	Azanian People's Organisation
BCM	Black Consciousness Movement
CBM	Consultative Business Movement
CC	Central Committee
CCB	Civil Co-Operation Bureau
CND	Campaign for Nuclear Disarmament
CPC	Coloured People's Congress
CIHS	Central Indian High School
CODESA	Convention for a Democratic South Africa
COSAG	Concerned South Africans Group
COSATU	Congress of South African Trade Unions
COSAWR	Committee on South African War Resistance
CP	Conservative Party
CPSA	Communist Party of South Africa
DP	Democratic Party
DTA	Democratic Turnhalle Alliance
EPG	Eminent Persons Group
FA	Freedom Alliance
FRELIMO	The Mozambican Liberation Front
GDR	German Democratic Republic
IDASA	Institute for a Democratic Alternative in South Africa

IFP	Inkatha Freedom Party
IP	Independent Party
IPRD	Internal Political and Reconstruction Department
IRA	Irish Republican Army
IUEF	International University Exchange Fund
MCW	Military Combat Work
MDM	Mass Democratic Movement
MK	Umkhonto we Sizwe
MPLA	People's Movement for the Liberation of Angola
MPNP	Multi-Party Negotiation Process
NAM	Non-Aligned Movement
NDR	National Democratic Revolution
NEC	National Executive Committee
NIC	Natal Indian Congress
NIS	National Intelligence Service
NLA	Natal Legislative Assembly
NLF	National Liberation Front
NPC	National Peace Committee
NSC	National Statutory Council
NUS	National Union of Students
NWC	National Working Committee
OAU	Organisation of African Unity
PAC	Pan Africanist Congress
PAFMECSA	Pan African Freedom Movement of East, Central and South Africa
PFP	Progressive Federal Party
PLO	Palestine Liberation Organization
PMC	Politico-Military Council
PMSC	Politico-Military Strategy Commission
RC	Revolutionary Council
RENAMO	The Mozambican National Resistance
RPMC	Regional Politico-Military Council
SABC	South African Broadcasting Corporation
SACP	South African Communist Party
SACPO	South African Coloured People's Organisation
SACTU	South African Congress of Trade Unions
SADF	South African Defence Force
SAIC	South African Indian Congress
SANROC	South African Non-Racial Olympic Committee
SARU	South African Rugby Union
SASCO	South African Students' Congress
SATIS	South Africa – 'The Imprisoned Society'

SAYRC	South African Youth Revolutionary Council
SCP	Soviet Communist Party
SSC	State Security Council
STST	'Stop the Seventy Tour'
SWAPO	South West Africa People's Organisation
SWATF	South West African Territorial Force
TEC	Transitional Executive Council
TIC	Transvaal Indian Congress
TIYC	Transvaal Indian Youth Congress
TRC	Truth and Reconciliation Commission
UCL	University College of London
UDF	United Democratic Front
UDI	Unilateral Declaration of Independence
UN	United Nations
UNISA	University of South Africa
UNITA	National Union for the Total Independence of Angola
UNTAG	UN Transition Assistance Group
USSR	Union of Soviet Socialists Republics
WCC	World Council of Churches
Wits	University of the Witwatersrand
ZANU	Zimbabwe African National Union
ZAPU	Zimbabwe African People's Union